Jean Genet

Jean Genet's significance within twentieth-century theatre has long been understated. This timely book, the only introductory text in English to Genet's plays currently in production, presents an overview of an influential and controversial writer, whose work prefigured many recent postmodern and post-colonial developments in theatre and performance studies.

The volume offers philosophical, historical, political and aesthetic readings of Genet's plays in order to render the complexity of his theatre exhilarating, rather than intimidating. It goes on to explore ways in which different directors, designers and actors have approached his writing. A spectrum of productions spanning 60 years, from 1947 to 2007, illustrates the sheer range of theatrical styles that Genet's texts inspire.

Reflecting on his early life and later political activism as well as the key plays, David Bradby and Clare Finburgh provide a comprehensive discussion of a playwright and theorist whose work caused riots in France, and whose writing represents a unique synthesis of life and art.

David Bradby (1942-2011) was Emeritus Professor of Drama and Theatre Studies at Royal Holloway University of London. He was the UK's leading specialist in modern French theatre, writing several seminal works on the subject, including *Modern French Drama* (1984, 1991) and *Le Théâtre en France* (2007). He was also a prolific translator of French dramatists, including Michel Vinaver and Bernard-Marie Koltes.

Clare Finburgh is Senior Lecturer in Modern Drama at the University of Essex. She has co-edited *Genet: Performance and Politics* (with Carl Lavery and Maria Shevtsova, 2006) and *Contemporary French Theatre and Performance* (with Carl Lavery, 2011). She has published many articles on Genet, and on a range of contemporary French and Francophone theatre-makers including Valère Novarina, Noëlle Renaude and Kateb Yacine.

ROUTLEDGE MODERN AND CONTEMPORARY DRAMATISTS

Series editors: Maggie B. Gale and Mary Luckhurst

Routledge Modern and Contemporary Dramatists is a new series of innovative and exciting critical introductions to the work of internationally pioneering playwrights. The series includes recent *and* well-established playwrights and offers primary materials on contemporary dramatists who are under-represented in secondary criticism. Each volume provides detailed cultural, historical and political material, examines selected plays in production, and theorises the playwright's artistic agenda and working methods, as well as their contribution to the development of playwriting and theatre.

Volumes currently available in the series are:

J. B. Priestley by Maggie B. Gale
Federico Garcia Lorca by Maria M. Delgado
Susan Gaspell and Sophie Treadwell by Jerry Dickey and Barbara Oziebo
August Strindberg by Eszter Szalczer
Anton Chekhov by Rose Whyman
Future volumes will include:
Mark Ravenhill by John F. Deeney
Caryl Churchill by Mary Luckhurst
Maria Irene Fornes by Scott T. Cummings
Brian Friel by Anna McMullan
Sarah Kane by Chris Megson

Jean Genet

Routledge Modern and
Contemporary Dramatists

David Bradby and Clare Finburgh

Routledge
Taylor & Francis Group

LONDON AND NEW YORK

First published 2012
by Routledge
2 Park Square, Milton Park, Abingdon, Oxon OX14 4RN

Simultaneously published in the USA and Canada
by Routledge
711 Third Avenue, New York, NY 10017

Routledge is an imprint of the Taylor & Francis Group, an informa business

British Library Cataloguing in Publication Data
A catalogue record for this book is available from the British Library

Library of Congress Cataloging in Publication Data
Bradby, David.
Jean Genet / David Bradby and Clare Finburgh.
p. cm. -- (Routledge modern and contemporary dramatists)
Includes bibliographical references and index.
1. Genet, Jean, 1910-1986--Criticism and interpretation. 2. Genet, Jean,
1910-1986--Dramatic production. 3. Genet, Jean, 1910-1986--Stage history. I.
Finburgh, Clare. II. Title.
PQ2613.E53Z574 2012
842'.912--dc22
2011022249

ISBN: 978-0-415-37504-7(hbk)
ISBN: 978-0-415-37506-1(pbk)
ISBN: 978-0-203-09891-2(ebk)

Typeset in 9.5/12 pt Sabon by
Saxon Graphics Ltd, Derby DE21 4SZ

Printed and bound in Great Britain by
TJ International Ltd, Padstow, Cornwall

Contents

List of Illustrations

Acknowledgements

We should like first to thank series editors Maggie B. Gale and Mary Luckhurst, who have followed this project patiently from the beginning, and have provided invaluable advice on both its content and its form. Niall Slater at Routledge has replied unfailingly and with promptness to our requests. Our colleagues at the Royal Holloway, University of London and the University of Essex have provided support, for which we are grateful. For their intellectual input, we should like to thank Christophe Brault, Colin Chambers, Michel Corvin, Maria Delgado, Albert Dichy, Frédéric Fisbach, Terry Hands, Carl Lavery and Tim Mathews. The Genet archives at the Institut Mémoires de l'Édition Contemporaine have been a constant source of invaluable information over the years. For help in finding illustrations and for providing publishing rights, our grateful thanks are extended to Cristèle Alves Meira, Claire Amchin, Dieter Blum, Thibaut Corrion, Yann Dejardin, Jake Green, Sébastien Rajon, Tate Modern, Victor Tonelli, Aurélie Renaud, Agnès Vannouvong and Pascal Victor. Finally, the period during which we have written this book has not been easy for reasons, some joyous, some much less so. We should therefore like to thank our families for their unending patience, support and interest. This book is dedicated to them.

Part I
Life, politics and play-texts

1 Life and politics

Jean Genet is an elusive and enigmatic figure. This is partly because he worked to make it so, and enjoyed building legends around his origins. More than most novelists or playwrights, he deliberately undermined everyday assumptions about stable identity, both his own and that of others. When giving interviews, which he did only rarely, he responded to direct questions with oblique answers and would often draw attention to what might lie hidden behind the answers he offered. He also enjoyed challenging his interlocutors with paradoxical statements, like his one-time mentor, the French playwright, film-maker and artist Jean Cocteau. He seldom indulged in self-consciously clever aphorism dear to Cocteau, such as 'I am the lie that always tells the truth,' a phrase the latter used recurrently. But Genet liked to mystify his own assertions, and would warn interviewers to treat everything he said with suspicion. To Hubert Fichte, for example, he said:

> GENET: ... If I'm alone I may speak a little truth. If I'm with someone, what I say is never completely accurate, I lie.
> FICHTE: But lies are doubly true.
> GENET: Ah yes. Discover the truth that lies within them. Discover what I wanted to hide when I told you some of these things.
>
> (Genet 1991: 176; 2004: 151, translation modified)

Coming from someone who had written a great deal in the confessional style, this statement is, and is intended to be, intriguing. When reading Genet, especially his early works of autobiographical fiction, one has constantly to be alert to what he was seeking to hide and what to reveal: in his life, just as in his fiction, the boundaries between real and imagined events are playfully unstable.

The key events in Genet's life have been recorded in several different versions, with the result that some uncertainties can never be resolved. No doubt this is fitting, given his resistance to conventional ways of thinking about identity. Throughout his life, Genet worked hard to maintain a distance between himself and conventional society. For example, he took care to avoid accumulating possessions and seldom had a fixed home, living a vagabond existence in various kinds of temporary accommodation. He could not have featured in the Sunday newspaper series which prints a photograph of the author's study, since he never possessed one. He was always on the move, and tended to gravitate towards cheap hotels close to the railway station of whatever town he found himself in. For Albert Dichy, director of Genet's archives and editor of many of his late writings, 'Genet's entire work is one long declaration of war.... There are two sides, two camps: on the one hand the world; on the other, Genet himself' (Dichy 1997: 21). In order to maintain his distance from commonly accepted moral codes, Genet made a virtue out of betrayal: he betrayed friends and foes alike and once wrote that it had cost him an effort to betray his friends but that it was worth it (Genet 2002: 888).

The story of Genet's life is further complicated by the fact that those who have written about him, beginning in 1952 with French Marxist-existentialist philosopher, novelist and playwright Jean-Paul Sartre, have mostly framed their accounts within their own theories of how he came to be who he was. These accounts differ not only from one another but also from Genet's own version of his life story, and so it is no simple matter to set out the events of his life. These problems were well understood by his biographer Edmund White who, while admitting that 'there's something very elusive about a life', nevertheless succeeded in constructing a plausible and highly readable account (White 1994). The details that follow here are mostly drawn from White's biography, and the reader is referred to its 820 pages for more expansive elaborations of the facts, as far as they can ever be known, and for judicious accounts of the varying possible interpretations of the elements that are disputed.

Genet's birth certificate states that he was born in Paris, at the Tarnier Childbirth Clinic at 89, rue d'Assas on 19 December 1910. His mother, Camille Genet, was single, aged 22, and his father unknown; she was to die less than ten years later at the height of the great Spanish influenza epidemic that killed millions in the winter of 1918–19. But she had little influence on the young Jean, since she looked after him only for the first seven months of his life, and then abandoned him to the care of the Hospice des Enfants-Assistés on 28 July 1911. Edmund White points out that Genet himself, in *The Thief's Journal* (*Journal du voleur*), gives a different first name (Gabrielle) for his mother, and a different street number for the hospital in which he was born (White 1994: 9). So from the very beginning, key facts are disputed. The young Genet was officially declared a ward of the *Assistance publique* (public welfare service) and sent to its fostering agency in Saulieu, which placed him with Eugénie and Charles Régnier in the small rural village of Alligny-en-Morvan (ibid.: 5–11). His foster-father was a carpenter and his foster-mother ran a small tobacconist's shop. They undertook to bring up the baby boy until he should reach the age of 13, in return for which they received a monthly payment from the State. The family was pious, and the child was brought up as a Catholic: he was baptized in September 1910 and took his first communion in 1922. The Régnier family house was situated between the church and the village school. Genet appears to have responded well to the opportunities for instruction offered by both institutions: 'Genet was teacher's pet but also helped the abbé at mass and sang in the choir' (ibid.: 17).

So a few of the basic facts at least are unambiguous: Genet's first 13 years were spent in the country, where he was cared for by a foster family, was brought up in the Catholic faith and was a good pupil. At the conclusion of his primary schooling, when his year-group took the standard examination to qualify for the certificate of primary education, he passed out first in his district, the only one to receive the grade of *bien* ('good'). But how was this experience received by the growing boy? The various accounts by Genet himself suggest that it was far from being a fulfilled childhood. His status as a foundling meant that he was always stamped as an outsider: the foundlings wore a special uniform which marked them out in the village. Many of the families who took them in treated them as little better than slaves, even though Genet was more fortunate, and seems to have been well cared for by Eugénie Régnier, at least in the early years of his placement with her. Another pointer to an unfulfilled childhood is the fact that he began to steal at an early age, something that is emphasized both in Genet's own accounts and in the recorded memories of others in the same village.

His early thefts provide a classic example of the contested interpretations of Genet's childhood. Sartre, his first biographer, painted a vivid scene, much quoted since, in which the boy's thieving was made the occasion of a public humiliation. At this point, in Sartre's existentialist interpretation, Genet made the foundational choice which brought into being the character he was to become: he decided that if society chose to brand him as a thief, he would accept the label and would devote himself to pursuing everything that was the opposite of a moral code founded on the sanctity of property (Sartre 1952: 61–88). Edmund White, however, can find no hard evidence that such a public humiliation really took place. In his view, the formative experiences on the development of the young Genet were those of love given and then withdrawn: first, the loss of his mother at seven months, then being cherished by his foster-mother, only to be displaced in her affections in 1918 (still only seven years old) when her own son returned from the trenches suffering from a wounded leg. With hindsight, White sees Genet as 'eternally suspended between the two systems', namely the Nietzschean will to self-definition through creating his own value system on the one hand, and the Christian ideal of renunciation, poverty and transcendence of the merely material through spiritual adventure on the other (White 1994: 43).

Genet's early novels, which all contain a strong autobiographical element, emphasize the possibilities of transcendence as found in the traditions of the Catholic saints' lives. Their titles make this plain:

Our Lady of the Flowers (*Notre-Dame-des-Fleurs*), *Miracle of the Rose* (*Miracle de la rose*); and their focus is on moments when grim or painful physical realities are transformed into ecstatic visions. The concept of sainthood was never absent from Genet's writings, albeit subverted in many different ways, and he embodied a very Catholic scorn for material security combined with a permanent awareness of death. In his last interview (for the BBC) in 1985, when asked how he spent his days, he answered: 'Well, I shall reply as St. Augustine did: "I'm waiting for death"' (Genet 1991: 306; 2004: 265). The evident attraction of saintly renunciation on Genet, which retained its power from childhood to old age, sits curiously with the dominant tone of his early prose writings, in which he was fond of depicting himself as a 'tough guy'. Doubtless these two apparently contradictory qualities both found their origin in Genet's abiding sense of the separation between himself and the rest of society, a separation that he sought to emphasize, not to eradicate. This emphasis no doubt explains his appeal to other artists who see themselves as outsiders, and his construction as gay icon in the 1970s and 1980s. From playwright Heiner Müller, whose mix of poetic inventiveness and political engagement rivals that of Genet, to US punk rock singer and poet Patti Smith, and sexually subversive photographer Robert Mapplethorpe, Genet has inspired artists the world over.

The quality that all accounts of the young Genet agree on, is his fertile imagination. He was free to borrow books from the school library and became a passionate reader from an early age. He read the French classics as a matter of course, but his great love was for boys' adventure tales, especially those of Paul Féval, a nineteenth-century author who specialized in cloak-and-dagger stories of daring criminals. His titles include *Les Mystères de Londres* (*The Mysteries of London*); *Le Roi des gueux* (*The Vagabond King*); *Le Mendiant noir* (*The Black Beggar*).[1] All those who knew him in his first 13 years testified to his love of books and to this was added the attractions of popular films when travelling cinemas visited the village, beginning what White calls 'his life-long infatuation with film' (White 1994: 26, 27).

It was not only the content and the images of popular fiction that exerted their fascination on the growing Genet. He also experienced an enthralment with the stuff of language itself. White picks out many examples of his delight in word-play and the association of ideas that comes from repeating words in such a way that one slips into another. For example, he transformed his childhood friend Solange Comte into *la comtesse* Solange ('Countess Solange') and loved to play on words, as in the example from *The Thief's Journal*: 'My life must be a legend, in other words, legible, and the reading of it must give birth to a certain new emotion which I call poetry. I am no longer anything, only a pretext' (Genet 1982: 98). As Edmund White states in the first line of the introduction to his biography, 'Genet had remarkable powers of self-transformation' (White 1994: xxxix), and in these two sentences from *The Thief's Journal* we see how he enjoyed playing with language in pursuit of self-transformation: he announces his intention to transform his life into something that can be *read*, a text that will not only be 'leg-ible' but will have a 'leg-endary' quality, thus making his lived experience into nothing but a 'pre-text' – an excuse for, but also the preliminary to, a text directed at readers. Genet's own versions of his childhood are thus all coloured by his early intention to confabulate his own legend, turning his life into fiction, and any understanding of how Genet experienced his childhood years must take account of the profound link that he saw between childhood and writing. His first books were all semi-autobiographical accounts of young men, sometimes very innocent, sometimes less so, but all facing the harsh facts of life, desire and death and the power struggles that are a part of all human relations at every level of the social hierarchy. In an interview given towards the end of his life he stressed that, for twentieth-century authors at least, to write was always to speak of childhood, citing Proust as the leading example of this (Genet 1991: 277; 2004: 239).

Although he had demonstrated his remarkable intelligence and aptitude for school work, no provision was made for him to attend secondary school. However, his scholastic success did allow him to escape the fate of the other orphans of his year-group, which was to be put to farm work as soon as their primary schooling was complete. Instead, arrangements were made for Genet to begin an apprenticeship as a printer at a residential college near Paris. To be sent to this college was quite a privilege, but after only a couple of weeks he ran away, announcing to his fellow students that he was off to America or to Egypt, where he would get a job in a cinema (Dichy 2002: lxxx). He was picked up by the police a few days later in Nice. In April 1925 the public welfare officers gave Genet a second chance, placing him with René de Buxeuil, a blind composer of popular songs living in Paris, who had asked if they could supply him with a boy to help him get around. Little is known of exactly how Genet reacted to his new position, but it seems that he took the opportunity to learn all he could about writing songs and poetry. In an interview, Buxeuil also stated that the adolescent had already decided to write his memoirs under a false name (Moraly 1988: 28).[2]

Genet spent longer in the Buxeuil household than he had at the printing college. It was not until six months had elapsed that he stole some money and was sent back to the welfare service. He then underwent psychiatric observation at the Saint-Anne clinic in Paris. The psychiatrist's report detected 'a certain degree of weakness and mental instability' (Dichy 2002: lxxx) and recommended that he be placed with a youth organization. He was confided to a charitable institution whose mission was to assess the youths placed in its care and decide what sort of work they were capable of doing. Genet lasted two months before running away and being picked up by the police in Marseille and returned under police escort to Paris. But he soon ran away again, was picked up on a train heading for Bordeaux, and was imprisoned for three months at La Petite Roquette, a prison for adolescents awaiting trial, in which a rule of absolute silence was enforced. After this, he was given a last chance by the authorities, who placed him as a farm hand with a peasant family near Abbeville in the north of France. But he ran away yet again and was arrested in Meaux in July 1926 for travelling on a train without a ticket. He was sentenced to be detained at the youth penitentiary of Mettray in the Loire Valley until he reached the age of majority, 21.

The life of the boys at Mettray was governed by strict military discipline. Every moment of the day, from when they were woken (at five in the summer and at six in winter) to when they went to bed at nine, was accounted for, mostly with repetitive manual tasks; the punishments handed out for the smallest infringements were so harsh that many of the inmates attempted suicide, some successfully. In his interview with the BBC, Genet remarks that the discipline was so severe that he was surprised that the French authorities found responsible men willing to take on the work (Genet 1991: 299; 2004: 258). Paradoxically, Genet appears to have achieved a kind of happiness there. It was his first experience of living in a closed society in which the rules of normal, heterosexual family life were set aside in favour of a different kind of power structure. Each new inmate was assigned to one of the so-called 'families', but these were families in name only. They consisted of dormitory blocks in which 30 boys would sleep, in hammocks, under the supervision of an older inmate singled out for this role and known as the 'senior brother' (*frère aîné*). From nine at night until the following morning, they were shut in and left to their own devices. In this atmosphere, the way to survive was to accept the role of young 'squire' to one of the more powerful, older boys. Genet appears to have taken well to this regime and to have enjoyed the rituals of submission and domination that flourished there. Looking back on the experience, he emphasized its theatrical quality: 'I believe that the relationships between the senior brother (the one placed in authority) and the other boys like me (whose relation was one of submission) produced a performance which the warders viewed with pleasure' (ibid.; translation modified). This emerges with great clarity in Genet's first and only completed film *Song of Love* (*Un chant d'amour*, 1950) and his play *Deathwatch*.

White emphasizes the erotic delights that Genet discovered, perhaps for the first time, at Mettray, and believes that it was his two and a half years there that did most to shape his future as a writer. He quotes Genet as saying that it was at Mettray, at the age of 15, that he began to write.[3] He then makes the interesting claim that 'for Genet "writing" was more a habit of mind, a way of sorting out powerful emotions, than of crafting sentences' (White 1994: 85). White's emphasis on the way the young Genet's feelings were shaped in this adolescent prison contains an important insight:

How did he organize his feelings at Mettray? In precisely the same way that he would later animate his novels – around the themes of honour and treason, of domination and submission, of authenticity and dissembling, of fidelity and flirtation. In

Mettray's medieval hierarchy Genet learned to be the page, the cabin boy, the vassal, even the coquette. He felt for the first time the quick, intense desire of rivalry, love and loss.

(ibid.).

White argues that Genet's writing began as action rather than reflection, growing out of the behaviour he adopted in response to the interplay of powerful feelings aroused in him by the experience he underwent at Mettray. In 'The Criminal Child' ('L'Enfant criminel'), a text written for a radio broadcast in 1948 (but censored at the last minute), he celebrated the rigours of Mettray and deplored the campaign by prison reformers that had led to its closure. He expressed his admiration for young boys learning to devote themselves to evil, declaring: 'As for me I have chosen to be on the side of crime' (Genet 1979: 388–9). It is worth remembering that at this time homosexuality was a crime, with the result that Genet was bound to feel outlawed by right-thinking society. His way of overcoming this was to glamorize it and to make it into a positive choice, going far beyond the attitude taken up by many other homosexuals at this time. As Dichy expresses it, he declared war on society (Dichy 1997: 21). This was to enhance further his reputation as a counter-cultural icon among later artists.

Despite the romantic glamour he attributed to the rigorous life at Mettray, and his delight in being part of an exclusively male, criminal society, with its special *argot* and its own rituals, Genet's itch for travel must have made this penitentiary existence hard to tolerate. He ran away once, after a year and a half, and finally escaped for good in March 1929 by volunteering for the army. His unit was sent to Damascus in 1930 and to Meknes in Morocco from 1931 to 1933. This period of military service left him plenty of time to read, and he appears to have taken the opportunity. He later claimed to have read everything that fell into his hands, discovering the joys of pulp fiction and *Détective* magazine alongside the works of Dostoevsky, French novelist André Gide and many others. In 1934 Genet's period of engagement came to an end and he was at last free to wander as he had always wanted. He attempted to contact a number of writers whose work had impressed him by their willingness to deal with homosexual desire, notably Gide. He secured a meeting with Gide, appealing to him for financial help on this and several subsequent occasions. He then travelled through France to Spain, spending some time in Barcelona and seeking out bars and cheap hotels in the rundown *barri gòtic*, where he encountered a range of underworld characters, many of whom are described or embroidered upon in *The Thief's Journal*.

A year later, he signed up for four more years in the army. This time he was transferred to the elite Moroccan Colonial Infantry Regiment, a company that saw itself as the rival of the French Foreign Legion. Genet later claimed that he had been in the Legion, but this was just an example of how he preferred, as White has it, 'glamorous near-truths' to the supposed facts. He spent eight months at the Regiment's barracks in Aix-en-Provence before he felt the pull of the open road again and deserted in June 1936. There followed a year of wandering in central Europe, which took him to Italy, Albania, Yugoslavia and Austria. He was arrested several times for theft and other infringements, and was expelled from both Albania and Yugoslavia. He took refuge in Brno, Czechoslovakia, where he requested political asylum. In January 1937 he was taken under the wing of the local League of the Rights of Man and spent some months living with one of the members of the League, Lily Pringsheim. He appears to have left a number of manuscripts with her, though these are now lost (Dichy 2002: lxxxii). He made a little money by giving French lessons to the wife of a Jewish industrialist, Anna Bloch, to whom he became very attached, maintaining a correspondence with her for some time. These letters too were lost for decades, but came to light after his death and were published in 1988.

He then returned to France via Poland, Germany and Belgium. Back in Paris, he was arrested for theft, discovered to be a deserter and condemned to eight months in prison. In the subsequent four years, while France underwent military defeat and occupation by the German army, Genet remained in or around Paris and was arrested eight times for theft – usually of small items, especially books. He sometimes sold the books he had stolen at one of the small *bouquiniste* stalls on the banks of the Seine in Paris. During his frequent stays in prison he began to write, trying his hand at all three literary genres:

prose with *Our Lady of the Flowers*, drama with *For 'the Beautiful One' (Pour 'la Belle')*, whose title later changed to *Deathwatch (Haute Surveillance)*, and poetry with 'Le Condamné à mort' ('The Prisoner Condemned to Death'), his first work to be published (a small print run of 100 copies at his own expense) in 1942. Both works demonstrate Genet's extraordinary mastery of style, employing the most exquisite classical French to express passionate emotions that leap off the page with striking authenticity. 'The Man Condemned to Death' is a poem of 65 regular four-line verses celebrating his love for Maurice Pilorge, a man condemned to the guillotine who was executed in 1939. Its juxtaposition of classical versification with explicit images of gay sexual gratification in a startling mixture of literary and low-life vocabulary charmed Cocteau when he read it, and paved the way to Genet's escape from the cycle of repeated crime and imprisonment.

The prose works he wrote at this time, part autobiography, part fiction, were his way of affirming the life he had chosen to lead. They celebrate life on the margins and glamorize those whom most people would think of as despicable: pimps, murderers, robbers. Genet often pointed out that popular thrillers, detective fiction and films about daring crimes did exactly the same thing, while illogically ensuring a conclusion in which law and order are respected after all. He claimed that his work was more 'honest' in exploring the attractions of criminality without condemning it at the last minute. These writings were his way of affirming his identity as a radical outsider. From the first page of *Our Lady of the Flowers*, he addresses his reader as *you* (*vous*) and attributes to the reader all the values shared by bourgeois society. He then proceeds, quite deliberately and explicitly, to draw this bourgeois reader into a state of mind in which s/he finds her/himself seduced by people and events that s/he would normally condemn as evil. The prose is sumptuous, especially in the passages where it recreates for the reader a scene of ordinary prison life transformed by the power of Genet's imagination into an ecstatic vision, drawing strongly on traditional Catholic iconography. At several points in the narrative, Genet explicitly comments on his love of imposture, theatricality, transvestites. Through the power of his prose, he transforms his prison cells into places of erotic adventure and spiritual enlightenment, where those condemned to death for the worst crimes may suddenly be transfigured and garlanded with flowers as in the appearance of some medieval saint.

Looking back over the various legends of his life, which Genet carefully constructs through his writings up until 1945, one is still struck by their originality and their protean quality, which makes them resist straightforward psychological explanations. For Genet specialist Jean-Bernard Moraly, the key to understanding Genet's project lay in his determination to master a literary idiom that would allow him to give lasting shape to the figures that thronged his fertile imagination. For Sartre, Genet chose his status as thief, homosexual and outsider as the only way available to him of affirming his freedom in the face of the oppression he experienced as a foster-child. For White, Genet's homosexuality and his thefts are intimately linked: the first sexual experience of the effeminate boy (as Genet is described in official reports) is to

> 'steal' the gestures of his idol.... The first act of homosexual love, then, is impersonation, but since he knew of the taboo, Genet links the guilt of theft to the guilt of homosexuality, which is another way of stealing, another form of forbidden appropriation.
>
> (White 1994: 38)

White disputes the theory of a progression in Genet's work, commonly accepted ever since it was proposed by Sartre, from the closed, private world of poetry to the more open form of the novel, and finally to the public, political nature of his plays. He disagrees with Sartre's Marxist-existentialist view that Genet's later writings, which tackle the world stage, treat more public or social concerns than his earlier works. White argues that, being conscious of being placed in a false position – a false son, a false pious choirboy, a false villager – Genet acquired an early understanding of social role-play. We have already noted Genet's comments on the theatrical nature of life at Mettray. White maintains that everything about his formative years developed this theatrical sensibility, and puts forward the view that

Theatre is the root form behind all of Genet's work; he had already written several scripts for the stage and screen before his first published works.... Genet conceived of conflict as theatrical. In a sense, he could never afford the luxury of inner strife or philosophical doubt. For him, there was a single reality, the world of power relations in society, and it oppressed him. His first task was to learn how to manipulate this reality through guile or charm or even sometimes intimidation – in short, though play-acting.

(ibid.: 39)

The manuscript of his first play, *For 'the Beautiful One'*, was completed in October 1942, having been written during a six-month spell in prison for the theft of books. It therefore pre-dates much of his prose work. Early in 1943 Genet was introduced to Cocteau, who had read and admired 'The Man Condemned to Death'. Cocteau was charmed, and offered to find ways to publishing more work by this unexpected young writer. When Genet was caught again, in May 1943, stealing a rare edition of poems by Verlaine, Cocteau organized his defence and testified in his favour before the court. During his stay in prison he worked on *Miracle of the Rose*. Released, and almost immediately caught once more stealing books, Genet spent the rest of the year in the Santé prison in Paris working on the manuscripts of five plays, since lost: *Hélioglobale*, *Journée castillane*, *Persée*, *Don Juan* and *Les Guerriers nus* (Dichy 2002: lxxxiii). Cocteau continued to act as Genet's guardian angel, and it was through him that Genet came to have *The Maids* (*Les Bonnes*) produced by Louis Jouvet in 1947. To be put on by Jouvet was a great honour: he was one of the most celebrated directors, known for having introduced work by both Cocteau and Jean Giraudoux to French audiences in the inter-war period. Genet was dazzled by the concern shown him by Cocteau, a mercurial figure, who had managed to remain in favour both with the Nazi authorities and with avant-garde writers and artists. He was influenced by him for the rest of the 1940s and copied him closely for a few years before falling out with him (see White 1994: 222). From Cocteau, he learned to construct a poetic persona that could claim the freedom of the creative artist as justification for behaviour that would otherwise be censured. Cocteau encouraged him to work across a wide range of artistic disciplines including poetry, prose and drama. Like Cocteau he wrote a ballet, and like him, Genet also attempted to make films.

Paris in 1944, in the months leading up to its liberation from German occupation in August, experienced a fever of literary and theatrical activity. A young generation of writers, of whom the most prominent were French left-wing playwright and novelist Albert Camus and Sartre, seemed to incarnate a new view of the world, stripped of all illusions, one that was in tune with a period when the whole population had experienced violence in one form or another, and when many of what the French had thought of as their traditional values had been found wanting. The opening of Sartre's play *No Exit* (*Huis clos*) in May 1944, for example, was seen as heralding a new style of existentialist theatre. Genet attended one of the first performances in the company of Cocteau. In the view of Michel Corvin and Dichy, co-editors of Genet's complete theatrical works, this exposure to Sartre's play influenced Genet's rewriting of *Deathwatch* (Corvin and Dichy 2002: 1016).[4] *No Exit* had been published a few weeks earlier in the eighth number of the literary review *L'Arbalète*, the same issue in which a chapter of *Our Lady of the Flowers* had appeared. In the atmosphere of a city where survival was a desperate struggle and where the distinction between criminals and heroic resistance fighters was sometimes blurred, the emergence of new work by a convict writer seemed somehow fitting: in the restricted circle of the Paris literary world, the name of Jean Genet 'was on everyone's lips' (White 1994: 287). By the time of the Liberation, most of Genet's major prose work was complete, and publication followed fairly rapidly. In 1946 *Miracle of the Rose* came out, followed in 1948 by the first official edition of *Our Lady of the Flowers*, previously available only in a clandestine edition (brought out at the end of 1943 by Robert Denoël but carrying no publisher's name). Meanwhile, impressed by the enthusiasm of Cocteau and of his stage designer Christian Bérard, the celebrated director Louis Jouvet agreed to stage *The Maids* at his theatre; after much rewriting, the text, together with *Deathwatch*, was published in March and April 1947 in the literary revue *La Nef*, and *The Maids* opened on 19

April 1947 at the Athénée theatre. *Deathwatch* followed at the Mathurins theatre in February 1949 (see Chapter 4 for accounts of both productions). In the meantime, Genet had become a celebrity. He was invited to script a ballet, *'adame Mirror*, performed by the Ballets de Paris at the Marigny theatre in May 1948, and in July of that year a petition signed by 45 writers and artists, headed by Cocteau and Sartre, was sent to the French President Vincent Auriol requesting that a special dispensation be granted to waive his possible imprisonment as a serial offender; the public pardon was ultimately delivered in August 1949.

In the course of the next five years, Genet once again spent time travelling around Europe and appears to have experienced something of a mental crisis. This was partly due to the publication in 1952 of Sartre's exhaustive essay on him as Volume 1 of his complete works. Genet felt crushed by the comprehensive existentialist psychoanalysis to which he was subjected in this book – he told Cocteau that he and Sartre together had turned him into a statue and they had subjected him to a kind of psychological castration (White 1994: 438). Around the same period, he had an experience which appears to have brought about a change of direction in his sense of his relationship to society at large. The period of the late 1930s and 1940s had been, for Genet, a time when he partly discovered and partly constructed an identity for himself as an outsider to mainstream society, one that depended on his ability to celebrate gay and criminal subcultures through his writing. He was able to maintain a distance, at least in his imagination, from the political and social upheavals caused by war, occupation and resistance, because he lived as someone with nothing at stake – nothing to lose and nothing to gain from the battles between fascists and anti-fascists. In fact, of course, he was in serious danger of being sent to a concentration camp (as many prisoners were); he only escaped this fate in 1944 through the intervention of Cocteau and other such protectors, who were convinced of his exceptional literary talent.

The image he had built up for himself relied precisely on this notion of his exceptional outsider status. Moreover, his writing had restricted itself to celebrating a closed-off world – that of the criminal underclass and of convicts confined within the walls of their prison. The one film he completed, *Song of Love*, was made in 1950 at the conclusion of this period; it stands as perhaps Genet's most extreme celebration of how the convict's imagination may, paradoxically, be liberated by confinement to a bare prison cell, transforming him into something approaching a medieval anchorite. In the film, the convicts depicted are very conscious of being spied on by the warders and respond by openly manifesting their contempt and hostility. Genet's whole mental and spiritual development, from childhood until his late thirties, depended on establishing his radical separation from and indifference to social norms and to the vast majority of the population. His own narrow world, enhanced by his transformative flights of fancy, and the richly expressive language he fashioned in order to express its fascination, was sufficient. He did not need to look outside. Now, however, with the ending of wartime conditions, in which normal social conventions are inevitably set aside, and with his growing recognition, Genet found himself obliged to take notice of the wider world. He began to realize how successful Cocteau was at keeping in with fashionable society, and became disillusioned with him. When the publication of Sartre's monumentally long study was the literary event of 1952, Genet found himself thrust still further into the public eye. Where many writers would have been delighted to have achieved such recognition, Genet found it crushing. Being defined so exhaustively by Sartre, he felt he had become a fixed character – just what he had been attempting to avoid all his life. He went into a depression.

His experiences during this period seem to have come to a head one day in an episode that he only wrote down in detail some dozen years later, attached to a fragment of an essay about Rembrandt, but which occurred some time in the early 1950s (the precise date is nowhere recorded). The experience was so radical as to make him feel that his whole outlook on the world had changed. It involved an encounter in a third-class railway carriage in Provence. His description of the event uses very forcible language to express his sense of disintegration:

> Some sort of putrefaction was corroding my former vision of the world, like gangrene. When one day, in a carriage, watching the

passenger seated opposite me, I had the revelation that every man *is worth* every other, I did not suspect ... that this would bring about such a systematic disintegration.

(Genet 1968: 21).

The passenger in question was not especially remarkable; Genet adds that he looked very ordinary, even ugly, and describes his moustache and mouth as revolting. But as their eyes met, he experienced a shock – he felt that the legendary singularity he had constructed for himself, his separation from the common herd, was dissolving into a disturbing awareness that in fact there was nothing of any significance to differentiate one human from another: all were interchangeable (ibid.: 22).

This moment of revelation seems to have crystallized a sense of the need for a new direction in his imaginative and fictional response to the world he lived in. His lush, private fictions, written in the form of intimate dialogues with the reader, gave way to a more public art form: when he began to write again, he was to concentrate on theatre, producing in the second half of the 1950s his three major plays: *The Balcony* (*Le Balcon*); *The Blacks* (*Les Nègres*) and *The Screens* (*Les Paravents*). Whereas the dramas in the early plays had concerned small, intimate groups, the action of these three plays involves the whole of society at every level, from royalty to revolutionaries, and extends to most social institutions – the police, the law courts, the army, the church, the political class, the press. Only the educational establishment is spared, perhaps because it was precisely here that the seeds of Genet's literary life were sown. Once he had started writing again, Genet worked fast, completing the first versions of *The Balcony* and *The Blacks* as well as the one-act *She* (*Elle*) in 1955. In the same year, he began to sketch out *The Mothers* (*Les Mères*), later to become *The Screens*, on which he continued to work for the next two years, completing a first version in 1958. He then rewrote it almost entirely between 1959 and 1961, while also drafting another new play *The Penal Colony* (*Le Bagne*), which he never completed.

Towards the end of 1955, he met Abdallah Bentaga, described by White as 'the lover who would leave the deepest mark (one might say scar) on him' (White 1994: 509). The child of a German mother and

Algerian father, Abdallah was an 18-year-old circus performer, a juggler and acrobat. Genet, who was entering into the period of his life when he could live off his royalties, paid for Abdallah to have high-wire lessons and followed him around Europe as he trained and then performed on the tightrope. Inspired by Abdallah, Genet wrote 'Le Funambule' ('The Tightrope Walker'), a mixture of love-letter, prose poem and reflection on the perils of life as an artist. To ensure a stable base for Abdallah's developing career, Genet even took a flat in Paris for a time, instead of living, as he preferred, in hotel rooms. Having found a new voice, as it were, Genet seemed more content to play his part in the Parisian arts world. He set a certain distance between himself and the gay circle around Cocteau, and encountered other strong creative personalities who influenced him in their turn. Among these was the Paris-based Swiss artist Alberto Giacometti, for whom he sat, and subsequently wrote an appreciative essay, *The Studio of Alberto Giacometti* (*L'Atelier d'Alberto Giacometti*). Another was Roger Blin, the ascetic theatre director who had been responsible for the first productions of Beckett's *Waiting for Godot* and *Endgame*. Blin was to direct the first productions of *The Blacks* (1959) and *The Screens* (1966). In Blin, Genet discovered someone who shared many of his views and ways of dealing with the world: a profound commitment to the oppressed and dispossessed, together with a strong antipathy to political groupings, systems and ideologies.

As well as following Abdallah's progress, Genet was now being solicited for permission to perform his plays. *The Maids* was given the first of many professional revivals by an influential Russian-born actor-trainer, Tania Balachova, in 1954 at the théâtre de la Huchette and was produced in English by Peter Zadek in 1956. Genet travelled to London for this production, where he met the director Peter Brook. Brook wanted the rights to direct *The Balcony* in Paris, since Zadek was already planning a London production for 1957 – Brook would finally succeed in 1960, the same year that the play also received its New York première, directed by José Quintero (see Chapters 4 and 5 for discussions of these productions). Since 1948, Bernard Frechtman had been translating Genet's works into English and had also acted as his agent in the United States. *Our Lady of the Flowers* quickly became a key novel for the young generation of oppositional poets

Figure 1   Alberto Giacometti, *Jean Genet*, 1954 or 1955, oil on
canvas. Tate, London, 2011.

know as 'the Beats', and in the course of the 1950s Genet's American
earnings grew steadily. In Frechtman he had an admirer who devoted
himself full-time to translating his work, representing his commercial
interests, and making sure that his work was at the forefront of
avant-garde literary developments in North America. Genet was thus
brought into contact with a very wide range of people, all of whom
had an interest in his work. He began to visit Greece, which for some

years became his favoured place of retreat when he found the demands of translators, producers, agents and admirers too much. He had signed a deal with the prestigious French publishing house Gallimard for the publication of his complete works early in the 1950s, and from then on he treated the publisher as his personal bank. He constantly demanded advances on his royalties, and whatever country he found himself in, if he was short of cash, he would seek out the local representative of Gallimard and expect money.

The period of the late 1950s was one of intense political upheaval in France. The war in Algeria, where French troops had been trying to contain an independence struggle and maintain direct rule from Paris, was building to a crisis. In 1958, this crisis was resolved by General de Gaulle returning to power: in 1959 he presided over the inauguration of a revised constitution which became the Fifth Republic. De Gaulle met fierce opposition, and was nearly overthrown by an army-led coup, but in 1962 he succeeded in bringing the war to an end and granting Algeria its independence from France. Beforehand, however, there were regular terrorist attacks in Paris and a siege atmosphere in which intellectuals took sides with either the independence fighters or the French army. In 1960, for example, a famous manifesto known as *The Manifesto of the 121* (*Le Manifeste des 121*) was published, including the signatures of 121 left-wing writers and creative artists in France, protesting against the use of torture by the French army in Algeria and insisting on the right of the Algerian people to self-determination. The government marked its displeasure at such intervention by banning all those who had signed from working on any of the state-owned broadcasting stations, a ban that lasted for several years. The manifesto was published in *Vérité pour*, a clandestine newsletter which also encouraged French soldiers to desert and declared its support for the Algerian independence fighters. Genet was unwilling to sign, but gave practical help: when Francis Jeanson, who published *Vérité pour*, had to go underground, Genet was one of those who provided him with a hiding place. Genet also encouraged Abdallah to desert when he was called up for French military service (White 1994: 511), with the result that Abdallah had to live and work outside France for several years.

Genet's view of the writer's political responsibility at this time was clear, and stated on many occasions, most notably in the prefaces to *The Balcony* and *The Blacks* (see Chapter 3). He considered that the task of theatre was not to advocate political solutions, not to condemn injustice, but to present images of the power of evil, so formidable as to create a kind of explosion in the minds of its audience. He claimed that power always hides behind theatricality, and that therefore the only way to expose its workings in contemporary society is to push that theatricality to its limit. Genet's understanding of what is meant by 'theatricality' is complex, and very relevant to contemporary debates about 'liveness' in performance (see Bradby 2006). Moreover, the complex relationships he builds between symbolic imagination and political reality in his plays have become exemplary for new approaches to political theatre (see Finburgh *et al*.: 2006: 55–91). His three major plays of the late 1950s all explore the consequences of political oppression. *The Balcony* calls into question the enduring myths of class power and revolution in the West; *The Blacks* deals with the postcolonial struggle to resist the cultural and linguistic hegemony of the former colonial power; *The Screens* goes much further: as well as depicting Arabs in revolt against French rule, it satirizes the French army in terms so extreme that its first production, in 1966, four years *after* the conclusion of hostilities in Algeria, provoked riots in Paris and questions in parliament (see Chapter 6). None of these are plays in the classical sense of the term; they are not organized around a central story or event in the way that *Deathwatch* and *The Maids* had been. They are best described as ceremonies: ceremonies designed to exorcise and transform. They could be seen as strategies for overcoming the oppression of the figures they depict, all of whom have been deprived in some way of their subjectivity and forced to live through the eyes of others.

Although the idiom of these plays differs considerably from the prose works of the 1940s, there are many links between them. Two of the most evident are Genet's use of direct address and his interest in transformation. Just as his first prose work had begun with the phrase, 'Weidmann appeared to *you* in the five o'clock edition' (Genet 1951: 9), so the late plays all contain characters who make a direct appeal to the audience. In *The Blacks*, Genet goes so far as to include a prefatory note in which he specifies that his play, written by a white man, is intended for a white audience; in the unlikely event of the audience being entirely black, a white person should be invited every evening: 'The organiser of the show should welcome him formally, dress him in ceremonial costume and lead him to his seat, preferably in the front row of the stalls. The actors will play for him' (Genet 2002: 475; 1960: 4). At frequent points in the play, the character named Archibald, who acts as a Master of Ceremonies, addresses the audience directly, as in his opening speech which concludes, 'We embellish ourselves so as to please you. You are White. And spectators. This evening we shall perform for you' (Genet 2002: 480; 1960: 10). Similarly, *The Balcony* concludes with Madame Irma's direct address to the audience: 'You must go home, now – and you can be quite sure that nothing there will be any more real than it is here' (Genet 2002: 350; 1991a: 96).

Genet's fascination with the process of imaginative transformation of place or person finds its natural outlet in theatre, and all of the late plays make explicit reference to the most fundamental feature of all play-acting: that a person puts on a costume in order to 'become' someone else. This is most strikingly presented in the opening scene of *The Balcony*, which shows a man taking off the costume in which he has just enacted his fantasy of being transformed into a bishop; and this is followed by two scenes depicting first a judge and then a general who turn out to be a false judge and general who dress up in the appropriate costumes for the thrill that the power-play affords.

The most political of the three plays is *The Screens*, since it depicts the revolt of Arabs against colonial settlers and their army, who are satirized in various ways. And yet this is no simple declaration of support for the anticolonial cause, since the Arabs too appear ridiculous and impotent. The sense in which this play may be seen to make a political comment is extremely complex, and Chapters 2 and 3 are devoted to exploring *The Screens* and Genet's other plays in detail. The relationship between the events depicted and the political realities of revolution, decolonization and liberation in the world of the late 1950s is not a simple one. But Genet was undoubtedly sincere when he wrote, in his foreword to the second published edition of *The Balcony*, that political problems need to be resolved by political action in the real world, and that problems explored in creative works should never be resolved in the imaginary realm: 'On the contrary, let evil explode on stage, show us naked, leave us haggard and if possible with no recourse except to ourselves' (Genet 2002: 261; 1991a: xiv, translation modified).

This was the period when Genet was becoming known all over the world, and was constantly being solicited for his advice about how to solve the production problems posed by his plays. He wrote a series of declarations about how they should be performed, of which the most detailed are letters to Roger Blin about the latter's production of *The Screens* (Genet 2002: 815–76; 1972: 7–60). Although an invaluable source of insight into how Genet viewed the theatre, these provide no easy answers to the practicalities of mounting the plays. Instead they constitute a meditation on the status of the work of art, its limits and its possibilities. These are supplemented by a number of other short writings on theatre that Genet published around this time, notably 'The Strange Word...' ('L'Étrange Mot d ...'), first published in 1967 in no. 30 of the prestigious French review *Tel Quel* (Genet 2002: 879–88; 2003: 103–12). But although these essays, letters and reflections demonstrate a very close engagement on the part of the author with questions of acting, of theatricality, and the many ways in which meaning is generated in performance, Genet mostly avoided attending rehearsals. When *The Blacks* was first staged in Paris in 1959, he even avoided attending the production itself, despite its considerable success. He later saw Blin's revival of the play in London and was so impressed that he put a note into the published edition of the play saying that Blin had achieved perfection, and that all future editions of the play would be obliged to include photographs of the original.

In 1959 Abdallah fell from the tightrope and injured his knee; he then began training for a horseback act, but Genet, who felt that his high-wire performance (under Genet's own guidance) had been an act of genius, became less interested in his career. He continued to support Abdallah financially, while transferring his passionate interest to the racing-car driver Jacky Maglia. Genet had known Jacky since he was a child; as an adolescent, Jacky had begun to steal cars in order to impress Genet, who responded by buying him cars of his own and financing his motor-racing career. He even consented to spend time with him in England, a country where he never felt comfortable, in order to buy him a Lotus and to see him race. Staying in Norwich, he acted as witness to Jacky's marriage to a local woman, signing his profession on the church register as 'thief' ('voleur') beneath that of her father, a policeman (White 1994: 536). Although Genet never entirely lost contact with his former lover, Abdallah reacted badly to the interest Genet was lavishing on his new protégé, and became increasingly depressed, finally committing suicide in 1964. His death had a profound effect on Genet, who reacted to the event by tearing up all his manuscripts and taking a vow never to write again (ibid.: 544). A year later, Jacky Maglia had a serious accident and was never able to race again. A third disaster followed in 1967, when Frechtman committed suicide. Genet had put his affairs in the hands of a certain Rosica Colin, cutting Frechtman out of his previous role as agent for all the English-language translations of his work. That year Genet too made his most determined suicide attempt (ibid.: 570). The deaths of those close to him perhaps made him indifferent to the way in which he was internationally fêted as one of the greatest dramatists of the century. Or was it precisely this sense of entering into the world of acknowledged 'success' that so depressed him? We have no sure way of distinguishing truth from falsehood where Genet's private motives are concerned: he remains forever suspended in a world of ambiguous potentialities.

The final phase in Genet's life was one of direct political involvement, and can be said to date from 1968, when he returned to Paris from a visit to Japan in May and found himself caught up in the near-revolution of that year. He subsequently visited Chicago, where he joined his admirers William Burroughs and Alan Ginsberg in demonstrations against the Vietnam War. He maintained his vow never to write again, publishing no new fiction, poetry or drama, but he began to engage in direct political action and to write political articles. In 1970 he returned to the USA at the invitation of the Black Panthers, a radical group fighting for Afro-American citizens' rights. He travelled around giving lectures on the condition of African-Americans, before visiting Brazil to see a celebrated production of *The Balcony* by Víctor García, who had previously directed *The*

Maids in a production that Genet much admired (see Chapter 4). Here he wrote his first major article in favour of black activists who had been put on trial in the USA. Back in France, he became involved in work defending immigrant workers, taking part in demonstrations and writing in their defence. He continued to follow the liberation struggles of African-Americans closely, and also visited Beirut, Damascus and Amman. However, he was still wary of becoming part of the French intellectual establishment. In 1971 he said:

'I don't want to be an intellectual. If I publish something about France, I'll strike a pose as an intellectual. I am a poet. For me to defend the Panthers and the Palestinians fits in with my function as a poet.'

(ibid.: 653)

In 1972 he visited the Middle East again, writing a long article on the Palestinians, which set him on the path of what was to become his last major book, *Prisoner of Love* (*Un captif amoureux*). Such political/poetic involvement was to continue for the remainder of his life, given additional urgency in the early 1980s after he witnessed an atrocity in Beirut in September 1982. The Israeli army had entered the city in pursuit of Palestinian forces, and the next day, when Genet and his host Layla Shahid were prevented by the Israelis from leaving their apartment, Phalangist forces moved into the Palestinian refugee camps at Shatila and Sabra on the outskirts, where they massacred the inhabitants – men, women and children. Two days later, Genet was able to enter the Shatila camp, posing as a journalist. Immediately afterwards he flew back to Paris and spent the next month writing 'Four Hours in Shatila' ('Quatre heures à Shatila'), an extraordinarily moving account of the horror he had witnessed (see Finburgh 2002). The book that Genet went on to write in the last years of his life expresses his sense that his own fate is somehow linked to that of the Palestinians. He writes of his own experiences and of his feelings for the dispossessed refugees he had come to know and love, and he also evokes a number of outsize, legendary characters. But as White points out, the style is very different from that of his early prison novels: 'The genre established by Genet [in *Prisoner of Love*] is a curious mixture of memoir, tract, stylized Platonic dialogue based on actual conversation, allegorical quest, epic' (White 1994: 723). In this book he brings together his poetic and political concerns, writing of the joy in life, the freedom and the triumph of the will that he discovered in these people, although they were deprived of everything normally thought of as 'human rights', and he links it to his own ascetic quest to rid himself of possessions and status. As Carl Lavery points out, *Prisoner of Love* includes the description of an experience of revelation not unlike that which Genet had experienced in the railway carriage in the early 1950s, when the singularity he had cultivated up until that point seemed to dissolve into an awareness of his interchangeability with the whole of humanity. But where that first epiphany had been grounded in horror and disgust, the new revelation was of 'a cosmic happiness or affirmation' proceeding from a similar sense of existing as just one human among humans (Lavery 2003: 167). Genet writes:

> The happiness of my hand caressing a boy's hair will be known by another hand, is already known, and if I die this happiness will not cease. 'I' can die, and what has permitted this 'I', what has made possible the joy of living, will perpetuate that joy of living without me.
>
> (Genet 1986: 424)

In his last decade his rhythm of life was interrupted by several treatments for cancer of the throat, but he continued to travel and to write. In 1985 he agreed to give a last interview, for BBC Television. In the same year he completed the manuscript of *Prisoner of Love* and was 'consecrated' when for the first time one of his plays, *The Balcony*, directed by Georges Lavaudant, entered the repertoire of the Comédie-Française, France's most prestigious national stage. Genet died on 15 April 1986 in a small Paris hotel room. In his will, he left his royalties to be divided between three people: Jacky Maglia, an old circus friend of Abdallah's named Ahmed, and a friend he had made in Morocco during the last years of his life, Mohammed el Katrani (White 1994: 731). He asked for his body to be taken back to Morocco, where he was buried in Larache, in a plot overlooking the sea.

This introduction to Genet's life and works is followed by five chapters. Chapters 2 and 3 present Genet's play-texts; chapters 4, 5 and 6 analyse key productions of the texts and raises issues surrounding productions.

As this chapter states, Genet wrote one ballet and around a dozen plays, some of which have never been retrieved. Of the eight plays published in the definitive collection of Genet's theatre, the Pléiade edition of his *Théâtre complet* (2002), the following are translated into English: *Deathwatch*, *The Maids*, *Splendid's*, *The Balcony*, *The Blacks*, *The Screens* (*Elle* and *Le Bagne* are not translated). Each play would merit a book-length study in itself, so we do not lay claim to providing comprehensive accounts of each and every one. Instead, we devote substantial space to works which, as university teachers, we feel inspire the most original and creative responses from students, whether in their practical or their academic work. *The Maids* and *The Balcony* therefore receive considerable attention. We also provide sustained discussions of more complex works like *The Blacks* and *The Screens*, which are habitually avoided at university level, owing to their lack of an obvious narrative through-line, or dominant subject matter. We hope, therefore, that our clear explications of these plays' philosophical, political and aesthetic considerations – which draw on a range of theoretical sources from Sartre's existentialism to Hans-Thies Lehmann's 'postdramatic' theory – and the historical contextualization we provide, will render the complexity of these plays exhilarating rather than intimidating. Finally, we have considered certain plays to be more 'minor'. Genet revised *Deathwatch* continuously over the duration of 40 years, no doubt testifying to the fact that he was never satisfied with it; and he never wanted *Splendid's*, *Elle* or *Le Bagne* to be published. These plays are therefore either treated briefly, or mentioned tangentially. Conversely, Genet's profuse theoretical writings on theatre (1972 and 2003), and some of his novels, are discussed in detail when we feel that they shed light on plays and productions.

The clear and concise presentations of Genet's play-texts included in the book's first half provide a useful starting point from which then to explore the ways in which different directors, designers and actors have staged these plays. This is the first comprehensive English-language account of his theatre in production. Genet's plays have been staged many hundreds of times over the past 60 years, from Paris to Tokyo, from London to São Paolo. In addition, many of his theoretical texts and essays, for example 'The Tightrope Walker' or 'Four Hours in Shatila', and even his novels, have been dramatized.[5] Rather than providing an inventory of productions, the second half of the book has specific research aims. First, it includes a spectrum of productions – over 30, from 1947 to 2007 – to illustrate the sheer range of theatrical approaches and styles that Genet's texts inspire. Of the scores of productions we could include, we select some because of their groundbreaking originality, for instance Víctor García's *The Maids* (Chapter 4) or Roger Blin's *The Screens* (Chapter 6). We choose others not necessarily because they are seminal or exemplary, but because discrete elements of the production shed useful dramaturgical light on a particular play, and could therefore provide future theatre-makers with useful means with which to approach Genet's theatre.[6]

Secondly, the second half views Genet's multiple stage directions, comments, prefaces and letters as a vastly rich resource for anyone approaching his play-texts from either an academic or a performance perspective. Some directors, for example Sébastien Rajon, whose *The Balcony* is discussed in Chapter 5, follow Genet's directions to the letter; others, like Philippe Adrien, whose *The Maids* is described in Chapter 4, are more circumspect:

> One asks oneself constantly what [Genet] means, the difficulty being how to interpret the deluge of directions he gives in his various texts entitled 'How to play *The Balcony... The Maids...*'. He prides himself on providing a user's manual, but the majority of his directions are in no way concrete. Rereading 'How to play *The Maids*', I said to myself that a text like that could justify a rebellion from a director.
>
> (Adrien 2008: 151)

Genet's directions are certainly often recondite and unhelpful to anyone seeking a practical guide to staging his plays. Genet himself would no doubt admit this, since he ends his preface to *The Balcony*,

'Maybe I'm not making myself clear?' (Genet 2002: 262; 1991a: xiv). On the occasions when Genet's directions were flouted, he expressed delight rather than contempt, writing to Patrice Chéreau, director of *The Screens* in 1983:

> It was most pleasant for me, yesterday, to see *The Screens* uprooted from my own vision and placed in yours, even if I sometimes had the impression I was being slightly tortured or ill-treated. Don't be mistaken: I was very happy.... Patrice, you have interpreted me, not betrayed me.
>
> (Genet 2002: 953)

Rather than being inconsistent, Genet's stage directions are perhaps intentionally ambiguous, in order to resist being prescriptive and consequently to invite the colourful plurality of varied artistic responses to which this book bears witness.

Note on translation

In this volume, quotations from Genet's plays are referenced in the following way. A page reference to Genet's final French version of each play, published in the 2002 *Théâtre complet*, is followed by a reference to an English translation, where this exists. In cases where translations for quotations are not available, for example because passages of the original play have been omitted from the English translation or because works have not been translated, we have translated the text ourselves. By providing bilingual references for each quotation, we hope that this volume will constitute an invaluable research tool for French scholars, theatre specialists and performance practitioners alike.

2 Key early plays

The Maids, Deathwatch, Splendid's

The Maids

What happens in The Maids

The curtain goes up on *The Maids* to reveal two female actors. One is in her négligée, screaming at the other about her gloves. No exposition, no explaining: spectators have to work out who this is and why she acts and speaks in such tragic tones (as the stage direction specifies). They are only utility rubber gloves, the kind used for household tasks, but during the first speech, the second actor, who wears a simple black maid's dress, plays with the gloves as if they were fashion items. This seems strange – it will be the first clue, for the alert spectator, that all is not what is seems. Having been ordered to take the gloves back to the kitchen, the Maid does so and, on her return, addresses the first actor as 'Madame'. It seems clear, then, that the scene depicts a mistress in conversation with her maid, and this is how the action continues for the next ten pages. The dialogue between the two actors is now violent, now intimate: it embodies abrupt changes of tone, which have a disturbing effect, administering a succession of jolts to whatever meaning the spectator is beginning to read into the scene. And all the time the actions appear strangely unreal – for example, while the servant is arranging the folds of the gorgeous evening gown she has just helped Madame to put on, she unexpectedly receives a vicious kick in the face. Madame addresses her servant as Claire and veers between tender expressions of interest, to insults about her smell. Claire appears equally unpredictable: she too veers between submissive care for her mistress and arrogant, even brutal treatment of her.

This scene is interrupted, after about 15 minutes' playing time, by the sudden ringing of an alarm clock. The tone of the actors' exchanges alters immediately. The intense tragic air is dropped for a more subdued one described in the stage direction as 'a sad tone of voice' (Genet 2002: 171; 1989: 46).[1] The first words spoken after the clock has ceased are: 'Let's hurry! Madame'll be back.' Some of the audience may have realized, before this point, that these actresses are portraying, not a mistress and her servant, but two servants, one of whom has been playing the role of mistress. To add to the confusion, the one who had been addressed as Claire up to this point now addresses the former Madame as Claire. In the next ten minutes or so of playing time it becomes clear that the one initially playing the servant is not Claire but Solange, and the one initially playing Madame is in fact Claire. Thus, everything that Claire has been saying, in the role of Madame, she has been saying, in a way, to herself, which underlines the fact that the Maids' hatred of their mistress is matched by their self-loathing. Their recriminations are again interrupted by a bell. This time it is the telephone. It is a friend of Madame's, 'Monsieur', who has just returned from temporary imprisonment. The audience learns that he had been incriminated on the strength of 'anonymous' letters of denunciation that had, in fact, been written by the Maids.

Soon afterwards, Madame herself returns and behaves in an outrageously self-indulgent manner, casting herself in the role of faithful lover, prepared to follow Monsieur to the ends of the earth, and patronizing her servants. This brings the play to its halfway point. The structure has been set up: the two Maids, trapped in their roles of submission to Madame and her lover, are attempting to devise schemes and ceremonies through which they might transcend their oppressed situation and achieve liberation. The remainder of the play will show how their scheme of denouncing 'Monsieur' comes to nothing and further limits their freedom of action so that they end by having to turn to a self-destructive finale.

Role-play

The action so far consists largely of a series of confusing role-plays. Genet's choice of structure for this play was startlingly modern in 1947. Not that role-play was a novelty in itself. But dramatists had traditionally used the device to reveal some hidden truth to their spectators, whereas Genet uses it to confuse them. He deliberately trails false clues and builds up erroneous assumptions in their minds, the better to overturn them. This allows him to draw his audience into an atmosphere in which it becomes impossible to establish a simple contrast between the 'true' and the 'false', and the audience's natural willingness to collaborate with the actors in their construction of an imaginary world is turned against them.

This confusion of identities in the first half of the play can be seen as the result of a careful layering of identities by the playwright. The two Maids are being shown to be living a very particular kind of existence – one that they share with oppressed people of all kinds, experiences that will be explored in greater depth in Genet's later plays. They are painfully conscious of seeing themselves through the eyes of others, and that entails experiencing themselves as 'other'. Rather than feeling secure in the knowledge of who they are, able to observe the world from a stable viewpoint, they are forced to acknowledge that they are interchangeable and expendable, shaped not by their own will but by the demands, or even just the whims, of the mistress who controls them. So in the layering of their identities Genet shows us, first, the status of the unmarried young woman obliged to seek employment in a bourgeois household; second, the dream (Madame's dream) of the devoted servant who wants nothing more than to see her mistress happy; third, the invention of a ritual ceremony which involves aping the mistress in her absence, and which is destined, however obscurely, to undermine and destroy her power. Possessing nothing but their own dispossession, the two Maids are obsessed with dreams of revenge and annihilation, and this obsession involves Claire being possessed by the figure of the absent mistress and Solange being possessed by the figure of faithful servant Claire.

But their state of dispossession also leads them into ferocious fits of jealousy *vis-à-vis* one another. Shortly before the alarm clock rings,

Solange briefly slips out of her role as Claire, and accuses Claire of wanting to steal the affections of the milkman Mario – apparently a desirable young man whom they both fancy. Their litany of hatred for Madame suddenly undergoes a shift, and they slip into abusing one another. Claire has to call Solange back to the game, and to her assumed identity of Claire, and as she does so the stage direction states that she is 'panic-stricken' (Genet 2002: 170; 1989: 44). In fact their mood throughout seems to be on the verge of panic or hysteria. The purpose of the ceremony, as they call it, is to give them release, and they repeatedly allude to this hoped-for release in terms that recall drug-induced ecstasy or sexual climax. The dramatic dialogue at first appears strangely directionless – they just seem to be talking about themselves, their situation and how they want to change it – but the audience gradually begins to understand the dramatic drive underlying their discussions: they are trying to talk themselves into a state of transformation where they can escape their constricted existence and become what they are not: free agents.

For in Genet's theatre, the function of representation is not to show the world as it is, but rather to show the exaggerations and distortions through which our imaginations try to construct the desired image of ourselves and the forces that shape those imaginary selves. Sartre explains this in a piece he wrote on *The Maids*: 'Claire can be Madame only if she seems Madame in her own eyes. Solange's becoming Claire represents the astounding effect of a reflective consciousness turning back on itself and wanting to perceive itself as it appears to others' (Sartre 1952: 687; in Genet 1989: 26).

Sartre's existentialism and The Maids

When Genet was writing *The Maids*, he was already being promoted by Sartre as an important new star in the French literary sky. It would be some seven years before Sartre's monumental study of Genet, *Saint Genet, comédien et martyr* (*Saint Genet, Actor and Martyr*) was to appear (1952), but Sartre already saw in Genet the living illustration of his own existentialist theory of consciousness. Sartre argued that, as human beings, we cannot avoid the awareness that we are conscious of something – whether ourselves or other people and things. We may long for the unreflective state that characterizes the vegetable and mineral world, but we cannot escape the knowledge that the human being is not a fixed, stable essence. Instead, it is constructed over the course of its existence. The most important factor shaping our consciousness of the world is what Sartre terms 'being-for-others', that is to say the various kinds of behaviour we routinely adopt because of what we know others expect of us. Sartre's analysis was influential on the thinking of Franz Fanon, the critic of colonial mentalities in North Africa, who argues, for example in *Black Skin White Masks* (1952), that the most persistent evil of colonialism is the way it obliges any colonized people to see themselves as the colonial masters see them. Thus, in particular, the colonized peoples of Africa mentally digest the colour associations of the colonial masters, identifying black with evil and white with good. Genet was to develop these ideas in his later play *The Blacks*. But already in *The Maids*, he shows how the mistress has colonized the minds of her two servants. Sartre explains this:

> The maids are relative to everything and everyone; their being is defined by its absolute relativity. They are *others*. Domestics are pure emanations of their masters and, like criminals, belong to the order of the Other, to the order of Evil. They *love* Madame. This means, in Genet's language, that both of them would like to *become* Madame, in other words to be integrated into the social order instead of being outcasts.
>
> (Sartre 1952: 681; in Genet 1989: 17)

Thus the Maids' repeated protestations of devotion to Madame can be seen to be the product of their desperate longing to share the existence that is hers, rather than the expression of simple human affection. They are painfully aware of how Madame patronizes them and treats them just as it suits her changes of mood, with no consideration for their feelings, but they still see that her existence is deeply desirable, relative to theirs. And at the same time as they 'love' their mistress, they also hate her, as many of their speeches demonstrate. Sartre's explanation continues:

They *hate* Madame. Translate: Genet detests the Society that rejects him and wishes to annihilate it. These spectres are born of the dream of a master; murky to themselves, their feelings come to them from outside. They are born in the sleeping imagination of Madame or Monsieur.... When he presents them before the footlights, Genet merely mirrors the fantasies of the right-minded women in the audience. Every evening five hundred Madames can sing out 'Yes, that's what maids are like', without realizing that they have created them, the way Southerners [in the USA] create Negroes.

(ibid.)

Sartre's comments on the response of Genet's audience can be seen to relate very precisely to the circumstances of the play's first production in 1947, discussed in Chapter 4. It is worth noting the accuracy of his detailed account of how Genet's Maids' minds work. They are tortured by the awareness of how their mistress imagines them: this is why they have devised the ritual enactment, with which the play opens and closes, as a way of trying to conjure away and destroy this state of being inhabited by feelings and ideas that are not truly their own, but are imposed on them from outside. However, the way out is not easy to find as, even when they play at being Madame, they are still conforming to an image she has imposed – 'they are still being played *by her*', in Corvin's words (Genet 2002: 1066).

It is clear that, in *The Maids*, Genet's subject is not simply the plight of domestic servants. Nor is it just a reworking of the famous case of the Papin sisters (see Edwards and Reader 2001). This crime story was notorious in France at the time and would have been familiar to his readers and audiences. The case involved two sisters, domestic servants just like Claire and Solange, who in 1933 murdered the woman who employed them and her daughter in a particularly gruesome manner. It has given rise to a number of novels, films and a psychoanalysis by Jacques Lacan. The subject of *The Maids* was clearly suggested to Genet by this case but, although he starts from the same situation, his play quickly departs from the historical facts: instead, it becomes an investigation of the mind of the outcast. Its dynamic combination of love, hatred, fear, self-loathing and desire for escape from imprisonment and exploitation in a condition imposed by others, could be seen to hold good for the criminal, the colonial or the homosexual, as much as for female domestics.

In the early 1940s, writing his novels of prison life, Genet had been more concerned to address the condition of the criminal without worrying much about what the bourgeois reader might think. But following his official pardon by the President of the Republic (1949), and his friendship with Sartre and his circle, Genet had been brought into close contact with the middle-class intellectual circles of Parisian society (see Chapter 1). His plays, written over the next decade, show him concerned to draw this group of people into his reflections on society. It was crucially important to the success of *The Maids* that it was first produced in a fashionable Paris theatre, with a cultured and well-heeled clientèle, many of whom would certainly have had domestic servants in their employ. The typical Paris apartment for well-off members of the middle class came with a *chambre de bonne*, or maid's room; these were always located on the top floors of the block, while the apartments of the families they serviced would be on the lower floors. Today, most of these *chambres de bonne* have been sold off and turned into 'studio flats' but in the 1940s even quite a modest middle-class ménage would normally employ at least one maid to do the daily cooking and cleaning. The purpose of Genet's dramatic writing is thus not only to celebrate the lives of outcasts, it is also to show the interdependence of the powerful and the dispossessed in any human society, and to confront the right-thinking bourgeoisie (as Sartre termed them) with the reality of this interdependence and, hence, with their own complicity in the state of those they condemn.

Rivalry and jealousy

In Genet's play, much of the dramatic excitement is generated by his choice to have two maids rather than one. This enables him to set up a tensely competitive atmosphere between the two, which gives energy and drive to the dialogue. They are in competition for everything: for Madame's favours, for the seduction of the milkman, for the right to decide how to enact their role-plays, and for keeping one another on course as they build up this ceremony the aim of which is to do away with Madame and her power over them. Halfway through the first sequence of the game, before the alarm bell rings, Solange gets carried away by her expressions of hatred for Madame, and slips into a wild denunciation of Claire, culminating in the words 'Solange says to hell with you!' (Genet 2002: 170; 1989: 44). This is a terrible false step in the ceremony, since Solange is supposed to be Claire, and Claire has to call her urgently to order. The incident is the audience's first clear demonstration that the apparent subject of the dialogue (Madame discussing with her Maid what dress to wear) hides a passionate and ferocious struggle going on under the surface between the two sisters. Until this point it has been carefully veiled, but here the veil is momentarily lifted.

Through their long rehearsals of rebellion against their mistress, the Maids aspire to achieve such intensity in their litany of hate that they finally reach a state of ecstasy or escape. This is first explicitly invoked shortly before the passage just quoted:

> SOLANGE *(in ecstasy)*: Madame's being carried away!
> CLAIRE: By the devil! He's carrying me away in his fragrant arms. He's lifting me up, I leave the ground, I'm off.... *(She stamps with her heel.)* And I stay behind.
>
> (Genet 2002: 169; 1989: 42)

On this occasion the ritual enactment of their ceremonial role-play fails to reach its ecstatic climax, and Claire expresses the frustration of not achieving fulfilment, but ultimately both will succeed, by accepting that the only way they can vent their hatred is to turn it on themselves.

The transformation game

Claire and Solange both refer on frequent occasions to the 'game' in which they invest so much of their emotional and imaginative energy. It is worth remembering that the word Genet uses for this, *jeu*, has a double meaning in French: both game and acting (just as the noun 'play' in English means both an act performed in a game and a text performed in a theatre). Playing a game, putting on an act, simulating in order to show up an underlying truth is one of the great commonplaces of contemporary theatre. It is usually associated, as in Luigi Pirandello's work, with the attempt to impose one's own special interpretation of a given event. But the games played by the characters in Genet's dramatic world have a more radical intent: they aim to transform the very realities with which they play. Solange makes the point with force and economy when she cries out, 'The game! Will we even be able to go on with it? And if I have to stop spitting on someone who calls me Claire, I'll simply choke! My spurt of saliva is my spray of diamonds!' (Genet 2002: 138; 1989: 52). The condensed image of the globules of spit transformed into precious jewels expresses the outsize ambition that Genet nurtures for his theatre.

In order to grasp exactly what kind of transformation Genet attempts to set in motion through the 'game' or 'ceremony' of *The Maids*, it is important to consider the preface he wrote to the first publication of the play in 1954 by the publisher Jean-Jacques Pauvert. This preface, now known as 'Letter to Jean-Jacques Pauvert', is not reproduced in the English translations of the play, but is included in a collection of Genet's writings, *Fragments of the Artwork* (2003). The general tone is one of disillusionment – with writing, with his own play and with western theatre in general. It was composed when Genet was suffering from a sense of the futility of all his writing, for which he partly blamed the crushing effect of the publication of Sartre's monumental *Saint Genet, comédien et martyr*, but which may also be attributable to his experience in the railway carriage (see Chapter 1).

Genet's preface complains that the western actor (in contrast with the performer in Chinese, Japanese or Balinese theatres) is only interested in constructing a realistic character – s/he is unwilling to 'become a sign laden with signs' (Genet 2002: 816; 2003: 37, translation modified). Genet contrasts his approval for Eastern theatre, described as 'ceremony', with his scorn for western theatre of psychological character study, which he terms puerile masquerade (ibid.). For him, the actor should seek to be as distant as possible from what s/he represents, aspiring to become the metaphor of what is enacted. The only example of this commonly encountered in western society, he argues, is the Catholic Mass: 'theatrically speaking, I know nothing more effective than the Elevation of the Host [by the priest at the climax of the mass]' (Genet 2002: 817; 2003: 38). Why does Genet need to reach back into his memories of his past as an altar boy to articulate his vision of what theatre should be? It is because this is the one example he can think of in which the force of the common belief among the congregation (for congregation, read audience) is sufficient to effect a transformation. As the priest elevates the Host and the congregation prays, the bread and wine are transformed into the body and blood of Christ (quite literally, in the traditional Roman Catholic understanding of this). This mystic transformation is brought about by the observation of specific ritual actions completed in the presence of people who believe in the efficacy of the transcendent power invoked.

Genet concludes his preface by recounting a story he claims to have heard from 'a young writer', that points in the same direction:

> Five or six kids were playing war games in the park. They were divided into two troops and were preparing the attack. Night, they said, was coming on. But the sky showed it was midday. They therefore decided that one of them would be Night. The youngest and frailest, transformed into something elemental, became the Master of the Fray. 'He' was the Hour, the Moment, the Ineluctable. He approached, it seems, from a long way off with the calm of a natural cycle, but weighed down with the sadness and solemnity of the gloaming. As he drew near the others, the Men, became nervous and uneasy ... The boy was arriving too soon for them. He was before his time, so by common consent the Troops and the Chiefs decided to eliminate Night, and he returned to being a soldier on one of the sides ... It is only on the basis of this formula that theatre could thrill me.
> (Genet 2002: 818–9; 2003: 39–40, translation modified)

This short preface gives few precise details about the play itself, but does explain what kind of dramatic power Genet believed western theatre might be capable of wielding in the right conditions. The figures of maids and mistress in his play, like the figures of the state in *The Balcony* or the figures of Blacks in *The Blacks*, are not to be taken to represent the reality of servitude, power or slavery, but its image. They are reflections of the images in the minds of their audiences and, insofar as they present the social hierarchies that structure our western societies, they become, in Genet's word, 'signs' onto which the audience projects its own image of social roles and power relations. Having been excluded from right-thinking bourgeois society, Genet sets up dream societies, which he can possess through play or ceremony. In this way he can transform and subvert images of reality, even though he may have no immediate or direct effect upon it.

Power struggles

These considerations provide a key to understanding all of Genet's theatre, and are especially relevant to *The Maids*, a play whose action consists largely of the two sisters' attempt to play out to its conclusion a ritual whose purpose is to change the power relations in their household. The power struggle has two different aspects, which interweave and thus add to the complexity and tension of the drama. The first aspect is the obvious one of revenge: Claire and Solange search for ways of settling scores with Madame for the state of subjection in which she keeps them. One method is to write an anonymous letter to the police accusing Monsieur of various crimes. Even for a plot such as this, in which many events appear more like dream than reality, this may appear excessively far-fetched. But a mere two years after the end of the Second World War it would not have seemed so. During the occupation of France by the German army (1940–4), the population was encouraged to report anyone suspected of activity hostile to the rule of the Nazi Reich. This resulted in an astonishing number of letters of denunciation by ordinary people, seeking to settle scores with their neighbours. With these memories still raw, the imprisonment of Madame's lover on the basis of an anonymous letter of denunciation would not have appeared improbable to the play's audience. Ultimately, of course, the sisters aim not just to wound Madame, but to kill her, which they plan to achieve by putting poison in her tea. But their whole condition as servants impedes their attempts to make a reality of this dreamed act of revolt, hence the importance of the ceremony they perform, whose purpose is to put them into a kind of trance in which their conditioned scruples can be overridden.

The second aspect of the power struggle played out in *The Maids* is the love-hate relationship between Claire and Solange. As the action unfolds, the audience gradually comes to see how the apparent interchangeability of the two Maids is yet another aspect of their loss of personal identity. Their individual names are of little significance, since their beings are so utterly subsumed into their function as household servants and the humble objects of Madame's charity. About halfway through, they reveal that they take it in turns to play the role of Madame in their 'game', and their strengths and weaknesses in this role become another source of rivalry between them. And it is at this point that Solange admits to having failed to act when she might easily have stifled Madame in her sleep (Genet 2002: 176; 1989: 56). It seems that the fantasy enactments of the ceremony played out by the Maids every day have proved to be all too powerful in one sense: they have transformed their image of Madame into something untouchable because it is so powerful *as an image*. In order to escape their conditioning, they have tried to build themselves up through the imaginary role-play, but their very success works against their ability to destroy the real Madame, since it builds her into a powerful image, and an image (as will be shown even more clearly in Genet's later plays) can never be eliminated, even if the bearer of the image were to be killed.

It only adds to their frustration to see that Madame herself is able to achieve some of the transforming power that they so desperately long for. Solange exclaims, 'Look, just look at how she suffers. How she suffers in beauty. Grief transfigures her, doesn't it? Beautifies her? When she learned that her lover was a thief, she stood up to the police. She exulted' (Genet 2002: 176; 1989: 57). Meanwhile, they are left behind, comfortless, with the desolate awareness that even to one another they are repellant:

SOLANGE: I want to help you. I want to comfort you, but I know I disgust you. I'm repulsive to you. And I know it because you disgust me. When slaves love one another, it's not love.
CLAIRE: And me, I'm sick of seeing my image thrown back at me by a mirror, like a bad smell. You're my bad smell.

(Genet 2002: 179; 1989: 61)

As Sartre explains, they can only 'be' the person that they see reflected in the eyes of those around them. This means being patronized by Madame or being recognized by one another as loathsome, helpless creatures, struggling for purchase in the slime at the bottom of the social heap.

By this point, nearly halfway through the play, the complexities of the dramatic situation have been revealed through a series of dramatic surprises, and the two Maids find a brief moment of comfort in recognizing their hopeless condition. There is a line that could have come from Beckett's *Waiting for Godot* (written at the same time as *The Maids* was first performed, it was not seen on stage until 1953):

CLAIRE: Hers is false. [*A long silence.*] Do you remember? Under the tree, just the two of us? Our feet in the sun? Solange.
SOLANGE: I'm here. Sleep. I'm your big sister.

(Genet 2002: 180; 1989: 64)

But the mood cannot last, and it passes almost before it has settled. Claire denounces sleep and nostalgia as weakness and insists that she and her sister maintain their resolve to poison Madame's tea, discusses the Phenobarbital that they will use, and urges her sister to be joyful: they must laugh and sing, since murder is unspeakable. It is at this moment that Madame returns.

Enter Madame

By bringing in his third character halfway through the play, Genet keeps the audience guessing what will happen next. In the second half, he employs the suspense method common in crime thrillers – the thrillers that Genet so enjoyed reading as a young man and to which the Maids also allude. Will Madame drink the poisoned tea or not? This common device for enhancing suspense, together with the two bells that go off unexpectedly (the alarm clock and telephone) show Genet still employing models drawn from popular drama, even while developing an ornately poetic style of dialogue that owes a great deal more to the examples of Cocteau and the French classics than to popular crime writing.

Madame's late entry also allows Genet to unsettle the audience still further, as it attempts to get to grips with the vertiginous instability of all the characters. Madame repeats many of the words we have already heard the Maids say – for example the melodramatic desire to follow her lover 'from prison to prison, on foot if need be, as far as the penal colony' (Genet 2002: 182, 167; 1989: 67, 39). Has Madame picked up phrases she has heard from the Maids, or were the Maids just very accurate in mimicking Madame? The question is never answered, but the way that Madame conditions her Maids, and the Maids in turn help to create the personality of Madame, is revealed through a sequence of dialogue in which she constantly changes her opinion about what has happened to herself and her lover. In this she shows that she too is unstable as a character, constantly trying out new poses, revealing herself to be at the mercy of how she appears to others, and lacking any fixed centre. In that respect she is exactly like the two sisters. The one important difference is that her independence is guaranteed by social hierarchy and so she is free to alter her expressions and opinions with every new whim, whereas the Maids lack this freedom.

The rapid mood swings exhibited by Madame have a curious effect in this section of the play, as the more changeable she appears, the more 'unreal' she seems. Sartre writes of Genet's deliberate aim to 'de-realize' his characters. According to Sartre, Genet was writing a disguised homosexual drama and would have liked the roles to be played by boys (Sartre 1952: 679; in Genet 1989: 13–14. See Chapter 4 for a discussion of this point). As the audience watches the interplay of mutual dependence between Madame and her servants, they see, in Sartre's words, 'being chang[e] ... into appearance and appearance into being' (ibid.: 679; ibid.: 14). Each of these imaginary characters, twisting and turning under the pressure of situations they find intolerable, becomes de-realized so that the audience can only see the interplay of imaginary symbols – or 'signs laden with signs' as Genet himself expressed it. The reason why this emerges with such startling clarity at this point is that the Maids' behaviour has until now been conditioned entirely by their schemes to be rid of Madame. The absent Madame has thus become, for the audience, the reality against which they have to measure the behaviour that they are given to observe. However, Genet shows Madame to be even more false, even less 'real' as a person than the Maids. Several times in the course of this scene she spots some fresh evidence left over from the Maids' ceremonial game, such as the fact that Claire is wearing make-up, and each time this happens the audience is reminded afresh of the earlier ceremony and of its intense reality, in contrast to the manifest artificiality of what is happening to them now.

The final ceremony

When Monsieur telephones to say he has been released, Madame suddenly changes tack, abandoning the role of desperate woman reliant only on her two faithful retainers. She slips back into the role of fun-loving woman-about-town. Solange is sent out for a taxi and Claire is left alone, desperately trying to make Madame drink her tea, which the Maids have duly poisoned. But although Solange takes as long as she can before coming back with the taxi, Madame refuses to drink the tea – she is playing the over-excited lover, anticipating a champagne reunion with Monsieur. Once she has flounced out, the two sisters are left alone again for the last third of the play, as they had been for the first half (Madame is on stage for less than a quarter of the play). In this final section the Maids realize that their stratagem to incriminate Monsieur is bound to be discovered, and at last they find the resolve required to play their game out to the end. They agree that the time for preliminaries is over and Solange articulates openly the ultimate aim, transformation: 'Let's get right into the transformation. Hurry up! Hurry up! I can't stand the shame and humiliation any longer' (Genet 2002: 191; 1989: 85). Claire signals her agreement by putting on the white dress that had been discussed in the first sequence of the play, not 'disguising' herself as Madame this time, but simply pulling it on over her black dress; and Genet's stage direction specifies that the black sleeves should show underneath, reminding the audience of the superimposition of mistress on maid.

It is Solange who first achieves the ecstatic transformation for which both had been yearning in the first section of the play. In a lengthy bravura monologue, she imagines herself making a proud, self-confident speech to her employer and to the police and then going to the scaffold, after having strangled her sister (dressed as Madame). She is exalted, she is free from the necessary submissiveness of the servant, she proclaims herself 'Madame's equal'. But this too is revealed as yet another flight of the imagination when Claire re-enters, still wearing the white dress, and addresses Solange once again as Claire, demanding to be served her tea. In another reversal of the balance of power, Solange suddenly collapses and seems too frightened to do as Claire asks, but Claire gradually calms her sister and imposes her will on her, obliging her to say the words 'Madame must have her tea' and to give her the poisoned cup, which she drinks, while Solange (as Claire) pronounces their final ecstatic speech of escape:

> SOLANGE: … Madame is dead. Her two maids are alive: they've just risen up, free, from Madame's icy form. All the maids were present at her side – not they themselves, but rather the hellish agony of their names. And all that remains of them to float about Madame's airy corpse is the delicate perfume of the holy maidens which they were in secret. We are beautiful, joyous, drunk, and free!
>
> (Genet 2002: 199; 1989: 100)

The transformation has taken place. The poison has been turned against themselves, yet they have succeeded in destroying the inherited image of the maid as subservient and faithful. They have substituted a new image, one that they term 'holy', just as they had dreamed of the violent deaths associated with saints halfway through the play. They have become 'the eternal couple of the criminal and the saint' (Genet 2002: 179; 1989: 63).

Deathwatch

Genet's first play – stages of composition

The first version of *Deathwatch* dates from the time when Genet was starting on the composition of his first literary works in prison. Set in the same world as that of his early prose writings, it is very different from *The Maids*. By looking at the differences, we can see how far Genet's dramatic writing changed between 1942 and 1947. Just like his novel *Our Lady of the Flowers*, the play is set in prison and its characters are drawn straight from the world of delinquents and criminals that the young Genet had come to know so well in the years since he was sentenced to Mettray in 1926. He makes no attempt to transpose the experiences of oppression and imprisonment to a different context (as in *The Maids*), nor does he seek to extend the action to other social situations (as in his later plays). The play is organized around the same themes as those identified in his prose writings by White: honour and treason, domination and submission, authenticity and dissembling, fidelity and flirtation (see Chapter 1). The characters are also similar to those found in *Our Lady of the Flowers*: three convicts, locked up in the same cell and so forced into intimacy with one another, all seeking to satisfy different needs in this restricted world.

The play has never been performed as frequently as *The Maids*, *The Balcony*, *The Blacks* or *The Screens*, which is probably because of its deliberately limited scope: it takes us inside the mind of Genet the young thief, trying to establish some sort of honourable place for himself in the tough world of convicted criminals. But it offers no ultimate solution to the dilemmas it evokes, and contains little hint of relevance to life outside its own very special situation. It seems that Genet himself was never entirely satisfied with the play. Corvin and Dichy have discovered ten different versions, spread over 43 years, and note that Genet's last rewriting of the play was in 1985, a few months before his death (Genet 2002: 993). As in *Our Lady of the Flowers*, the plot is structured around a moment of transcendence in which a prisoner, condemned for murder, is touched by a kind of grace, and revealed as possessing a strange beauty, though not one he has chosen.

The other two prisoners struggle with one another for his approval and attempt to emulate his evident superiority, but fail.

The different stages through which the play went show how Genet gradually stripped down and concentrated the action, making a virtue of the confined setting of the prison cell and using it to increase the atmosphere of tension, rivalry and violence. In his first draft, the play was in three acts and included a key scene in which Green Eyes, the charismatic murderer, is let out of his cell and goes to the visitor's room to meet his woman. In later versions, this scene is cut and the whole action is restricted to a single act, having a circular or spiral structure, since it both begins and ends with a violent struggle between the other two inmates of the cell: Maurice and Lefranc. At the start of the play, Green Eyes has just pulled the two apart, preventing any serious injury from taking place. At the end, they once again spring at each other and this time Green Eyes does not intervene as Lefranc strangles Maurice. The action taking place between these two crisis points shows the three circling around one another, seeking domination or submission, proclaiming their fidelity or attempting to seduce one another, reflecting on their own sense of authenticity, or lack of it, and facing up to their own solitude as condemned men.

Genet's prose writings, which *Deathwatch* resembles in many ways, develop a detailed chronicle of what happens to human beings when condemned to prolonged imprisonment. They show how inmates spontaneously construct their own hierarchies. In some ways the values on which these hierarchies are built are similar to those in the society from which the prisoners have been exiled. For example, strength, vigour, charisma, sexual potency are all admired. But where success in bourgeois society is also measured in terms of wealth, longevity and the accumulation of possessions, success in Genet's prison world is measured in the extremity of the crimes committed and the convict's absolute commitment to evil. The most glamorous figures are the murderers, those who go proudly to their death on the guillotine (not finally abolished in France until 1981). But it would be wrong to think that Genet's admiration goes to thugs or bruisers, determined to impose themselves on others by brute force. On the contrary, and paradoxically, Genet's murderers have something of the quality of saints. This is certainly true of Green Eyes, the prisoner to be guillotined for murder in *Deathwatch*, who speaks of his crime as a gift from God: 'I didn't want what happened to me to happen. It was all given to me. A gift from God or the devil, but something I didn't want' (Genet 2002: 31; 1989: 160).[2]

Sartre's existentialism and Deathwatch

Even more strongly than *The Maids*, *Deathwatch* shows the influence of Sartre on Genet at this time. In 1944–5, as Paris was liberated from German occupation and a new mood swept through the capital, Sartre's *No Exit* enjoyed tremendous success with critics and audiences alike. Its three characters, incarcerated forever in a hell of their own making, became a powerful symbol for the restrictions of the war years. The play was seen as a call to avoid, in the newly liberated France, the hypocrisies and betrayals that had played into the hands of the occupier. Genet's play resembles Sartre's in its central situation: three people, locked in together against their will, who struggle to dominate one another. It also resembles it in its central theme: the search for authenticity in the midst of false appearances, dissembling, treachery and hypocrisy. In both plays, the characters enact a series of attempts to convince one another of their force and integrity while in fact disguising certain things from the others. In both, the tension rises to the point where one of the characters attempts to murder another. Here the resemblances in plot cease, however, since in Sartre's play the murder fails – the characters are already dead, so they can resolve nothing by murder, but are caught in an eternal vicious circle. But in Genet's the murder succeeds, and indeed the whole status of murder and of the murderer becomes the central focus of the play's conclusion.

In the first manuscript, then entitled *For 'the Beautiful One'* and dating back to 1942, the act of murder is presented as the defining action in a man's life, through which, if he assumes it, he acquires a hard, irreversible outline. Not only Green Eyes, whose crime was committed some time before, and was the cause of his imprisonment, but also Lefranc, who murders Maurice at the end of the play, accedes to the status of *un dur* (a hard man) and is welcomed by Green Eyes as *frangin* (little brother). By time time Genet rewrote the play for publication in 1947, he had established a clear distinction between the crimes of Green Eyes and Lefranc. For Green Eyes, the murder had been a moment of grace – something given to him from God or the devil (as quoted above) rather than something he had willed. For Lefranc, the murder of Maurice, committed in order to raise himself to the same level as Green Eyes, fails, and instead of a brotherly embrace from Green Eyes he receives only scorn and a speech that reveals that Lefranc has failed in his attempt to become *un dur* (a hard man):

> GREEN EYES: You don't know the first thing about misfortune if you think you can choose it. I didn't want mine. It chose me. It fell on my shoulders and clung to me. I tried everything to shake it off. I struggled, I boxed, I danced, I even sang, and, odd as it may seem, I refused it at first. It was only when I saw that everything was irremediable that I quieted down. I've only just accepted it. It had to be total.
>
> (Genet 2002: 31; 1989: 161)

In this crucial difference between the versions of 1942 and 1947, one can no doubt detect the influence of Sartre. The existentialist philosophy that Sartre had developed in his writings of the 1940s, notably *Being and Nothingness* (*L'Être et le néant*) and his novel *Nausea* (*La Nausée*), proposed a theory of human behaviour in which most actions are undertaken from motives that are other than what they seem. Since human consciousness is dominated, Sartre argues, by consciousness of the judgement of others, most human actions are undertaken in a state of what he termed *bad faith* (*mauvaise foi*): the desire to influence the all-important judgement of those around us and thus achieve a defined character. The only way to avoid this is to be able to act in some sense gratuitously: that is, without any consideration for the judgement of others. Not surprisingly, Sartre's novels contain almost no examples of people who achieve such authenticity, though they abound in studies of the manifold ways in which people indulge in bad faith. In the distinction between the murders of Green Eyes and Lefranc, a distinction that was only introduced into the play in the rewritten version of 1947, there is a perfect example of the difference between authenticity and bad faith as theorized by Sartre. Green Eyes's crime has a certain authenticity because it was 'given' to him – it was an action he subsequently assumed, and for which he accepted responsibility, but it was not committed to achieve a particular end. Lefranc's murder, on the other hand, was committed in order to justify his claim to be as hard as Green Eyes and to persuade him to accept him as his 'brother'. In this, he fails.

Genet's early fictional themes

As well as the influence of Sartre, this altered ending to *Deathwatch* reflects Genet's own development as a writer. As White indicates, Genet's early writing was a way of expressing his admiration for hardened criminals and his desire to be accepted in their company, as well as his love of the prison system in which he had come to take a kind of perverted pleasure. In *Deathwatch*, Lefranc keeps a collection of photographs of famous murderers hidden in his mattress (Genet 2002: 17; 1989: 128). In particular, there is discussion of Weidmann, the same murderer who is mentioned in the first line of *Our Lady of the Flowers*, and who was the last man to be guillotined on a public square in France (1939). The other murderers named here – Soklay, Vaché, Angel Sun – also feature in *Our Lady of the Flowers*, in which Genet the narrator mentions that he keeps a collection of their photos, cut out of magazines. So Lefranc can be seen to share some of Genet's own characteristics as he struggles to work out how he can live with a degree of self-respect in the world of criminals and how he can achieve a place, or role, in the structured hierarchy of prison society. But the more he wrote, and the more he was recognized for his writing, the less Genet was tempted by the kind of irremediable criminal gesture that Lefranc hopes will secure him a defined character and status in the prison. In fact, the difference between the two versions of *Deathwatch* illustrates Genet's change of heart, as he moves from an initial fascination with the charisma of the murderer to an understanding that this kind of misfortune cannot be chosen, only assumed, and that his own means of escape from the status of petty criminal that he shares with Lefranc will be through the power of his imagination and his growing ability as a storyteller.

In his later plays, then, Genet discovered how to use his own experiences of rejection, rebellion and imprisonment in order to explore the myriad ways in which societies reject, oppress and imprison those whom they cast in the role of 'other'. But *Deathwatch* is a transitional work, in the different versions of which one can see Genet doing two things that were to be essential for his future as a playwright. First, he was placing himself back in his initial position as convict: it is from his fundamental understanding of what it is to be on the bottom rung of the social ladder that everything else in his writing proceeds. Second, he was digesting Sartre's theories of the nature of being, and preparing to move beyond them. Corvin and Dichy see the play as a demonstration of this learning process that Genet was undertaking in the 1940s. They characterize Maurice, Lefranc and Green Eyes as merely 'pawns being manoeuvred around the existential chess-board' (Genet 2002: 1022).

Struggle for control leading to murder

The conflict enacted in the play consists of a struggle for control as each of the characters attempts to impose his desired view of himself on the other two, and of an ultimate realization of loneliness as the two left standing at the end realize their irremediable solitude. Lefranc is the main motor of the action, since his desire to impress Green Eyes and his jealousy of Maurice motivate the majority of the changes taking place in the dynamic between the three cellmates. After his initial attempt to strangle Maurice, Lefranc tries to provoke a reaction from Green Eyes by praising the strength and charisma of another convict, Snowball. This attempt fails, but Lefranc has more success in getting a reaction in relation to the impending visit of Green Eyes's woman. Green Eyes has received a letter from her, but as he is illiterate, he relies on Lefranc to read it to him, just as he had relied on him to write to her before. He does not trust Lefranc, suspecting that he has used the letter as a way to try to 'steal' his woman. In the first version, the imagined rivalry over this woman outside the prison has a much larger place. In the version of 1947, it becomes merely the pretext for mistrust and power play between Lefranc and Green Eyes.

Maurice interrupts these arguments by making provocative approaches to Green Eyes. His behaviour reveals that his main weapon in the power struggle is his good looks and ability to attract Green Eyes. In the intensity of the emotions that fly around the cell, Maurice makes it clear that he sees himself as the rival of the woman in Green Eyes's affection and swears that he will murder her if he gets out of jail. Meanwhile, Green Eyes refuses to be drawn into the game of seduction and counter-seduction, reminding the others that he is a condemned man and hence completely alone. They succeed, however, in persuading him to recount the crime that put him in prison and he does so in a mood of increasing ecstasy, in which he evokes both the attempt to avoid the calamity of a capital crime and also the fascination he held over others:

> But if you'd seen me before, with my hands in my pockets, and with my flowers, always with a flower in my teeth! They used to call me ... Would you like to know? It was a nice nick-name: Paulo with the Flowery Teeth! And now? I'm all alone.
>
> (Genet 2002: 15; 1989: 124)

As in *Our Lady of the Flowers*, the image of the criminal is beautified by the association with flowers, and there is something deliberately incongruous in the evocation of the murderer's teeth adorned with lilacs.

Finally, when the Guard announces that Green Eyes's woman has come to visit him, Green Eyes refuses to go, and tells the guard he can 'have' her. The treatment of the woman is entirely instrumental throughout – not once is she thought of as having any feelings or rights. In the all-male world of the prison, she is seen purely as a possession, a trophy to be handed around according to the whim of the moment and a mere marker of the possessor's status. This is one of the features that make this play a lesser work than those that followed: in these, especially in *The Screens*, Genet wrote some unusual and profound roles for women. In *Deathwatch*, they might as well not exist as human beings. The play concludes with another long sequence in which Lefranc and Maurice struggle for supremacy and for the approval of Green Eyes, who gradually withdraws into his own sense of solitude, remote from their concerns.

When he had completed the first version of the play, still dependent on Cocteau to promote his writing and get his work published, Genet intended the part of Green Eyes for Jean Marais, Cocteau's lover and a leading *jeune premier* of stage and screen. But Marais rejected the part, and Cocteau's influence on Genet waned as Sartre's grew, as evidenced in Genet's revision of the play. However, Cocteau's influence during the last two years of the German occupation of Paris, 1942–4, seems to have led Genet to devote much of his energy to writing plays. Embarking on his new literary career, he appears to have completed five plays in addition to *Deathwatch*, and to have begun work on a study entitled *Theatre, Dreams and Prison* (Corvin and Dichy in Genet 2002: lxxxiii). All of these early works have been lost. However, it seems likely that all would have resembled *Deathwatch* in their concern with how to transform the social stigma of the convict or outcast into something privately glorious and glamorous. In his introduction to the English edition of *Splendid's*, White quotes an interview that Genet gave to a Spanish literary magazine in 1969 in which he explained that his early works, mostly written in prison, were addressed to a solitary reader, one who would feel furtive or shameful about acquiring a book by the notorious Jean Genet, and who would therefore savour it in secret. This would have applied to his early plays as well, since at this time he had no experience of theatre production, and approached drama as just another literary genre alongside poetry and prose. But he went on to say,

> … when I set about creating my [later] plays, I had to write for spectators in a group. I had to change my mental technique and to know that I was writing for a public which each time would be visible and numerous.

White concludes that 'the personal, homosexual content of the novels [and plays and poems] had to be translated into the public, heterosexual terms of the later plays' (White 1995: x–xi).

Splendid's

Splendid's is the last play that Genet wrote before the drought of
several years that preceded his embarking on *The Balcony* and
The Blacks in 1955. It was intended for a radio performance in
1948, but Genet was not satisfied with it and decided it should
never be published or performed. In 1953, Frechtman saw him
tear up the manuscript and declare that he wanted the play to be
ignored. However, it later turned out that a copy had been kept in
the files of Marc Barbezat, his publisher, and thus the play
was rediscovered and published after Genet's death (in 1993). The
story it tells is of a group of seven gangsters, and one former
policeman, who have kidnapped the daughter of an American
millionaire and have holed up on the seventh floor of a luxury
hotel. Without intending to, one of the gangsters has killed the
heiress, and so the group have nothing left with which to bargain as
they face the massed police who have surrounded the hotel. In order
to make them believe that she is still alive, one of the gangsters dresses
in her evening gown and emerges on the balcony holding her sequined
fan. But there is no real escape for them and so, eventually, they
decide to shed their tough image and hand themselves over to the
law.

Splendid's is correctly considered by White to be a transitional
piece, situated halfway between Genet's extremely personal,
autobiographical writings of the late 1940s and the broader, more
public canvas of his three great plays of the late 1950s. It is clearly
linked to the early work through its themes and characters: like
Deathwatch, it deals with a group that is exclusively male, and its
dynamic emerges from the struggles for domination, and dreams of
escape, that are played out within this group. It also shares with
Deathwatch the theme of homoerotic attraction exerted by people
who are willing to assume responsibility for acts that go beyond the
limits of socially acceptable behaviour, often destroying lives, whether
those of others or their own. By deploying a cast of eight, Genet made
the interplay of these struggles more varied and complex than in
Deathwatch, since more permutations are possible with a group of
eight than with one of three (or four including the guard).

However, despite having a larger cast, *Splendid's* at first glance appears to retain the respect for the classical unities of time, place and action that also seemingly and deceptively characterizes *The Maids* and *Deathwatch* (see Chapter 4 for a discussion of 'deceptive classicism'). In Genet's later plays he was to break free from such restraints, developing his own unique approach to dramatic space and time. The setting he specifies for *Splendid's* is, in fact, even closer to classical models than those for *The Maids* or for *Deathwatch*, but it is also a transitional space. It is described as 'Un hall, au 7ᵉ étage d'un grand palace. À droite et à gauche les portes des chambres. Au fond des fenêtres reliées par un balcon. Lustres. Luxe. Tapis' (Genet 2002: 217). In Neil Bartlett's excellent English translation this becomes 'A hallway, on the seventh floor of a palatial hotel. To the left and to the right, the bedroom doors. At the back, windows connected by a balcony. Chandeliers. Carpets. Luxury' (Genet 1995: 3). As Bartlett astutely points out in the preface to his translation, this is a perfect twentieth-century version of the antechamber in the royal apartments so common in Racine's plays. That Genet chooses to write *palace* (rather than *hôtel*) strengthens the sense that he wishes to echo classical settings, combining both the grandeur and the anonymity of an indeterminate space situated *between* royal apartments.

Transitional setting

This setting may be seen as transitional in the way it differs from the settings of *Deathwatch* and *The Maids*. Both of those plays were set in places having clear social associations: 'a prison cell' for the first and 'Madame's bedroom' for the second. Because of their identifiable locations, these plays have too often been performed within the realist-naturalist tradition, whereas Genet in fact specifies in the stage directions to *Deathwatch* that 'the entire play unfolds as in a dream' (Genet 2002: 5; 1989: 103). The stage direction for *Splendid's*, similarly, is carefully devised to function as a dream space, an 'in-between' space of the imagination, in which all kinds of transitions, transformations and treasons are facilitated.

The indeterminate quality of this neutral space points forward to the setting of *The Balcony*. Both 'le palace' of *Splendid's* and the

House of Illusions of *The Balcony* share the associations of luxury with an atmosphere in which people go to escape, briefly, from their limited, ordinary lives. The central role of the balcony in both settings, discussed at length in Chapter 5, further underlines the way in which *Splendid's* may be seen as a forerunner of Genet's later work. The use of language also looks forward to the unique linguistic register that characterizes Genet's late plays. As in all his writing of the 1940s, the influences are eclectic: detective fiction written for the popular market and gay slang of the Parisian underworld combine with lines reminiscent of the classic French authors. There are echoes of Racine in the recurrence of poetic lines that fit the metrical definition of the alexandrine (12-syllable line interrupted by a caesura), and the influence of Cocteau is evident in the way that the most ordinary objects are given numinous powers. This eclectic idiom has proved to be influential on the generation of young French playwrights who began to work in the 1970s and 1980s, of whom Bernard-Marie Koltès is an outstanding example.

Transformation

Another important link between *Splendid's* and the later plays, marking it off from *The Maids* and *Deathwatch*, is its treatment of the theme of transformation. The two earlier plays were focused tightly on the moment when a character attempted to transform her/himself into another by means of the most irrevocable action – suicide or murder. In *Splendid's* the emphasis has altered, subtly, towards travesty and betrayal, which were to preoccupy Genet throughout the rest of his life. The French word used by Genet is *le travestissement*, which has a wide range of associations in French, covering drag, cross-dressing, dressing-up, parody and misrepresentation. Each of these associations finds enactment in the play. Not only is it clearly a parody of *film noir* and gangster fiction, but it also parodies the classical theatre. Misrepresentation is key to the dramatic action, as the point of view on the events in the hotel varies between that of the gangsters inside and that of the media outside (relayed through the regular interventions of the voice of the radio commentator). Moreover, the gang's main concern is not whether they will get out alive, but whether their actions are being misrepresented to the outside world. Everything they do is guided by their perceptions of how they are being represented.

This comes to the fore at the climax of the play, when most of the gang decide to give themselves up rather than fight to the death. Their motives are clearly articulated, first by Bravo, who explains that it will be an action carried out in order to disturb and alter the image of this gang of desperate outlaws that the radio commentator has been constructing:

> ... so as to play one last dirty trick on the police, on Justice, on the Rich, on the Nice, one last filthy trick: to take some shit, to take all of their bullshit and smear it right over the all too pretty image they have of us.
>
> (Genet 2002: 242; 1995: 41)

A few lines later, Bob confirms this motive: 'I for one have had it with being what they've made me be' (Genet 2002: 243; 1995: 42). This reminds us of how far Genet's thinking was dominated by Sartrean existentialism at this time. Nevertheless, and despite its debt to Sartre, the final *travestissement*, or self-betrayal, of the gang is dramatically original: there is nothing else to compare with it in the theatre of Genet's time. It shows his imagination already working on the theme of identity, self-definition and its betrayals, a pattern that was to find its ultimate expression in Saïd in *The Screens*.

Genet may perhaps have rejected this play because he felt its reflections on identity were too dependent on Sartre's ideas. The year he tore it up, 1952 was the year when Sartre's monumental study of him appeared, the year when he felt crushed under its weighty theorizing. Perhaps the rather simple binary opposition between the police and the criminals no longer satisfied him at a time when he was beginning to see how he might use drama for an investigation into identity in more complex terms – terms that did not remain locked in the private imagination, however original, of his characters, but that took account of the public social and political dimensions. Postcolonial cultural theorist Edward Said has written about this aspect of Genet's work, calling him a 'traveller across identities':

Identity is what we impose upon ourselves through our lives as social, historical, political and even spiritual beings. The logic of culture and of families doubles the strength of identity which, for someone like Genet, who was a victim of the identity forced on him by his delinquency, his isolation, his transgressive talents and delights, is something to be resolutely opposed.

(Said 1995: 238)

Splendid's presents a group of people, each of them struggling to make sense of their identities in the terms here expressed by Said. All could be seen as standing in for different aspects of Genet himself: each one, in his own way, struggles against the identity imposed upon him by outside forces, and thus the gangsters may be seen as forerunners of the Blacks in the play of that name, and the Algerians in *The Screens*. What is lacking in *Splendid's* is the political dimension so evident in the last three plays.

Conclusion

These three early plays show Genet discovering his unique voice as a dramatist. Metaphorically, he breaks out of the world of the prison cell, and sheds some of his fascination with the great criminals and some of the whimsically poetic vision he had learned from Cocteau. Broadening his world view, he begins to apply his oblique vision to society at large and to the power games that are played out on the stage of history. At first his vision of interpersonal relations is heavily dependent on the existentialist theory developed at the time by Sartre. But there are already signs that he is less interested in the impossible search for authenticity that preoccupied Sartre in the late 1940s, and more drawn by his fascination for the possibilities of transformation in all its forms (including betrayal) and the complex links between political power and the force of the human imagination.

3 Key late plays

The Balcony, The Blacks, The Screens

The Balcony

The brothel and the image of power-play

The Balcony opens with a sequence of peep shows. The audience is put in the position of a group of people who have come together for the voyeuristic thrill of observing what goes on behind the closed doors of a brothel. But Genet disappoints those who might have been hoping for anything resembling a live sex show. Instead, he deflects the device of the imaginary visit to the brothel so as to lead his audience into a meditation on the nature of power. Each of the first three tableaux shows us a figure of authority – first a bishop, then a judge, then a general. These roles are lovingly, extravagantly built up on stage through the use of costumes and properties. Each of these authority figures is aided by a girl from the brothel, whose job is to flatter the Bishop, Judge or General by confirming his power. She is there not just to satisfy his sexual demands, but also to play out an elaborate, pre-established ritual enabling him to subdue her by his assumed authority.[1]

The audience quickly understands that this is all just make-believe: the figures on stage are not what they seem. They are ordinary men who come here in order to indulge their fantasies by playing these roles. The play's opening thus recalls that of *The Maids*, where we were shown the interplay between two servants as one of them assumed the role of mistress. But whereas in the earlier play we saw one of the Maids dressing up and playing out the part of Madame for

15 minutes before she was brought up short by the sounding of the alarm clock, the action of *The Balcony* starts at the end of such a scene. The Bishop is not putting on but removing his costume: his allotted time in the brothel is already up and he is being urged to hurry by two women. One is the prostitute who has been playing the part of the Sinner in need of the Bishop's absolution; the other is Madame Irma, the owner and manageress of the establishment. Madame Irma refers to her domain as a 'House of Illusions', since it offers clients a range of different roles that they may play out. It appears to have been suggested to Genet by a brothel he knew in Barcelona in the 1930s, which went by the name of *El Gran Balcón*.

Madame Irma's prostitutes are trained to tease, tantalize and, in the end, pleasure their clients by playing up to the fantasy role that they have chosen. In the case of the Bishop in Tableau One, the audience witnesses the afterglow of pleasure experienced by the man who imagines himself as a bishop, recalling the moment when he administered absolution and the face of the girl was lit up with repentance for, as he says, '... our sanctity was created for that very reason, that we might forgive her those very sins. Even if it were only make-believe' (Genet 2002: 267; 1991a: 4, translation modified). In other words, for him to feel himself to be fully a bishop he needs the Sinner to demonstrate her dependence on him. This ontological condition is made clearer in Tableau Two, when we see a man dressed as a judge, who is paired with a thief. The Judge's fantasy consists of sentencing the Thief for her crimes, but she is reluctant to go through with the game according to his desires, and teases him by pretending that perhaps she has committed no crime at all. This threat reduces the Judge to a trembling heap since, as he explains:

> My existence as a judge is an emanation of your existence as a thief. You'd only have to refuse – but you'd better not ...! To refuse to be who you are – what you are, and therefore who you are – for me to stop existing ... for me to vanish, to evaporate. Burst. Volatilised. Denied.
>
> (Genet 2002: 275–6; 1991a: 13, translation modified)

For the Judge's satisfaction to be achieved, the girl playing the Thief must not only admit to having committed the crimes in question, but must also accept the sentence meted out. In other words, it is a condition of the Judge's existence that the criminal should acknowledge him as such and accept his right to pass judgement.

Following the tableau with the Judge comes the tableau with the General. Here the fantasy imagined by Genet is more humorous. It is relatively easy to understand how the Bishop depends on the Sinner and the Judge on the criminal, but how to express the social necessity of military power? It is done by making the General dependent on his horse, which does duty for a whole army. The girl in this tableau has to pretend to be his faithful steed, carrying him into battle before ending up following his funeral procession after his death. For ultimately, the dream of each of these three men is to achieve the finality conferred by death. While they live, their desired existence as bishop, judge or general is in the hands of those who are willing to acknowledge them as such. But once they have entered the changeless domain of death, their being will be fixed: the General on his equestrian statue remains forever a general, no matter what subsequent generations may think of his military exploits.

The fourth and last of the opening sequence of peep show tableaux shows a little old man dressed as a tramp, who tries to offer a bouquet of flowers to a girl who whips him scornfully. After the lyrical evocations of desire fulfilled that characterize the first three tableaux, this one stands out by its brevity: it contains only two lines of dialogue, in which the Little Old Man seeks reassurance that there are lice in his wig and the Girl assures him there are plenty. The Little Old Man shows the reverse side of the first three: where they had sought to play out roles of exalted power and prestige in society, the Little Old Man finds satisfaction in total abjection. This, too, is a condition that has no absolute or objective status, but is conferred only by the scorn of others: he is dependent on the girl who whips him in the same way that the man playing the Judge is dependent on the girl who acts the part of the Thief.

The politics of desire

The Balcony is a political play, but a very unusual one. It deals, not with political programmes for reform, nor with a given way of ordering society, but with political *desire*. In conventional political discourse, power is mostly thought of as a constraint. It is a force on which limits must be set, sometimes one that must be overthrown. This is the dream of Roger and his group of rebels. They are outraged by the self-sufficiency of the established powers and attempt to overthrow them in order to replace them with a power structure that will be more responsive to the will of the masses. But Roger is to find that the archetypal figures who embody power – the Queen, Bishop, Judge and General – are untouchable. This is because of the obscure nature of political desire, as it is revealed through the action of the play. The fact is that these elites, though hated by many, are *desired* by many more. The effect of the first three tableaux was to show the deep roots of such power symbols in the collective psyche, and their obscure appeal. For as the story of Roger's defeat unfolds, Genet suggests that most people in fact desire to be dominated.

This begins to be explored in Tableau Five, where the centre of interest shifts from the clients of the brothel to those responsible for creating the grand illusions put in place to satisfy those clients' desires. After the brief glimpses into the workings of the House of Illusions provided by the first four tableaux, this is a long one, perhaps over-long. In it we see Genet revelling in the lyrical evocation of the inventiveness that lies behind the illusions. The dialogue between Madame Irma and her most trusted girl, Carmen, twists and turns, so that it is quite hard for the audience to follow its unfolding reflection on the relations between reality and illusion. In his notes on how to perform *The Balcony*, Genet was insistent that this tableau mark a sharp change of tone:

> In the first four scenes almost everything should be played in exaggerated fashion, although there are some passages in which the tone should be more natural, thus making the exaggeration seem more outrageous. In short, no equivocation, but two opposing tones.

On the other hand, from the scene between Madame Irma and Carmen until the end, the thing is to discover a narrative tone that is always equivocal, always shifting.

(Genet 2002: 258; 1991a: xi)

This is a pivotal scene, then, and it is here that the audience begins to find the explanation for the tableaux they have just witnessed, and the perspective that will make it possible to understand what follows. Genet is too dynamic a dramatist to put a theoretical lecture in the mouth of one of his characters, as Sartre sometimes did in his plays such as *Lucifer and the Lord* (1951) or *Altona* (1959). Instead, he uses the rivalry that seems to exist between Irma and Carmen to generate a dramatic dialogue out of which emerges his fundamental insight, which is that all power masks itself behind theatricality. Ignoring Irma's scornful attitude, Carmen rhapsodizes about her time as a prostitute playing the part of Saint Teresa. The tableau that follows illustrates how the theatrical appearance on the balcony of the brothel inmates dressed up in their finery, has an overwhelming effect on events in the street outside: the symbolic power of the Queen, Bishop, Judge and General is sufficient to quell the forces of rebellion. But here we are treated to a lyrical evocation of Carmen's delight in theatricality that was entirely devoid of any desire to exert power. Being innocent of any such desire, it possessed a kind of purity. Carmen has experienced a pure ecstasy and Irma understands this. She uses the same imagery as the Maids, of taking off, becoming airborne, floating through the sky (Genet 2002: 293; 1991a: 30).

But though she understands and appreciates Carmen's desire to lose herself in this way, Irma's own motivation is very different. She is a remarkable figure, quite exceptional in Genet's theatre. She is a survivor. She is not even a little in love with death, and that alone marks her out from everyone else in the play. She is the master technician, the maintainer of systems, the real guarantor that life goes on. And she can do this because she has such a clear understanding of the need of human beings to deny reality in favour of illusion or, rather, to relate to their reality through their most cherished illusions. She understands that power is the prerogative of those who are able to manipulate this fundamental human tendency, and her satisfaction comes from standing outside and observing. It is she who speaks the final words of the play when, addressing the audience, she says, 'You must go home, now – and you can be quite sure that nothing there will be any more real than it is here ... You must go' (Genet 2002: 350; 1991a: 96). When Genet demands that, after Tableau Four, the performers of the play discover a new narrative tone 'that is always equivocal, always shifting', he indicates the kind of progressive revelation that the play should have on its audience: at first the distinction between play-acting and reality appears to be clear. In each of the first three tableaux, there are moments where the playwright specifies the need for the actors to break out of role, so as to emphasize the fact that they are playing out an imaginary fantasy. Irma and Carmen even comment on the fact that every scenario has to have one small detail that is false, so as to throw into relief the artificially-constructed nature of everything else. But from Tableau Five onwards, such distinctions are perhaps not as clear as they at first appeared. At the end of Tableau Five, the Police Chief makes his appearance. The rebellion in the streets of the city causes him very little concern. He is far more anxious to know whether any of Irma's clients has come to her brothel with the express desire to perform the role of Police Chief. Although in reality he is quite able to control the rebels, he will only have the sense of exerting 'real' power when his role has become an object of desire on the same level as those of the Bishop, Judge and General.

Immediately after this, in Tableau Six, we are taken into the public square beneath le Grand Balcon, where the revolutionary forces are drawn up under the leadership of Roger. He is engaged in a bitter struggle with his men, who want to take his lover, Chantal, with them so that she can sing to the rebel forces, thus strengthening their morale. She is quite willing to go with them, but Roger opposes this. He has rescued her from Madame Irma's establishment, where she previously worked, and he is leading a crusade to reject the seductions of glamorous power roles in favour of a more rational, democratic exercise of power. When his men argue that her singing on the barricades is more powerful than a hundred armed rebels, he cries, despairingly:

In order to fight against an image Chantal has frozen into an image. The fight is no longer taking place in reality but in the lists. Field azure. It's the combat of allegories. None of us know any longer why we revolted.

(Genet 2002: 312; 1991a: 73)

Despite his impassioned pleas, she insists on going with the men, leaving him in despair. Ultimately, the question of what possesses the greater 'reality', the imaginary power role or the forces of armed rebellion, is shown to be unanswerable: all power is rooted in an exploitation of theatricality, and the apparent opposites with which the play opened – fantasy and reality – are in fact inseparable. Genet made a great many pronouncements that clarified this understanding of power. In an interview in 1977, he said:

Power cannot do without theatricality ... power shelters behind some kind of theatricality, whether it is in China, the Soviet Union, England or France ... There is only one place in the world where theatricality does not hide power and that is the theatre.

(Genet 1991: 155; 2004: 131)

In other words, the reality of the exercise of power on external bodies cannot be separated from the images and desires implanted in the imaginations of those subjected to power.

The final stage in the equivocal power struggle between Roger, as leader of the revolution, and the Police Chief, as defender of the establishment, comes in Tableau Nine. At this point the rebellion has been quelled, with the assistance of the Envoy from the palace, by the appearance on the balcony of the brothel clients presenting the unruffled image of authority. The self-congratulations of Madame Irma and her clients are interrupted by the arrival, so long awaited by the Police Chief, of someone wishing to play out his scenario. It turns out to be the defeated Roger. Carmen leads him into the studio set aside for this scenario, which consists of a monumental mausoleum, inspired by the one that the military dictator General Franco was having built for him in Spain at the time when Genet was writing the play. Roger has concluded that, since he has been drawn despite himself into 'a combat of allegories', he will take the fight to the enemy's territory and try to defeat him at his own game. He puts on the costume of the Police Chief, goes down into his tomb but, at the last minute, makes a violent gesture that runs counter to the scenario by pulling out a knife and castrating himself. He does this exclaiming that in this way he will merge the Police Chief's destiny with his own. But, of course, the Police Chief is not damaged – quite the reverse. The action of Roger has had the opposite effect: it has confirmed the status of the Police Chief in the imaginary power hierarchy.

Lucien Goldmann, a celebrated Marxist sociologist, maintains that the play can be read as an illustration (doubtless unconscious on Genet's part) of the realization in western societies of the fact that real power has been wielded for a long time by capitalism's forces of order (primarily the police), even though people still imagine power being in the hands of traditional figures. The play explains, in Goldmann's interpretation, that this realization in fact comes about as a result of a period of revolutionary threat, culminating in the defeat of the forces of rebellion, and that this corresponds precisely to historical developments in western Europe between 1917 and 1923 (Goldmann 1966). Whether or not Genet would have endorsed this precise interpretation, it is clear that his play explores the universal human desire to live in an ordered society, where power is exercised according to what we feel to be our deep needs, and the uneasy sense that those who now exercise that power do so without legitimacy.

The Blacks

The first production by Roger Blin

In the autumn of 1954, the actor-director Raymond Rouleau was planning to start up a company of black actors in Paris, and asked Genet to write a play for them (Genet 2002: 836; 2010: 228). In the event, he failed to find sufficient actors to make up a company and, although Genet's first version of *The Blacks* was delivered to Rouleau within a year, it was not performed until October 1959, at the théâtre de Lutèce, where an all-black cast was directed by Blin (see Chapter 5). Genet's correspondence with Marc Barbezat makes it clear that the play thus emerged from the same burst of creative energy that also produced *The Balcony* and *The Screens* (1988). *The Blacks* was exceptional in Genet's *oeuvre*, however, since it was the one play whose first production satisfied him completely. The first text had been published by Barbezat in January 1958; following Blin's production 18 months later, Genet persuaded Barbezat to issue a revised text, including 33 photographs of the performance and a preliminary note expressing the wish that no future edition should be published without the photos of this production. This lavishly illustrated edition was re-issued several times over the next 20 years until, in 1979, Genet allowed his play to appear without the photographs in the publication of his complete works.

In the play's first published version, Genet had included the following very short introduction: 'One evening an actor asked me to write a play for an all-black cast. But what exactly is a Black? First of all, what's his colour?' (Genet 2002: 475; 1960: 3). This demonstrates the deliberate ambiguity at the centre of this play, and is a first clue to what Genet meant when he wrote 'it is not a play like the others' (Genet 2002: 1188). After Blin's production, Genet added an additional note, printed just after the one quoted here, in which he explains that the play had been written for a white audience and that, in the unlikely event of it ever being presented before an all-black audience, someone must put on a white mask and be ushered ceremonially to a seat in the front row, with a spotlight on them, so as to mark clearly the nature of the play (Genet 2002: 475; 1960: 4). In this way, Genet wishes to emphasize that the actors who appear on stage do not represent a realistic image of any particular black society: rather, they represent the phantoms that inhabit the minds and imaginations of white people, for whom the play is performed. It is worth noting that Genet's chosen title, *Les Nègres*, is a term that carries the same pejorative overtones as the English words 'Negroes' and 'Niggers'; his translator chose the more neutral word 'Blacks', but Genet's choice of *Nègres* shows that he meant the play to represent only Blacks *as seen by Whites*.

A play with no story

The play has no story in the conventional sense of the word. Its action consists of a sequence of carefully planned rites, whose purpose is to undermine and dissolve the status of the actors as 'Blacks': people whose being is defined by 'Whites' as being black, non-white, other, alien, inferior. Genet's way of presenting this can be seen to draw on Frantz Fanon's influential analysis of the racism that resulted from French colonization in North Africa, *Black Skins White Masks*, in which he wrote, 'The Black has two dimensions; one when he is with a person of his own race, the other when he is with a White. A Black behaves differently with a White and with another Black' (Fanon 1967: 17, translation modified). *The Blacks* is a ritual ceremony for dissolving the second of Fanon's 'two dimensions'. If the play were to be performed with no Whites present, this second dimension would not exist, and the play would lose its purpose.

When reading or viewing this play, then, we should not look for story or character, even in the limited sense that we found in *The Balcony*. Rather, we need to be alert to the replacement of dramatic action with ceremonial rite. This quality is what makes Genet a precursor of 'postdramatic' theatre. Hans-Thies Lehmann, the scholar responsible for launching the term 'postdramatic', acknowledges Genet's importance in pioneering this new form:

> Postdramatic theatre is the replacement of dramatic action with ceremony, with which dramatic-cultic action was once, in its beginnings, inseparably united. What is meant by ceremony as a moment of postdramatic theatre is thus the whole spectrum of movements and processes that have no referent but are presented with heightened precision; events of peculiarly formalized communality; musical-rhythmic or visual-achitectonic constructs of development; para-ritual forms, as well as the (often deeply black) ceremony of the body and of presence; the emphatically or monumentally accentuated ostentation of the presentation.
>
> (Lehmann 2006: 69)

These terms are useful in analysing and accounting for the power of *The Blacks*. 'Heightened precision' perfectly describes the opening stage direction in which the drawing of the stage curtain reveals how 'four Negroes in evening clothes ... and four Negresses in evening gowns are dancing a kind of minuet around the catafalque to an air of Mozart' (Genet 2002: 479; 1960: 7 translation modified). Genet specifies that 'the ladies' costumes – heavily spangled evening gowns – suggest fake elegance, the very height of bad taste' (Genet 2002: 478; 1960: 8). And the first character to speak, Archibald, demonstrates 'accentuated ostentation', as he plays the heavily ingratiating master of ceremonies, introducing the other characters and explaining the nature of the ceremony that is to follow: 'You are white. And spectators. This evening we shall perform for you ...' (Genet 2002: 480; 1960: 10). Lehmann's new vocabulary for analysing what happens in dramatic ceremonies is important, not in order to prove that *The Blacks* is a postdramatic play, but because it helps to show how Genet's restless creativity led him to test and question the limits of drama as understood at his time, and to discover solutions that were to pave the way for later avant-garde developments.

Genet was acutely conscious of the traps and opportunities for self-deception involved when a white European tries to write for black performers. In addition to his two prefatory notes he wrote a posthumously published preface in 1956. In this he traces the path of the moral ambiguities that lie in wait for the writer, and clarifies his claim to have written the play not *for* Blacks, but *against* Whites. Claiming to write *for* Blacks would involve the type of hypocrisy dissected in the following passage: 'Wanting to write for the Blacks would derive from that moral abjection that involves taking interest magnanimously, with understanding, in the weak; absolving one's conscience; abstaining from any effective action' (Genet 2002: 838; 2010: 230). On the other hand, he goes on to say:

> I had the right to try and wound the Whites, and through this wound, to introduce doubt. In fact, I think it is necessary that a scandalous act make them question themselves, worry them with regard to this real problem that causes no conflict in their souls.
>
> (ibid.)

The 'wound'

The first English critic to draw serious attention to Genet's preface, and to its importance for understanding *the Blacks*, is Carl Lavery, who sees the idea of the 'wound' as central to Genet's understanding of the world from the 1950s onwards (Lavery 2010: 49–101). Lavery traces this back to the experience that Genet had in a railway carriage (see Chapter 1), and claims that, in *The Blacks* especially, Genet's aim is to inflict a wound on the Whites in his audience:

> For Genet, a theatre that 'wounds' has the capacity to free the subject from the prison house of language and the fetters of discourse. The instantaneous gap that the Genetian wound opens in consciousness – although painful – is intended to produce a utopian space where authentic communication can potentially take place.
>
> (Lavery 2006: 74)

The effect Genet aims for thus goes beyond any allegorical meaning incorporated in the story and waiting to be extrapolated by the audience (as in the case of Brechtian theatre) and aims instead to destroy the very medium it uses, namely theatre, by drawing attention to the 'theatricality ... that power can never do without' and shocking the audience into a recognition of its own complicity in the oppressive power relations alluded to on stage. In this way, as Lavery writes, '*The Blacks* betrays its own dramatic logic (the replacement of the thing by the sign) and becomes a situation which, to adopt [Guy] Debord's language, starts on the far side of theatre' (ibid.: 75–6). This could be paraphrased by saying that the function of Genet's play is to assault white audiences. There is some evidence that this is indeed how the first audiences responded to it: the reviews were divided, and fellow playwright Eugène Ionesco walked out saying that he was not going to sit there and be insulted.

With historical insight, one can see that Genet's determination to focus unwaveringly on the underlying racism of all white colonialism was indeed one of the most original aspects of his work in the second half of the 1950s, especially in *The Blacks* and *The Screens*. This was a period in which, all over Africa, challenges were being mounted by indigenous populations against white supremacy embodied in colonial powers. In East Africa, for example, the Mau-Mau were fighting a determined war of liberation against the British colonial establishment, and in Algeria the *Front de Libération Nationale* was beginning to mount an armed challenge to the century-old French occupation of their country. No other European dramatist of the time understood so clearly the issues that were at stake, and no other dramatist confronted white audiences with their unreflective racism in so stark a manner.

What happens in The Blacks

In the opening minutes of the performance, after the audience has been suitably confused by the dancing to the Mozart minuet and its sudden interruption, the dialogue builds up a carefully orchestrated contradiction between a European audience's conventional expectations of what a company of actors has to do – improvise, learn lines, try to impersonate other characters – and the contrasting model of a 'rite', constantly referred to by Archibald, the Master of Ceremonies, in which none of these is important because only one thing counts: to follow rigidly what the ceremony lays down. The aim of the ceremony is only revealed gradually, but Archibald gives a hint when he says, 'by stretching language, we'll distort it sufficiently to wrap ourselves in it and hide' (Genet 2002: 488; 1960: 27). In other words, to free themselves from the 'dimension', as Fanon calls it, imposed on them by Whites, the Blacks must begin by distorting the language they have been forced to use.

Just as much of the dialogue of *The Maids* was generated by the disagreements between the two sisters about the tactics they should employ in their attempts to free themselves from Madame, so here the Blacks argue amongst themselves about the best way to carry out their rite. But they are not in fundamental disagreement about the purpose of the rite, which is to achieve pure hatred, purging themselves of any desire for what is white that has been inculcated into them by their colonial educators and missionaries. When Diouf, the voice of reconciliation, protests, Archibald puts him down violently, but accepts that he must have his say, since his speeches are scripted into the text:

> ARCHIBALD (*to Diouf, violently*) Once again you must know that you are wasting your time. Your arguments are well known. You will speak of reason and consensus: but we shall insist on irrationality and refusal. You will speak of love. Go ahead, since our speeches are allowed for in the text.
>
> (Genet 2002: 490; 1960: 29, translation modified)

By 'the text', Archibald means the sequence of the rite that the Negroes are there to perform, and whose multiple purposes will only gradually emerge as the play progresses. One of them, already stated, is to distort language, to find an alternative to the oppressive French language that has been imposed upon them. This will also involve finding alternative values to those enshrined within the French language and its cultural heritage. Thus, they will have to turn their backs on reason, on love, on all the profoundest assumptions underlying white civilization. The dialogue explores how hard this is. Village, for example, complains that he feels love towards Virtue, but Archibald reminds him that this is impossible in the context of their rite: 'You're a Negro and a performer. Neither of whom will know love' (Genet 2002: 495; 1960: 39). Archibald goads the others on in their enterprise to distort the language of the colonizer and discover alternative values. In this process Genet writes some of his most striking poetic speeches, for example Archibald's:

> I order you to be black to your very veins. Pump black blood through them. Let Africa circulate in them. Let Negroes negrify themselves. Let them persist to the point of madness in what they're condemned to be, in their ebony, in their smell, in their yellow eyes, in their cannibal tastes ...
>
> (Genet 2002: 502–3; 1960: 52)

And this great speech is followed by the 'Litany of the Livid', in which all the unpleasant and evil associations of the colour white are explored (Genet 2002: 504; 1960: 54–5).

Rejecting the 'white' value of universal love, the participants in the rite must struggle to discover absolute hatred. At its centre is the re-enactment of the murder of a white woman by Village. The catafalque placed centre-stage supposedly contains her corpse, and there is lengthy discussion about whether Village was attracted to her or not. This is important to Archibald, in charge of the rite, since he has to determine whether the crime was committed out of pure hatred: 'His crime saves him. If he committed it with hatred ...' (Genet 2002: 502; 1960: 51). The re-enactment continues with Village evoking the scene, until he comes to the point where he requires someone standing before him to represent the dead woman. Felicity designates Diouf, and he is ceremonially dressed in 'a blond wig, a crude cardboard carnival mask representing a laughing white woman with big cheeks, a piece of pink knitting, two balls of knitting wool, a knitting needle and white gloves' (Genet 2002: 503; 1960: 53). The dialogue explores the various ways in which black Africans are made to feel inferior to white colonizers, and especially how the colonial enterprise involves deliberately cultivating in the black mind the *desire* for whiteness and what it represents. As William Blake's poem so powerfully evokes it: 'I am black but oh my soul is white.'

This is interrupted by a character named Ville de Saint Nazaire, translated by Frechtman as Newport News. He comes in for a second time, to announce to Archibald that while this charade is being performed for the white audience, something altogether more important is happening off-stage: a fellow Black is being tried for betraying a black rebel to the white authorities, and is about to be executed. For the first time, the stage direction for Archibald reads: 'he has changed his voice. Instead of declaiming, he speaks in his natural tone' (Genet 2002: 517; 1960: 81). Speaking to Newport News, Archibald reverts briefly to Fanon's other dimension (the way the Black behaves when with a person of her/his own race). This point is made explicit in Newport News's dialogue at his next appearance when he says: 'But though we can put on an act in front of them (*pointing to the audience*), we've got to stop acting when we're among ourselves' (Genet 2002: 517; 1960: 82). Like his other entrances, this visit of Newport News is very brief, serving only to satisfy him that the diversionary ceremony continues.

An incomplete ceremony

The ceremony builds to a climax, but Village seems reluctant to complete it: his natural impulses lead him to be friendly, and he has to struggle to take on the hatred required of him by the rite. At this point, Felicity stands and delivers a magnificent rousing speech, beginning with the words 'Dahomey! Dahomey! To my rescue, Negroes, all of you!' (Genet 2002: 514–5; 1960: 76–7). Into this Genet has poured his ability to write intensely evocative, lyrical prose, here celebrating the millions of Blacks who have been dispersed around the globe by colonial powers in the course of history. After this comes the second main re-enactment of the evening, when the members of the Court attempt to exert their authority. Until this point they have been watching passively from a raised platform behind the stage (reminiscent of the balcony on which the courtly figures appeared in *The Balcony*). Now they decide that the Blacks must be punished, and they come down from the upper level to exert their authority. But immediately they feel ill at ease. Genet enjoys drawing on all the phantoms of fear fixed in the memory of the white colonial enterprise:

> THE GOVERNOR: (*hiccoughing after each word*) Stop in your tracks. Prudence, circumspection, mystery. All is swamp, quagmires, arrows, felines ... here, from the skin of their bellies the snakes lay eggs from which blinded children take wing ... the ants riddle you with vinegar or arrows ... the creepers fall madly in love with you, kiss your lips and eat you ...
>
> (Genet 2002: 523; 1960: 91–2)

Meanwhile the Negroes, under the balcony which the Court has not yet left, 'utter the sounds of the virgin forest: croaking of the toad, hoot of the owl, a hissing, very gentle roars, breaking of wood, moaning of the wind' (ibid.). After centuries of oppression, in which they have been taught to despise their skin, their culture and the land of their birth, their only recourse is to emphasize these things, to exalt and glory in the sounds of the 'virgin forest' that so terrify the Whites.

What follows is the final act in the rite, as the 'white' Court comes to pass judgement on the murder of the white woman, attempting to cow the Blacks with all the instruments of colonial law enforcement. The audience is reminded that this is, in fact, only a charade, as it transpires that there is no white corpse, not even a coffin, under the apparent catafalque at the front of the stage. Instead of being about a real body, the dialogue becomes concerned with definitions of beauty. The members of the Court invoke European concepts of beauty, while the Blacks continue their oppositional insistence on reversing these values. As Felicity says:

> To you, black was the colour of priests and undertakers and orphans. But everything is changing. Whatever is gentle and kind and good and tender will be black. Milk will be black, sugar, rice, the sky, doves, hope will be black ....
>
> (Genet 2002: 531; 1960: 106)

At last Newport News makes his final entry to announce the execution of the traitor and 'with a single movement, the members of the Court solemnly remove their masks. The audience sees the five black faces' (Genet 2002: 533; 1960: 111). The traitor has been executed, and Newport News announces that another freedom fighter has been appointed to continue the work of the one who has just been condemned to death:

> He's on his way. He's going off to organize and continue the fight. Our aim is not only to corrode and dissolve the idea they'd like us to have of them, we must also fight them in their actual person, in their flesh and blood. As for you, you were present only for display.
>
> (Genet 2002: 533; 1960: 112)

The word used by Genet for 'display' in the original is *la parade*, a word that was traditionally used in French theatre for the 'taster' show put on outside the theatre to encourage spectators to buy tickets for the real performance inside the theatre. The show we have just witnessed is thus reduced to the level of a distraction from the real drama happening elsewhere.

The play now moves rapidly through the final sequence of the rite, in which the Court members replace their masks and are ceremonially killed by the Blacks. They then get up again, as if in child's play, and Archibald makes his final speech, justifying the whole enterprise:

> My friends, allow me first to thank you all. You've given an excellent performance. (*The five members of the Court remove their masks and bow.*) You've displayed a great deal of courage, but you had to. The time has not yet come for presenting dramas about noble matters. But perhaps they suspect what lies behind this architecture of emptiness and words. We are what they want us to be. We shall therefore be it to the very end, absurdly.
>
> (Genet 2002: 541; 1960: 126)

The rite is finished and the audience is left with a last glimpse of Village and Virtue trying to invent a new way to talk about their love for one another that does not rely on the clichés of European love literature. The last words are Virtue's 'At least, there's one sure thing: you won't be able to wind your fingers in my long golden hair ...' (Genet 2002: 542; 1960: 128).

Thus the play maintains to the bitter end the underlying necessity for the Blacks to dissolve the image that white civilization has constructed, if they are to able to invent a new way of being. In his last play, *The Screens*, Genet was to attempt something similar in relation to the Arabs of France's North African territories. In this way, Genet's later, more politically targeted plays link with his first plays: they all present us with anti-societies. The worlds of prison, domestic service, brothel, black or Arab rebels are all defined by opposition to white, catholic, bourgeois norms of how society should be. This links back to Sartre's notion that we are dominated by our sense of 'being-for-others'. We see ourselves through the eyes of others and are painfully conscious of how they judge us. The Blacks, like the characters inhabiting all Genet's plays, are painfully aware that their existence and, more profoundly, their very consciousness, is conditioned by the scorn and contempt of others. These plays therefore set out to investigate the levels of interdependence that link the oppressed to the oppressor, and are all built around rites or ceremonies of metamorphosis in which the oppressed, by accepting and exaggerating their condition, aim to transform their shame into pride, thus changing the rules of the game and turning the tables on their oppressors.

The stage as 'de-realizing space'

Genet's original insight was to see how the game of theatre itself could be turned inside-out to achieve this aim of transforming shame into pride. For him, the stage is a *de-realizing* space that dissolves the reality of everything that appears within its frame. Of all his plays, *The Blacks* expresses this idea most bluntly, when Archibald comments on the function of theatre and the parallel status of actor and Negro: 'An actor… a Negro… if he tries to kill, destroys the reality of even his knife' (Genet 2002: 535; 1960: 114, translation modified). Hence, as Archibald never ceases to remind the other Blacks, the job of the stage is not to imitate life; anything that might tempt the white audience to see the performance as a mimetic representation of real life must be avoided. Instead, in keeping with the play's subtitle *clownerie* (clown show), they try to push their performance of white people's image of Blacks to such grotesque extremes that it explodes, becomes 'de-realized'. The technique is exactly the same as that appealed to by Genet when he points out that *The Balcony* is not a satire, but 'the glorification of the Image and the Reflection' (Genet 2002: 260; 1991a: xiii). Similarly, in his *Avertissement* (note) on the same play, he writes that the problems set out on stage should never be resolved on the imaginary plane because this will reassure the audience that the problems require no further action on their part. 'On the contrary, let evil explode on stage, let it show us naked, leave us haggard if possible, and with no other recourse than to ourselves' (Genet 2002: 261; 1991a: xiv, translation modified).

The change of emphasis that we find in Genet's last two plays, *The Blacks* and *The Screens*, lies in the way that they hint at a different kind of opening towards the future. They were written at a time of vigorous political discussion among colonized peoples all over the world, especially in French-occupied North Africa. In *The Screens*, Genet was to tackle the Algerian War of Independence head-on, and both this and *The Blacks* look forward to his later overtly political writings on behalf of the Black Panthers of the USA and the Palestinian liberation fighters.

The Screens

A political play?

Whereas in *The Balcony* the revolution takes place offstage, and in *The Blacks* the traitor is executed in the wings, in *The Screens* the revolution explodes before the spectator's eyes. Imperial power is dismantled by anti-colonial Arab insurgents, as the play progresses. Genet first published *The Screens* in 1961, whilst France was still fighting against Algeria's claims for independence. However, Genet never overtly references this historical event, since the Arab country in which he locates the play is not specified, and the colonial occupants' names range from Monsieur and Madame Bonneuil, who are undoubtedly French, to Sir Harold who must be English, Monsieur Blankensee, who could be Belgian, and Brandineschi, who sounds Italian. Blin, who directed the French première of the play (see Chapter 6), argues that Genet did not write *The Screens* in support of Algeria; he wrote it against armies: not just the French army, but all armies (Blin 1986: 201). Blin remarks that Genet warned him, 'Most of all, don't make my play left-wing' (ibid.: 202). Whilst the anti-imperialist thematics in *The Screens* can certainly be considered political, Genet does not align himself with party politics for, as he illustrates in *The Balcony*, both left- and right-wing politics are equally preoccupied with appearance rather than with transforming society.

A fractured narrative

The Screens is not a political play in any recognizable sense. It contains no tangible change in power dynamics, no inspirational hero, no substantial message. Genet had intended it to constitute the opening work of an immense cycle of seven plays entitled *Death II*. *Death I* would contain prose works, one of which is published as 'Fragments' (Genet 1990: 67–97; 2003: 19–35).[2] 'Fragments' is an appropriate title, since the few works that Genet composed for this intended opus resist unity, harmony and coherence. French novelist and critic Marie Redonnet describes *The Screens* as 'an epic smashed into tiny pieces' (Redonnet 2000: 197); François Regnault, dramaturg for director Patrice Chéreau's 1983 production of the play, would concur: 'Paths cross each other without meeting. Voices alternate without hearing each other. The usual coherence of subjectivity explodes. Innumerable characters materialize and dematerialize, leaving just enough time for an image to form' (Regnault 1983). *The Screens* is governed by no logical, linear narrative, Genet himself confirming this: 'People say that plays are generally supposed to have a meaning: not this one. It's a celebration whose elements are disparate, it is the celebration of nothing' (Genet 2002: 847; 1972: 14). Disintegration constitutes the organizing, or rather, disorganizing principle of *The Screens*.

The Screens fractures not just narrative coherence, but also conventionally recognized systems of value and morality. *The Balcony* and *The Blacks* already begin the deconstruction of categories such as truth and falsity. Just a few examples serve to illustrate how, in *The Screens*, Genet blurs the distinctions not just between true and false, but also between large and small, ugly and beautiful, high and low, comic and tragic, living and dead: the French Gendarme calls himself 'small', whereas he towers over the Arab women; characters die, notably the old villager Si Slimane and rebel leader Kadidja, but still converse with the living, who are separated from them by nothing more than the screens after which the play is named; stage directions instruct actors to look up, though the action takes place below; Saïd refers to Leïla as ugly, but describes her in the most lyrical terms, as a pile of dove droppings that accumulate into a statue (Genet 2002: 625, 617, 694, 646; 1962: 64, 55, 145, 87). Genet's adage that poetry is 'the art ... of using shit and making you eat it' applies to this last example, where the base and repugnant are represented by beauty (Genet 1953: 190). It also indicates the potential for transformation that lies at the heart of Genet's aesthetic, and notably of his theatre. Since categories and values do not have permanent or stable meanings, people and things can transform from one value to its opposite. Boundaries between conventional opposites are disassembled or destroyed just like screens. The radical equality engendered by Genet's concept of the 'wound' – where nothing of any significance differentiates one human, or one value, from another – levels all hierarchies and opposites.

With 16 sprawling tableaux, an expansive cast of nearly 100, and a panoramic spread of locations, *The Screens* is far too epic, kaleidoscopic and poetic to describe in terms of plot. Notwithstanding, certain narrative threads emerge, which we indicate here, to provide the reader with tangible reference points that, if nothing else, s/he can unravel.

The 'plot'

The 'Nettles Family' comprises Saïd who, because he is the poorest man in the region, has no choice but to marry the ugliest woman, Leïla. The story of Leïla, Saïd and Saïd's mother is set to the backdrop of an uprising against occupying colonial powers, led by the female fighter Kadidja, who is killed, and then by the old matriarch, Ommou. The Nettles Family lives in contravention not only of the colonial regime, but also of the insurgency, since they retreat into isolation and degradation. Running counter to their abjection is the activity of Warda, the Arab prostitute who dresses and decorates herself in sumptuous clothes instead of exposing herself, which would be more fitting to her profession. And running obliquely throughout the play are Saïd's relationships with his mother, Kadidja and Ommou, all of whom attempt to define and shape him (the play's original title was *The Mothers – Les Mères*). No plot-line or character dominates. Saïd, for example, is supposedly the hero, heralded as such by the revolutionaries, but unlike any classical hero is absent for much of the play.

The theatricality of power

Rather than being structured by plot, *The Screens* contains themes, metaphors and motifs that Genet weaves into its multicoloured fabric. Most notably, like *The Balcony*, *The Screens* treats the dynamic between appearance and power. As in *The Balcony*, the ruling regime – in this case an occupying colonial power – is revealed by Genet to be a fake façade behind which subsists nothing of substance. Here, this façade is represented visually by the paper-thin screens that dominate the play (for a detailed discussion of screens see Chapter 6). The colonial landowner Monsieur Blankensee wears padding to enhance his physical stature, explaining, 'it takes all that faking to impose ourselves' and admitting, 'my pad is the chief element of my prestige' (Genet 2002: 633, 645; 1962: 73, 85, translation modified). His friend, the plantation owner Sir Harold, is well aware, like the Bishop, Judge and General in *The Balcony*, that his image bears more impact than his reality. For this reason he leaves a giant stuffed replica of his glove to watch over his plantation workers in his absence, since this symbol of authority bears more clout than his actual presence. The colonial army, too, cultivates its outward appearance in order to impose its military might. The Lieutenant gives orders to his men:

> Good warriors, brave warriors, of course, but above all handsome warriors. So: perfect shoulders, rectified by artifice if necessary. Muscular necks. Work on your necks… by torsion, tension, contraction, distortion, suspension, compression, flexion, fluxion, masturbation… Hard thick thighs. Or seemingly so. Knee-high,… beneath your pants, put sandbags to swell your knees, but appear like gods!
>
> (Genet 2002: 639; 1962: 79, translation modified)

Evocative of Monsieur Blankensee, the soldiers bolster their thighs with sandbags. More important than their intelligence or strength is their image. Moreover, the more that colonial authority is threatened, the more the soldiers reinforce their image. The Lieutenant explains, 'It's not a matter of intelligence, but of perpetuating an image that's more than ten centuries old, that grows stronger and stronger as that which it represents crumbles' (Genet 2002: 675; 1962: 119). The Lieutenant's speech to his troops, just quoted, describes how the combatants must cultivate their image. Moreover, many of the Lieutenant's words are in themselves pure image, since they contain no real meaning. Paronomasia is a poetic device where words are selected according to their sound rather than their meaning. This is the case here, where Genet selects words according to their suffix '-ion', rather than because of their signification. Paronomasia can result in catachresis, where words make no semantic sense. For example, it is questionable whether some of the Lieutenant's exercises, notably 'distortion' or 'masturbation', will strengthen the soldiers' neck muscles. The Lieutenant's lecture speaks of appearance, and is itself but appearance, since it makes little real sense. Since the army preoccupies itself more with its image than with fighting the uprising, Sir Harold accuses it of masturbatory narcissism: 'The army's playing with itself, like a lad behind a fence' (Genet 2002: 634). Their colonial chevrons and polished spats become vacuous symbols. The French Sergeant admits this when he dies: 'The uniform, the stripes, the decorations and the officer's school diploma when you've got one! … And what's left? Emptiness' (Genet 2002: 711; 1962: 170).

As in *The Balcony*, not only the ruling regime, but also the oppressed population is obsessed with image. Warda conceals her decaying body and rotting teeth behind lavish robes and ornate hairpins. She compares herself to a coffin, thereby, like the Bishop, Judge and General in *The Balcony*, aspiring to the finality of death, where her image will be eternally fixed (Genet 2002: 584). The prostitutes, in Genet's words, become the visual echo of the colonial soldiers, since the main occupation of both is to primp and preen themselves (ibid.: 957). The revolutionary forces that seek to overthrow the regime are also infatuated with image. When they seize control, they simply perpetuate the same myths of power as the colonials they overthrew: they form a disciplined army that wears imposing uniforms, establish a military band, and raise a flag (ibid.: 689). Colonials and insurgents alike deck themselves in apparel, creating and disseminating their public image. In the play's closing tableaux, almost everyone has been killed in the anti-colonial war. Now the shifting vagaries of life cannot compromise or corrupt their images. The Sergeant is immortalized in a street name in Cahors, a town in France where his uncle makes mattresses (ibid.: 737). 'The whole world is ritualized,' says Genet in an interview (Genet 1991: 161; 2004: 137, translation modified). Neither colonials nor revolutionaries escape Genet's universalizing ontology of theatricality, which is highlighted by the fact that when they die, they all tear with surprising ease through the same paper screens and appear in the same space, one of the play's abiding images.

The revolutionaries' theatricality is confirmed when they follow the example of the colonials who have appointed the Sergeant as their figurehead, by nominating Saïd as their hero. The fact that *Sergeant* and *Saïd* bear the same initials and number of syllables, underscores this equivalence. As Genet states, the Sergeant is 'the counterpart, luminous by Western standards, of Saïd' (Genet 2002: 847; 1972: 14). The Sergeant's gleaming medals and impeccable discipline constitute the mirror reflection – no more or less artificial – of Saïd. The rebels champion Saïd because they perceive his thieving and degradation to be a defiant act against colonial law and order. Saïd has stolen the jacket of Taleb, his workmate at Sir Harold's plantation, and is imprisoned. His new bride Leïla, far from being delectable, is actively repulsive. When Saïd's mother asks where she is going, she replies, 'To wipe my nose in the garden, to wash away my snot and tears, and to comfort myself in the nettles' (Genet 2002: 594; 1962: 28). The Mother, rather than defending her son, implores Taleb to press charges against him (Genet 2002: 601–2; 1962: 35–6). Members of the Nettles Family thus debase themselves intentionally, and for this reason the revolutionaries celebrate them. Ommou's adulation of Saïd is clear: 'we're embalming your sordidness, your shittiness' (Genet 2002: 730; 1962: 192). A public holiday is announced in his honour, and the revolutionaries give the Nettles Family the epithet 'holy family' (Genet 2002: 707; 1962: 163). Colonial European, Christian emblems are simply replaced with different symbols and icons. The emulation of Christianity is emphasized notably when Saïd is described as floating in the heavens or walking on water, 'brow in the nebulae' and 'feet on the ocean' (Genet 2002: 731; 1962: 192). Ommou even talks of stuffing him, thereby preserving him like a holy relic or a hunting trophy (Genet 2002: 727). Saïd is disincarnated, transformed into a pure and empty sign whose appearance bears no relation to his reality.[3] The discrepancy is flagrant between the image the revolutionaries create of Saïd, and the reality of his puny stature and insignificant presence, when finally he arrives at the end of the play after having lost his way because he does not know his left from his right – hardly credentials for a hero. This does not deter the revolutionaries or their leader Ommou, who exclaims, 'If it were necessary to invent Saïd... If it were necessary word by word, here and there, to spit, to slobber a whole story... written or recited... to slobber the Saïd story' (Genet 2002: 732; 1962: 193). The revolutionaries produce an iconography that suits their narrative of dissidence, regardless of Saïd's reality. Like the insurgents in *The Balcony* who crown Chantal as their figurehead, revolutionaries in *The Screens* need an image to follow. And paradoxically, like the Negroes in *The Blacks*, the Arab revolutionaries, far from rejecting the image constructed by European colonial discourses, conform to it. By revering the Nettles Family, they reaffirm the racist stereotype of the thieving, filthy native who does not understand the positive values of social refinement and moral rectitude.

Eluding appearance

Nettles, after which the family is named, habitually grow beyond the bounds of a tended garden. The first syllable of the French for nettle, *ortie*, is 'or', homophone of 'hors', meaning 'outside'.[4] Saïd and Leïla are unique in Genet's theatre, since they elude image and type. Moreover, *Leïla* means 'night' in Arabic, and she is shrouded in obscurity both literally, because she is cloaked, hooded and veiled, and metaphorically, since her highly ambiguous character never shapes into an identity. For example, she appears subjugated, but never submits to Saïd, whose impotence she mocks (Genet 2002: 591; 1962: 25). At the end of the play she literally disappears, since all that remains is her hooded costume. She can be captured by no image.[5] Saïd is no less elusive. He refuses to conform to the image cast upon him by the revolutionaries, exclaiming, 'That's not me, Saïd!' (Genet 2002: 732; 1962: 194). His revolutionary zeal could hardly be more absent, his battle cry being, 'To the old gal, to the soldiers, to all of you, I say shit' (Genet 2002: 735; 1962: 197). He is an absent, unwitting, unwilling hero. He is uncategorizable and unfathomable. Ommou admits to him, 'it's become impossible to judge you. If no one has gone as far as you ...' (Genet 2002: 728; 1962: 189). Saïd and Leïla never arrive in the realm of the dead because their images never become fixed and definitive. The last words of the play are uttered by the Mother, who asks of her son, 'Then where is he? In a song?', to which Kadidja responds 'with a gesture expressive of doubt' (Genet 2002: 737; 1962: 201). He and his wife remain forever elusive.

In spite of their refusal to join the organized revolution, Saïd and Leïla are the true rebels. They systematically refuse to be domesticated by preconceived ideas of behaviour or ideology. In one of his comments on the play Genet explains that Saïd must even betray his betrayal. In other words, were his betrayal of his compatriots to become a predictable political programme, it would harden into a doctrine. Genet states that were he to rewrite the play, he might give tableaux titles such as: 'Saïd betraying – but by making a mistake so serious that the betrayal fails: the betrayal betraying Saïd' (Genet 2002: 682). Saïd even fails at betraying. But his failure is his success. Until his death, he never conforms to type or concedes to the constricting expectations of others. Only Saïd and Leïla escape the theatrical carnival of stereotypes that parades across Genet's stage.

Only Saïd and Leïla ensure the future of poetry, which transcends all cliché.

Part II
Key productions

Key proteins

4 Key productions and issues surrounding production
The Maids, Deathwatch

Introduction

This chapter discusses *The Maids* and *Deathwatch* in production across six decades, demonstrating the wide variety of theatrical approaches and styles that Genet's early texts inspire.[1] To understand why Genet's early plays engender such a diversity of artistic responses from directors, designers and actors, this chapter begins by considering the different and opposing dramatic traditions from which his theatre draws, notably French classicism, naturalism and Far-Eastern performance. In turn, it notes how the role played by plot and character in Genet's theatre is diminished, enabling a glittering array of other theatrical elements to take to the stage: scenography, costumes, objects, performance styles, which are discussed in detail in this second half of the book. It is all the more important to question the validity of a plot-based or naturalist reading of Genet's plays, given that the readership of this book is based principally in the UK and USA, where narrative-driven social realism dominates contemporary theatre.

Deceptive classicism

Deathwatch and *The Maids* might appear initially to display a certain classical unity. They respect some of the conventions of discipline and order that dominated French theatre during the seventeenth and eighteenth centuries, where a play had to adhere to a brief time span, single location, straightforward plot, and visual and verbal simplicity that avoided baroque display (Scherer and Scherer 1993). A comparison of the many drafts of both plays reveals how Genet progressively eliminated multiple temporalities, settings, sub-plots and secondary characters. Taking place over three days, located in both prison cell and visiting room, and divided into three acts, an early draft of *Deathwatch*, *Pour 'la Belle'*, is outwardly more disjointed than the final version. The posthumous 1988 edition, revised 40 years after Genet first conceived *Deathwatch*, is set in one cell and spans only a couple of hours. Genet pared down later versions of *The Maids* to an equally seemingly classical simplicity. Manuscripts dating from the mid-1940s, several of which are published and painstakingly compared by Corvin and Dichy in Genet's *Théâtre complet*, show how *The Maids* initially contained 12 characters and four acts, each situated in a different location. The final 1968 version contains only three characters (Claire, Solange and Madame), one location (Madame's bedroom), and a 24-hour time span (Corvin 2001: xiii). Genet's draft title for *The Maids* was *The Tragedy of the Confidantes*, and some critics argue for its status as pure French classical tragedy (Marchand 1997: 159; Chevalier 1998: 37–43; Puzin 1998: 24–46). Oreste Pucciani describes it as 'near-perfect, in the tradition of pure French classical tragedy', and even argues that it is divided, by the sound of the alarm clock, telephone, doorbell and slamming door, into five acts (Pucciani 1972: 22).

From this account one might assume that Genet simplifies time, space and narrative in order better to foreground plot which, according to French classical theatre, heavily influenced by Aristotle's *Poetics*, should be 'the source and (as it were) the soul' of a play, its principal unifying element (Aristotle 1996: Chh 4, 5, 8). Certain critics, for instance Michel Vaïs, see *The Balcony* as a turning point away from the classicism of Genet's earlier plays (Vaïs 1978: 171). However, the apparent conventionality of Genet's earlier theatre is deceptive. With their self-consciously literary, image-charged dialogue, which pirouettes vertiginously from one existential crisis to another, *Deathwatch*'s three cellmates, Green-Eyes, Lefranc and Maurice, leave the reader/spectator in a mist of philosophical ambiguity. At the end of an early version, written in 1947, Lefranc confesses his desire for Yeux-Verts openly (Genet 2002: 117). When Lefranc then kills the charmingly boyish Maurice, his motivation – his jealous, uncompromising passion for Yeux-Verts – is clear. The final, supposedly more classically structured version, however, displays none of this narrative clarity. Genet transforms *Deathwatch* into a poem that, rather than reflecting rationally on themes like submission, domination, abjection and saintliness, refracts them into a kaleidoscope of questions, as Chapter 2 recounts.

Equally with *The Maids*, also discussed in detail in Chapter 2, the streamlining of time and space in no way simplifies plot. At the end of the earliest draft of *The Maids*, written in 1946, Monsieur and Madame return home to find Claire lying dead on the floor in one of Madame's dresses, and Solange interrogated by the police. This version, which Genet describes in a letter as 'the most talkative one' (Genet 2002: 815; 2003: 36), provides a far more conclusive *dénouement* than the final one, which is superficially more 'unified', but where the two sisters' motivations and destinies are unclear.[2] Genet's early plays therefore offer none of the reassuring resolution and conclusion often implicit in French classical unity, even if they do inherit formally from that tradition. In Genet's theatre, drama, deriving etymologically from the Greek for action, is fragmented into sequences of isolated dramatic moments. To use the storyline of his plays as a guiding principle when staging them is thus likely to lead down dead-ends.

Counter-naturalism

Genet's early plays transcend the conventions of both French classicism, and also of naturalism. Naturalism maintains that humans are determined by their social environment. Naturalist theatre thus aims to observe scientifically people in their social milieu, which is then accurately reproduced, without fantasy or embellishment, in the set, costumes, dialogue and acting of a play (see Zola 1968).[3] Genet specifies that the cell in *For 'the Beautiful One'* be 'reproduced according to its real size: 3.5 × 3.5 m' (Genet 2002: 33–4). His sketch depicts a cell containing a tin jug, mug and plates, a washbasin and latrines, a chair chained to the wall, and an iron bed positioned under a copy of the prison rules. His scrupulous reproduction of a prison cell is replaced in the final version of *Deathwatch* by a visual simplicity that clearly attempts to distance itself from a naturalism that might limit his work to social comment: door, granite block bed bearing a couple of blankets, small window (ibid.: 5; 1989: 103). Instead of a naturalistic reproduction, Genet proposes a minimalist evocation. The costumes, too, are more than simple copies of prison uniforms. The cellmates are dressed in strident black and white; the guard's uniform is oversized (Genet 2002: 5; 1989: 103). With respect to *The Maids*, Genet insists that 'it is not a plea against the treatment of servants. I suppose there are unions for domestic workers – that is not my concern' (Genet 2002: 127). Instead of a theatre that 'reflects too exactly the visible world, the actions of men', Genet aspires towards a theatre of imagination, creativity, poetry (Genet 2002: 816; 2003: 37).

Plethoric theatre

Since plot and social theme do not provide the foundational structure of Genet's theatre, meaning is distributed across a plethoric array of scenic elements. Shortly before Genet began writing theatre, revolutionary French playwright and theoretician Antonin Artaud wrote, 'if in theatre the text is not everything, if lighting is also a language, theatre will uphold the notion of another language that utilizes text, lighting, gesture, movement, sound' (Artaud 1964: 209). From the beginning of the twentieth century in Europe, theatrical elements that had formerly been considered merely decorative were increasingly employed, in order to communicate meaning. Décor was no longer simply 'decoration'. Two theatre designers, British-born Edward Gordon Craig, and Swiss-born Adolphe Appia, elevated set and lighting to art forms which bore a stage presence to rival the play-text.[4] Genet appears to apply his radical egalitarianism, explained in Chapter 3 with respect to the 'wound', to objects too: 'Every object possesses its own magnificence, no greater or lesser than that of any other object' (Genet 1979: 35; 1988a: 67). Against an anthropocentrist tradition that prioritizes character or plot, Genet writes a theatre that affords significance to a host of theatrical elements: gesture, costumes, make-up, hairstyles, scenography, lighting, stage properties, music, acoustics, vocal tone and rhythm. Unlike in naturalist theatre, these elements are not enlisted simply to depict social class, cultural context or a historical moment. They become artistic ends in themselves. Brook explains how the visual in Genet's theatre bears as much weight as the verbal:

> [I]mage in his theatre never takes second place. On the contrary, the essence of his poetic thought is revealed via image. ... In this way, Genet incarnates, is part of, and essentially paves the way towards the most important direction in theatre today: theatre where word and image cannot be separated from each other.
>
> (quoted in Aslan 1973: 126–7)

Brook testifies to the fact that Genet contributes crucially towards the evolution of the twentieth-century art of *mise en scène*, where non-textual visual and acoustic features become key elements in theatrical expression.[5]

Critic Alain Bernard Marchand claims that a naturalist aesthetic dominates Genet's early plays, notably *Deathwatch* (Marchand 1997: 214). However, a handful of examples suffice to demonstrate the vital importance of every element on Genet's stage, and how these elements become symbols, rather than merely properties that set a scene. The only stage property that remains in the final version of *Deathwatch* is the Guard's 'bunch of keys' (Genet 2002: 21). These obviously denote his power and the inmates' powerlessness, since they lock the latter away. They also possess phallic overtones, for they are inserted into the keyhole which, according to Genet's stage directions, should be visible to the audience. His directions then suggest that Maurice caress the keyhole, while smiling (ibid.: 23). The keys and keyhole thus reinforce the homoerotic tensions simmering between the inmates. Not only properties, but also scenography is charged with signification. Despite the fact that the cell's contents are spartan, Genet describes how 'The walls of the cell are of hewn stone and should give the impression that the architecture of the prison is very complicated' (Genet 2002: 5; 1989: 103). The complex linear motif created by the brickwork continues onto the door and window, which are 'barred', and onto the prisoners' costumes, which are 'striped'. Like an etching from Giambattista Piranese's *Prisons* (1745–50), a profusion of crosshatched lines is scored across Genet's set, weaving a web that ensnares the prisoners. The rigid formalization of space might also evoke the panoptic prison structure analysed in *Discipline and Punish* (*Surveiller et punir*, 1975), an examination of the penal system by French philosopher Michel Foucault, which probably influenced Genet's 1985 redraft of the play. In a panoptic prison, cells surround a central tower from which the guard can observe all inmates at all times. Foucault describes how the cells are 'like so many cages, so many small theatres, in which each actor is alone, perfectly individualized and constantly visible' (Foucault 1979: 200). The sense of inescapability created by the linear motif is accentuated further by Genet's lighting design – 'As much light as possible' (Genet 2002: 6; 1989: 104) – with its connotations of unyielding surveillance.

Each scenic element across Genet's theatre bears multiple potential connotations. Flowers in *The Maids* are by no means simply decorative. Fresh-cut flowers indicate Madame's wealth since, as Claire notes when playing Madame in the 1947 edition, the flowers the Maids keep in their attic are made of paper (Genet 2002: 168).[6] Flowers also underscore class difference, as Madame tucks one behind Claire's ear in a condescending gesture redolent of when she casts her old dresses off on the Maids (Genet 2002: 154; 1989: 74). Since the flowers are sweetly scented and pretty, they also 'camouflage', in Solange's terms, the undignified and degrading position in which Madame maintains the Maids (Genet 2002: 131). When Solange-playing-Claire slaps Claire-playing-Madame, she exclaims, 'Madame thought she was protected by her barricade of flowers' (Genet 2002: 134; 1989: 45). Even though the flowers are fresh and not artificial, they still symbolize the falsity of Madame's airs and graces. Notably, the Maids have bought her mimosa, *mimosa* containing the verb 'to mime'. Flowers thus stress the show and theatricality of Madame's behaviour.[7] Finally, the Maids fill Madame's bedroom with an over-abundance of flowers, as if to transform it into a mausoleum. Madame senses the morbidity of their floral tribute, since her first words as she makes her flamboyant entrance are, 'There's no end to it! Such horrible gladioli, such a sickly pink, and mimosa!' (Genet 2002: 147; 1989: 66). And Claire mimics Madame's sentiments at the start of the play: 'You crush me with your attentions and your humbleness; you smother me with gladioli and mimosa' (Genet 2002: 130; 1989: 37). Here, Claire both imitates Madame, articulates the Maids' plot to murder Madame, and anticipates her own suicide. In Derridean terms, flowers in Genet's works disseminate their diverse meanings like pollen (Derrida 1972: 36). Moreover, the pollen spreads intertextually across Genet's *oeuvre*. Notably, two of his novels – *Our Lady of the Flowers* and *Miracle of the Rose* – feature flora in their titles; so too does Genet's name: *genêt* means 'broom', as philosopher Jacques Derrida notes in his extensive study of Genet, *Glas* (Derrida 1974: 205). Genet's plays become poems; and each element contained within the poem becomes a verse, bearing a multitude of meanings.[8]

Theatre semiotician Anne Ubersfeld explains that objects in theatre can either be utilitarian, for example a sword used solely for the purposes of a duel; or symbolic (Ubersfeld 1982: 180). Solange feels terrorized by the objects in Madame's apartment, believing that one or other of them will reveal to the police the fact that the Maids wrote a letter framing Monsieur: 'Everything will accuse us. The curtains marked by our shoulders, the mirrors by my face ...' (Genet 2002: 143). In 'The Tightrope Walker' Genet warns, 'I know objects, their nastiness, their cruelty, their gratitude too' (Genet 2002: 821; 2003: 69, translation modified). As critic Odette Aslan writes, 'Objects in Genet's works lose the notion of being simple accessories, becoming primary players' (Aslan 1972: 26). Words, objects, colours, sounds in Genet's theatre are symbolic, in that they signify in excess of their literal denotation, becoming saturated with signification. Keys and flowers are but two examples, discussed here to underscore how a naturalist production would betray the poetry with which Genet invests almost every element in his play.

The Maids in production

Louis Jouvet (1947)

The Maids was the first of Genet's plays to be staged. First performed
in April 1947, seven years before Beckett's *Waiting for Godot* and
four years before Ionesco's *The Bald Prima Donna*, *The Maids*, with
its anti-dramatic resistance to plot and anti-psychological rejection of
recognizable character, is one of the key plays of the *avant-garde*
movement that was to dominate French theatre during the 1950s and
1960s.[9] Ironically, then, its première at the théâtre de l'Athénée in
Paris, directed by Louis Jouvet, was a largely naturalist affair which
pitted the serving and ruling classes against each other.[10] In a 1944
debate on theatre Cocteau warned, 'The serious mistake in the theater
[*sic*] is to use a lot of chairs and armchairs and unnecessary flowers.
That makes for frightful disorder and a bogus naturalism' (in Sartre
1976: 50). Three years later, Jouvet appears to have made this
mistake, in order to render Genet's play more easily acceptable to
Paris's conservative bourgeois public (White 1994: 343).

Genet wrote 'How to play *The Maids*' in 1962, 15 years after the
first production of the play. Whilst often abstruse and contradictory,
the text provides some useful indications for staging the play:

> It is, quite simply, the bedroom of a woman who is a bit of a tart,
> a bit of a lady. If the play is staged in France, the bedroom should
> have a featherbed .... The bedroom should vary depending on
> whether the play is staged in Spain, Scandinavia, Russia. The
> dresses, however, must be extravagant, not pertaining to any
> fashion or period. It is possible that, for their role-play, the two
> maids deform Madame's dresses monstrously, by adding false
> trains, false ruffs. The flowers must be real, the bed real. The
> director must understand, for I cannot explain everything after
> all, why the bedroom must be more or less the exact copy of a
> woman's bedroom, the flowers real, but the dresses monstrous.
>
> (Genet 2002: 127)

The wealth of properties and furniture should denote the country in
which the play is staged. This gives the impression that, as with

naturalism, the production should enable spectators to draw comparisons with contemporary sociological issues. Moreover, as in the theatre of France's main exponent of naturalism, André Antoine, accessories like the bed and flowers should be 'real', rather than stylized. In keeping with yet another tenet of naturalism (see Zola 1968), Genet's décor comments on social class by emphasizing the discrepancies between Madame's and the Maids' wealth and comfort. Madame's luxury is visibly evident from the set, whereas the Maids describe their attic room as 'bare and mean' and remonstrate bitterly that it has 'no hangings to push aside, no rugs to shake, no furniture to caress ..., no mirrors, no balcony' (Genet 2002: 137; 1989: 50). The set, according to Genet, then, evokes a lady's bedroom from a recognizable place and period. The outfits in which the Maids dress, however, are associated with no particular fashion or era. He claims that the reasons for this are obvious. A director can presumably assume that the dresses should appear false, since the Maids concoct costumes for their role-plays out of random, clashing items from Madame's wardrobe. However, Genet's claims that his instructions are 'obvious' are somewhat disingenuous. A purely rational explanation both of his play, and of the stage directions, is rendered extremely complicated by the highly poeticized dialogue and obscure narrative. Since it is not clear why some aspects of the scenography and costumes should be naturalist and others not, productions of the play vary wildly.

Christian Bérard's rococo set for Jouvet's production comprised luxuriant drapes; chandeliers; lace and chintz wall panels adorned with gilt picture-frames and mirrors; Louis XV scroll-legged chairs bearing cherub arm-rests; a bureau with gilt inlay; ornate lamps; a chichi dressing-table decked with pots, powder-puffs, perfumes and a silver tea-set; a walk-in wardrobe brimming with evening gowns and hat boxes (for photographs see Boyer and Boyer 2006: 144–5). The Maids' simple black uniforms, and Madame's dress with its wasp waist and fox furs, typified the fashions of the day. Jouvet's production anticipated Genet's wish, expressed later in 'How to Play *The Maids*', that certain costumes adhere to a different register, in order to designate when the Maids enact their role-play. Notably, when one of the Maids played Madame, her neck-to-floor taffeta ruffs were the height of ostentatious bad taste.

Naturalism and realism habitually have recourse to metonymy, whilst more stylized forms like romanticism and surrealism employ metaphor (Jakobson and Halle 1956: 91–6). Jouvet's production resorted to metonymy, since it represented the bedroom by selecting and presenting features contiguous with a real bedroom: bed, dressing-table, etc. The colour scheme was the only element that might have been perceived as metaphorical. A sketch by Bérard shows the drapes and carpets in blood red and the ceiling and wall panels in duck-egg blue. Red might have foreshadowed the Maids' murderous intentions, and the rather overbearing combination of red and blue could have pointed to Madame's lack of taste and moderation, and/or the stifling atmosphere to which the Maids were subjected. The reception of Jouvet's production was cold, ironically because critics were baffled by its artificiality. Therefore, in spite of the faithful reconstruction of a bourgeois lady's bedroom and the psychological acting style, the poetry of Genet's play-text must have been evident to audiences, and must have sat awkwardly with the naturalist set (for a summary of reviews see Genet 2002: 1070–1; White 1994: 352).

Jean-Marie Serreau (1963)

The next notable staging of *The Maids* was French director Jean-Marie Serreau's June 1963 revival of his May 1961 production at Paris's Odéon-Théâtre de France. For this new version, the Maids were played by black female actors, Serreau thus marrying his two passions: contemporary playwriting and non-European performance traditions deriving mainly from France's former African colonies.[11] One critic complained that Serreau's essentially naturalist production betrayed the complex philosophical dimensions of Genet's play (Sandier 1963). For another revival of the play, in 1973 at the théâtre des Amandiers in Nanterre, Serreau seems to have refined his dramaturgy in philosophical terms, to reflect the play's questions of identity:

> Genet. We play. Theatre is the idea that we play in life, that we turn our daily existence into a theatre. … It is in a way a critique

of the falsity of our existence. We play a role to which we are not suited. Our personal life is in a way a failure, from which we try to escape.

(Serreau 1973).

When stating 'we play a role to which we are not suited', Serreau echoes Sartre, who writes in *Saint Genet*:

[Genet] affirms the priority of the object which he is to them over the subject which he is to himself. Therefore, without being clearly aware of it, he judges that the appearance (which he is to others) is the reality and that the reality (which he is to himself) is only appearance.

(Sartre 1952: 47)

Person derives from the Latin 'persona', meaning mask. To be a person is to wear a mask, to perform a role for an audience. In *The Blacks*, the 1959 staging of which (discussed in Chapter 5) no doubt influenced Serreau's 'black' production of *The Maids*, one character says, 'Let [Negroes] persist to the point of madness in what they're condemned to be, in their ebony, in their odor, in their yellow eyes, in their cannibal tastes' (Genet 2002: 503; 1960: 52). In Serreau's production, the Maids performed roles expected of them by a society that dictated not only the social position of a maid, but also that of a Black. Genet, however, warned that casting black actors only as the Maids, and not as Madame, would limit the play to a tract on racism, and ignore its broader philosophical scope (Blin 1986: 125).

The Living Theatre

The February 1965 production of *The Maids* at the Kurfürstendamm Theater in West Berlin, directed by the Living Theatre, the US performance group heavily influenced by Artaud, marked a significant departure from naturalism in the play's production history. The refusal of naturalism was clear from the start: all three parts were played by men. Apocryphally, Genet claimed that *The Maids* should be played by male rather than female actors. The only evidence for this exists in *Our-Lady-of-the-Flowers*: 'If I had to stage a play where women had roles, I would insist that these roles be played by male adolescents' (Genet 1951: 147).[12] Since this source is a novel rather than a theoretical essay or interview, and is therefore fiction, albeit 'autofiction' (Sheringham 1993: 202–45), it cannot be regarded as a stage direction. Notwithstanding, casting male actors in female roles in Genet's plays has now almost become *de rigueur*. In Japanese director Moriaki Watanabe's October 1995 production at the X Theatre in Tokyo, the Maids were played by men; in Argentinian director Alfredo Arias's March 2001 production at the théâtre de l'Athénée (by then renamed the Athénée-Théâtre Louis Jouvet), the director himself played Madame.[13]

Cross-casting provides an effective means with which to expose the gender ambiguities in Genet's *oeuvre*.[14] In an essay on the blurring of masculine/feminine identities, Elizabeth Stephens describes how the penis in Genet's work does little to reinforce heteronormative assumptions regarding masculinity:

> What is eroticized here is not the penis's unchanging stiffness, but on the contrary its tendency towards transformation, its metamorphosis from flaccid to tumescent, and erect to satiated. ... It is this potential for becoming that Genet's work focuses on.
> (Stephens 2004: 91)

Like all aspects of human identity, gender, for Genet, is unfixed, unstable and constantly open to transformation. 'I am like anyone else, essentially changing', says Genet in an interview (Genet 2004: 131). The idea that gender is a social, political, cultural or aesthetic construct rather than an innate essence, which has since been developed into the field of Gender Studies, was explored by the Living Theatre, since the female characters' femininity was enacted, role-played, by three heavily-built male actors in high-heeled shoes, black satin dresses, wigs and false breasts.

Cross-casting enables both an interrogation of gender and heightened theatricality. In his 1954 'Letter to Jean-Jacques Pauvert', discussed in Chapter 2, Genet expresses how he feels an affinity more to Far-Eastern performance traditions and rituals than to European acting styles, where the actor tends to efface her/himself behind the fictional character (Genet 2002: 815; 2003: 36). Naturalist acting is founded largely on the teachings of turn-of-the-century Russian theatre-maker and theorist Constantin Stanislavski, who describes how actors should find examples 'in life and recreate them on the stage' (Stanislavski 1980: 61). Genet deplores this technique, which he describes in his letter as complacent and unimaginative. He wrote this letter perhaps as a negative reaction to Jouvet's production, or to naturalist theatre in general. Genetian critic Jeanette Savona notes that instead of losing themselves in the fiction of the character, Genet's actors must heighten the spectator's awareness of the artifice of play-acting, through stylized gesture (Savona 1983: 86–7). In a letter to Frechtman, Genet recounts the impact that the Peking Opera had on him (Genet 2002: 951). In traditional Chinese theatre every item of costume, every colour, every gesture carries symbolic meaning: a table represents a bridge; the waving of blue flags is the sea (see Riley 1997). In both Chinese and in Japanese Noh and Kabuki theatres, every aspect of the production is heavily stylized. Costumes are ostentatiously sumptuous; dialogue is chanted or sung to musical accompaniment; movement, essentially comprising gliding across the stage and stamping, or in the case of Kabuki, dancing, is highly stylized (Gontard 1987: 10). The Living Theatre's co-directors, Julian Beck and Judith Malina, inspired by non-European acting traditions, borrowed abrupt gestures and sudden shrieks from Kabuki, and an incantatory use of voice from Tantric Buddhism. Voice and body were stylized, avoiding the kind of 'approximative' and complacent naturalist acting style that Genet admonishes. Moreover, since the three actors swapped roles each night, identification between actor and character became less likely (see Biner 1968: 110).

The Living Theatre's scenography complemented the non-naturalist acting. Far from reproducing Jouvet's bourgeois interior, the set resembled a chapel, complete with columns, and an altar laden with gladioli:

> An altar – the one about which Claire speaks. Everything is in black white or metallic. At intervals from each other, Ancient Greek columns, made from draped white velvet, the upper

corners gathered and fixed in the centre, to form capitals. The furniture – screen, bed, dressing-table, chandelier – was created by Jim Tiroff out of old bicycle wheels, curtain rails, metal bedsteads, iron frames.

(ibid.: 110)[15]

Whilst the acting highlighted the theatricality of gender, the set underscored the artifice of propriety – upright morals and behaviour acceptable to the middle classes. On the one hand, the difference in social status between Madame and the Maids was reinforced since, in keeping with the practices of classical theatre, Madame entered stage-left – conventionally reserved for nobility – and the Maids entered stage-right, where their kitchen was supposedly located. On the other, Madame's bed, dressing-table and chandelier were cobbled together from old bicycle wheels and iron bars – incongruous in a bourgeois interior – suggesting that behind her façade of genteel civility she was just as morally impoverished as the Maids were financially destitute. Madame's refinement was a performance that she play-acted in the same way that the Maids play-acted Madame.

The Living Theatre highlighted the notion that theatricality serves to construct the identities not only of people, but also of objects: items of junk literally became bourgeois furniture. Transformation defines Genet's entire *oeuvre* where, through poetry, what is socially regarded as repugnant is presented as beautiful. In his first interview, for *Playboy* magazine in 1964, Genet explains, 'poetry consist[s] in taking subjects taken to be vile into subjects accepted as noble' (Genet 1991: 17; 2004: 8). In 'The Tightrope Walker', he writes of 'this metamorphosis of dust into gold dust' that characterizes the circus, where a ring filled with sawdust becomes the place of awe and magic (Genet 2002: 825; 2003: 73). Indeed, as Chapter 2 has noted, Solange effects this metamorphosis in *The Maids*: 'my spurt of saliva is my spray of diamonds … You twirl a feather duster like a fan. You make fancy gestures with the dishcloth' (Genet 2002: 138–9; 1989: 52). The Living Theatre's renovation of refuse into refinery illustrated the theatricality that, across Genet's entire *oeuvre*, transforms identities, meanings and realities.

Víctor García (1969)

The Living Theatre announced a break from naturalism, which Argentinean director Víctor García – another Artaudian – took to extremes.[16] His 1969 Spanish production *Las criadas* premièred at Barcelona's Poliorama Theatre, later going on tour to the théâtre de la Cité Universitaire in Paris, where Genet saw it three times. García's scenographic design comprised a bare oval stage surrounded by 14 six-metre panels of polished aluminium (for photographs see Genet 2002: 1371–2).[17] The panels' mirrored surfaces cast multiple distorted images of the Maids and of Madame, La Señora. The only piece of furniture, a chrome clothes rail, was also reflective. Like flowers, mirrors are foundational metaphors in Genet's *oeuvre*. *The Maids* begins as Claire-playing-Madame 'pats her face' at the dressing-table mirror (Genet 2002: 129; 1989: 36); Madame has patent shoes in which Claire-playing-Madame forces Solange-playing-the-Maid to look at her miserable reflection (Genet 2002: 130; 1989: 37); Claire exclaims to her sister, 'I'm sick of seeing my image thrown back at me by a mirror, like a bad smell. You're my bad smell,' and when playing Madame she accuses the Maids of being, for the upper classes, 'our distorting mirrors, our loathsome vent, our shame, our dregs' (Genet 2002: 144, 159; 1989: 61, 86). Sartre describes identity in Genet's works as 'a hall of mirrors. The fact is that there are only reflections and reflections of reflections organized around a central reflection' (Sartre 1952: 598). The only validation of identity is provided by a mirror image, in all its ephemerality and impermanence.[18] García's scenography represented how identity according to Genet's philosophy is a dizzying multiplicity of reflected, refracted appearances.

The overbearing vertical panels encapsulated both the instability of identity, and a sense of confinement. Hardly any space existed between panels, affording the effect of a prison cell, heightened further by the beams that penetrated the cracks, like light through barred windows. In Genet's text, the Maids complain repeatedly that the atmosphere is stifling: 'I'm stifling. You're stifling me *(She wants to open the window)* Oh! Let's have some air!' (Genet 2002: 142: 1989: 57). They are metaphorically suffocated by their confinement. Whilst the Maids' room bears only a tiny skylight, Madame's floor-to-ceiling windows open onto a balcony, and the light breeze that sets her curtains fluttering invigorates the Maids (Genet 2002: 161; 1989: 93). Madame's windows therefore become a symbol of potential liberation. Solange exclaims, 'The wind exalts me!' and in the 1947 edition, the wind blows the French windows open just as she pronounces her diatribe on murdering Madame (Genet 2002: 159, 194). However, the set in García's production provided no such vain hope of salvation. The panels posing as La Señora's windows swivelled on pivots to reveal yet more panels, as if the windows had been bricked up. Furthermore, they echoed like slammed prison doors when the sisters thumped them in furious desperation. This sense of imprisonment has been conveyed by several other productions: in Dominique Quéhec's (January 1977, Maison de la culture, Amiens), Madame's window was heavily barred, opening onto a black void; in Philippe Adrien's (1996, discussed presently), the window was bricked up with breeze-blocks. In these productions parallels were perhaps drawn between the Maids' incarceration by Madame and the inmates' imprisonment in *Deathwatch*. The British film version of *The Maids*, (also discussed presently), appears less claustrophobic, since the camera takes the viewer into the street; to the Bilboquet café where the recently liberated Monsieur awaits Madame; onto Madame's balcony, where the wind blows through Solange's hair. However, at the end of the film, the same wind blusters through Madame's apartment, swirls through the dead Claire's gown, and snuffs out each candle in the bedroom, as the film fades to black. García's production was therefore no exception in portraying visually and atmospherically the Maids' state of literal and existential internment and hopelessness.

Whilst García's scenography was striking, his production was marked mostly by the three actors' performances. He explains:

> The play recommends a house full of flowers and perfumes ... I wanted my actresses to convey this house overfilled with flowers, this cemetery, mortuary, via their acting. I observed the behaviour of the three actresses, who had become three lost souls, and I established my layout for the stage in relation to this behaviour.
>
> (García 1970: 8)

For García, the scenography was to be created by actors' bodies occupying space, rather than by furniture and properties. In a footnote that Genet adds to the final version of the play, he states:

> Directors must elaborate a way of walking that leaves nothing to chance. The Maids and Madame move from one point of the stage to another by drawing a specific geometry that signifies something. I cannot say what, but this geometry must not be the result of simple to-ings and fro-ings. It will inscribe itself in space like, for example, a premonition inscribes itself in the flight of birds, the activity of life inscribes itself in the flight of bees, the activity of death inscribes itself in the practices of certain poets.
>
> (Genet 2002: 136)

Reminiscent of traditional Japanese theatre, the actors' movements must be calculated: like those of a migrating bird, pollinating bee or, in an indication that is, typically for Genet, no doubt intended to inspire rather than to instruct, a poet writing in the face of death. In accordance with Genet's recommendations, which he reiterates in 'How to Play *The Maids*' (Genet 2002: 126), the bodily movements of García's actors were choreographed into geometric and circular patterns, to the point of hieratic ritualism. Not only their bodies, but also their voices, resisted the complacency of naturalism. Their staccato diction encapsulated Genet's suggestion that 'their voices ... appear suspended or interrupted' (ibid.: 125). In addition, Solange-playing-Claire's voice was flat and monotone; Claire-playing-La Señora's was shrill. García employed a technique that he terms 'dehumanization', since it strips actors of their temptation to enact immediately recognizable human characteristics (García 1968: 71–9). The blatant stylization afforded the impression that their speech was scripted rather than natural, emphasizing further the idea that identity derives from performance.

During the staging of *Las criadas* Genet wrote a series of letters to French director Antoine Bourseiller, who incidentally staged *The Balcony* (November 1969) and *The Penal Colony* (April 2006). In one letter, Genet describes 'a voice that stops on one word, when it should stop on another; it is a question of finding the right word and the right voice ... a gesture that is not made in the right place at the right time' (Genet 2002: 903). In García's production no harmony was evident between the body's movements and the voice's utterances. Núria Espert who, alongside Julieta Serrano, played one of the Maids, explains the complexity of Genet's compound characters:

> The characters were so complex, that after a couple of days, [García] asked Julieta and me to carry out a task that consisted in radically cutting the play up into different levels. So number one would be Solange, number two Claire, number three Claire-Solange, when Claire plays Solange ... number five Claire playing Madame, six, when Claire playing Madame plays Claire (this is when Claire ridicules Madame without forgetting that she is Claire), seven, etc., up to twenty-five, thirty-two. We found forty-seven levels when we were working! We couldn't show them all – we would have needed an IBM computer.
>
> (quoted by Compte 1975: 262)[19]

Identity for Genet is composite; it comprises layers of images sedimented onto us by family, society, culture, religion. The incoherent movements and sounds emanating from García's actors shattered notions of identity as a unitary plenitude, presenting it as a crazed mirror of clashing reflections. Moreover, Genet critic Yvonne Went-Daoust adds a surrealist interpretation to this discordant aesthetic, stating that when dialogue is juxtaposed with unexpected gestures, it enables forgotten and singular areas of the unconscious to be liberated (Went-Daoust 1980: 140).

Genet's stage directions note that the Maids wear flat shoes whereas Madame wears high heels (Genet 2002: 129, 132; 1989: 41). In García's production Claire-playing-La Señora and La Señora herself wore platform shoes resembling hugely elevated Ancient Greek *cothurni*, on which they tottered across the steeply raked stage. This produced the double effect of rendering naturalist movement impossible and of accentuating La Señora's literal and social superiority over the Maids, which was underscored further by the metre-high headdress resembling an Ancient Greek *onkos* that Claire-playing-La Señora wore. This, and her silver robes that jangled with fake gold trinkets, restricted her movement further, again rendering stylized gestures obligatory. Under their plain black smocks the Maids wore black stockings and white knee pads, which served the practical purpose of protecting the actors' legs, and evoked those worn by servants who used to polish parquet flooring. Their prostrate clambering across the stage, again far from naturalist, occupied the horizontal plane, whilst La Señora, who first made her entrance by being lowered from the flies, occupied the vertical. The fact that the Maids slithered across the stage as opposed to walking upright – a characteristic that distinguishes humans from animals – and fought like dogs, stripped them of their humanity. When Claire drank the poisoned tea, she fell into a round shallow hollow at the front of the stage. This space – a kind of bear pit – stressed further the Maids' animality, especially since in the final scene they lay naked under the swathes of black satin material which posed both as the decadent Señora's sheets and as Claire's death pall (the pit also resembled a sacrificial altar).

Lighting, too, highlighted the Maids' base condition. They skulked out of the darkness at the start of the play and proceeded to lurk in the shadows, whereas when Claire-playing-La Señora first appeared, she rose from a circle of light centre-stage, and she and the real Señora were bathed in intense brightness throughout the play. The only time the Maids were fully illuminated was when they were tracked like animals or fugitives by a spotlight whose beam resembled a searchlight. Both set and lighting conspired to establish a hierarchy between servant and mistress, dominated and dominant, animal and human.

In 'How to Play *The Maids*' Genet states that the scenic design must vary according to whether the play is staged in Spain, Scandinavia or Russia. García located the play in an abstract, atemporal, ahistorical setting. However, he demonstrates his desire to reflect society in his art when stating, 'If I create violent spectacles, it's because they reflect our world of violence and fear' (García 1968: 76). His production certainly carried political potency, since the oppressiveness of the towering metal set and the actors' physical struggle to negotiate the inhospitable stage would have resonated immediately with Spanish audiences who, in the early 1970s, had lived under the military dictatorship of General Franco for over 30 years.[20]

At the time of the production García explained, 'I took the text as a guide, a screenplay that I could develop' (quoted by Olivier 1971). Whilst maintaining Genet's dialogue intact, García did not adhere in any literal sense to Genet's stage directions. He responded, in imaginative ways that Genet could perhaps not have anticipated, to the playwright's desire for scenography, lighting, costumes, movement and voice not simply to be accessories laid over the top of the text, but to contribute crucially to meaning production. For this reason, no doubt, Genet declared his admiration for this, arguably the most celebrated production of *The Maids* (Galey 1970: 13).

Alain Ollivier (1991)

In a characteristically contradictory manner, Genet itemizes the set and properties for *The Maids* in considerable detail, and at once admits that the director can dispense with them altogether:

> And if one wants to stage this play at Epidaurus? The three actresses could simply agree, before the start of the play and in front of the audience, on the nooks to which they would give names like: bed, window, wardrobe, door, dressing-table, etc.
>
> (Genet 2002: 127).

Were the play to be presented in the bare acting area of an amphitheatre, the actors could point to the imaginary location of each item of furniture. Genet reveals the paradox of naturalism: the more naturalist the play, the more artificial paraphernalia it requires. French director Alain Ollivier's September 1991 production at the Studio-Théâtre de Vitry, a nineteenth-century tinsmith's workshop in the Parisian suburbs, dispensed with the profusion of objects employed, for example, by Jouvet (see Cournot 1991).[21] Before the play began, the actors entered the stage – the wooden workshop floor. With chalk, one traced a square on the floor, denoting Madame's bureau, and placed the potentially incriminating key in the square. Another laid a square of material on the floor, denoting

Madame's dressing-table, and placed a necklace on it. The key and necklace were the only stage properties, along with large oblong stones stacked in two rows towards the back of the stage, upon which Solange placed a red and a white dress, and a pair of red shoes (for photographs see Genet 2002: 1373). Lighting was provided by hundreds of tea candles placed on planks just above floor level along three sides of the stage, affording the ritualistic atmosphere evoked by García's and many other productions. The most striking feature was the magical transformation of a plain wooden floor marked with chalk, into Madame's bedroom. In a text entitled 'The Criminal Child', Genet writes:

> 'Monsieur Genet', he said, 'the Management is obliging me to take these knives away from them. So I must obey. But look at them. Are you telling me they're dangerous? They're made of tin. Tin! You can't kill someone with that.' Did he not know that by distancing itself further from its practical usage, the object transforms itself, that it becomes a symbol? Sometimes, even its shape changes. One can say that it has become stylized.
>
> (Genet 1979: 385)

The director of the correction centre derides the young offenders when he discovers that their weapons are not real. For Genet, he has missed the point. Using their imagination, the children 'stylize' the harmless toys into weapons of mass destruction. This simultaneous belief and acknowledgement of the falsity of the situation should, for Genet, be the foundation of all theatre. He writes in his letter to Pauvert, '[A performance] is vain if I do not believe in what I see, which will stop – will never have been – as soon as the curtain falls' (Genet 2002: 818; 2003: 39). The simultaneous illusion of total presence, and its negation, constitutes for Genet the height of theatricality, which Ollivier achieved in his production.

Philippe Adrien (1996)

At one extreme, Jouvet reproduced all the trimmings of a lady's bedroom; at the other, Ollivier staged *The Maids* in a completely empty space. French director Philippe Adrien's production at the théâtre du Vieux Colombier in Paris drew from both naturalist and minimalist traditions, testifying to the play's aesthetic scope.[22] Adrien wanted to strike a contrast between the highly literary, artificial nature of Genet's text, and the plausible psychological performance style of his actors (Adrien 2008: 152). He seized upon Genet's brief but notable mention that the Maids 'have grown old' and that their faces are 'wrinkled' (Genet 2002: 125) to cast the young movie star Jeanne Balibar beside two female actors 20 years her senior (for photographs see Bradby and Sparks 1997: 102). The production thus added youth and age to the power dynamics (Adrien 2008: 154). Moreover, Madame's apartment contained 1930s art deco furnishings, every detail evoking an exclusive New York apartment, except for the black-and-white wallpaper that, upon closer inspection, seemed disquietingly to reproduce distorted skulls like those in Holbein's *The Ambassadors* (1533). Just as the Maids uttered the words 'the objects are abandoning us' (Genet 2002: 156), the entire set disappeared piece-by-piece into the walls, floor and flies (see Chevalier 1998: 111–12). The apparently naturalist set was converted into a poetic environment through recourse to dream, or rather nightmare, since the Maids were literally and metaphorically abandoned to their miserable, hopeless fate not only by Madame but even by the objects.

In the UK – the film version (1975)

The Maids has been staged more than any other of Genet's plays, not least in the UK. The first ever British production, which took place in 1952 at London's Mercury Theatre Club, was directed by the then British-based German director Peter Zadek, who subsequently directed *The Balcony* (see Chapter 5).[23] It was designed by British sculptor Eduardo Paolozzi, and performed in French. The UK-based Greek director and friend of Genet's, Minos Volanakis, staged one of the most significant UK productions, mainly because its legacy remains in cinematic form. Presented at the Greenwich Theatre in 1974 with the cream of British acting talent – Glenda Jackson, Susannah York and Vivien Merchant – it was adapted with the same cast for the screen by Christopher Miles.[24]

The principal difference between the play and film was the set. In the Greenwich production the stage, designed by Yolanda Sonnabend, was made from a huge piece of stretched canvas suspended just above the floor like a trampoline. York explains that the actors had to walk gingerly in their high heels, for fear of falling down (York 2003). As in García's production, the actors' mode of walking was thus necessarily stylized, though here the connotations were different. Rather than symbolizing power hierarchies, movement, according to York, reflected the characters' shifting identities, discussed in Chapter 2, since nothing underfoot was solid or certain.

In contrast, the visual aesthetic of the film version is at first glance, and not surprisingly for cinema, realist. Miles's adaptation represents a recognizable Paris: the exclusive Place Vendôme where Madame's apartment is located; the kepi-wearing gendarmes; the Peugeot police car screeching past a parked Citroën DS... However, as with Genet's play-texts, this realism is deceptive. Whilst the exterior represents the early 1970s Paris in which the film was shot, Madame's apartment becomes a timeless shrine to grotesque decadence. The cream dressing- and bedside-tables and bedsteads are complemented by the vases of pink and white flowers, themselves offset by the purple bedspread, mauve walls and lilac chandelier. When she enters, Madame's cream outfit matches her interior impeccably. This symphony of pastels is interrupted only by Madame's gold-coloured curtains, tablecloths, window handles and jewellery. The film's set is not simply a metonymical denotation of an upper-class apartment; it becomes a metaphor symbolizing the kitsch vulgarity of Madame's wealth in the same way, incidentally, as the 50 pairs of shoes in Marcel Delval's 1979 all-male production at the théâtre Varia in Brussels (Quirot 1989).

The film provides close-up shots of salient metaphors from Genet's play-text, notably, in one of the opening scenes, Solange's rubber gloves. These are significant in *The Maids* because Solange preens them like the feathers of a fan, turning 'sawdust into gold dust', to use Genet's expression. Moreover, gloves can be put on and taken off, symbolizing the non-essential nature of identity. In addition, hands are an essential part of the body in *The Maids* because Claire hand-writes the accusatory letter denouncing Monsieur, and Solange tries to strangle her sister with her bare hands and crosses them, as if handcuffed, at the end of the play. Like García's production, the film also recognizes the significance of mirrors. The first glimpse the viewer catches of Claire-playing-Madame is her reflection in the dressing-table mirror, in which Madame herself is also later seen, illustrating Genet's notion of human identity as appearance rather than essence. Details outside the apartment are also charged with metaphorical signification. At the entrance to Madame's building, with its rococo staircase and ornamental plinths, are stacked rubbish bags, intimating, like the Living Theatre's production, that behind Madame's decorum lurk corruption and degeneracy.

Other cinematographic techniques add symbolic signification. When Claire fantasizes about being sent to a penal colony for Madame's murder and, with her sister, becoming 'the eternal couple of the criminal and the Saint' (Genet 2002: 179; 1989: 63), she is filmed through a tulle drape, as if in a dream. Madame is filmed from the same angle when romanticizing about becoming Monsieur's partner-in-crime. Fantasy is key to the play: the Maids dream of Monsieur's incarceration and Madame's departure or murder; Madame, in a flight of fancy, sees herself as Monsieur's accomplice. The film's camerawork revealed how, in *The Maids*, not only identity but also reality itself is composed of image, daydream.

Acting in the film complements this non-realist, stylized visual aesthetic. Jackson explains that the actors maintained the acting style they had developed with Volanakis for the stage production (Jackson 2003). York confirms that the acting was far from naturalist. She explains how it was impossible to conduct psychological character studies of the Maids since they have no 'inner life'. They 'don't develop from speech to speech ... It's almost as though Claire talks and Solange goes into a quiet patch, and Solange talks and Claire goes into a quiet patch', clarifies York. Since Genet's characters do not seem to communicate, she concludes that 'the reality or the humanity of these characters is always questionable' (York 2003). The three actors' delivery reflects Genet's dehumanization of character – 'the abolition of characters' (Genet 2002: 816; 2003: 37) – since they appear distant, absent, their melodramatic rage, false pleasure and exaggerated affection devoid of genuine sentiment.

Costumes too carry symbolic value. When, in the final scene, Claire role-plays Madame, she wears a gown with pleats running from her neck to the ground. As she fans the dress out with her arms, she resembles a radiant sun. Her towering hair suggests the 1960s fashion for beehives, and also Marie-Antoinette's grandiose wigs, enabling comparisons between Madame's maltreatment of the Maids and the tyrannous abuse of the lower classes by Louis XIV, the Sun King. However, the dress, made from diaphanous voile, also evokes a dandelion clock which the wind that rushes through the apartment at the end of the film will blow to nothing; or else a carnation, like the one Solange crushes in her palm in a closing scene. Costume, connoting Madame's power and the Maids' powerlessness, therefore becomes as significant to meaning production in the film as it is in many of the stage productions.

The screenplay, written by Miles and Robert Enders, and based on Volanakis's translation, follows the 1947 version whilst at times abridging lengthier monologues. Genet redrafted his plays constantly, paying acute attention to the positioning of each word, syllable and stress. For example, the 1954 version begins with 'These gloves', and the final version with 'And these gloves'. Genet's arrangement of the dialogue frequently results in prose charged with alliterations, assonances and rhymes. Just one example is provided when Solange cradles her exhausted younger sister after the first ritualistic role-play:

CLAIRE   *plaintivement* : Solange?
SOLANGE   Mon ange?
CLAIRE   Solange, écoute

(Genet 2002: 145)

The rhyme between 'Solange', repeated twice, and 'ange' (angel) affords a sonorous quality to Genet's text that Volanakis's translation and Miles's and Enders's screenplay at times reflects. In the following example, 'Madame had her love song her dove song her milkman her lovers', the rhyme between 'love song' and 'dove song', and the repetition of 'her', which Jackson stresses each time she utters it, transform speech into incantation in a way that does some justice to

Genet's original dialogue. Though Genet's text often scans like poetry, in 'How to Play *The Maids*' he writes, 'As for the so-called "poetic" passages, they must be said as if they were completely obvious, like when a Parisian taxi driver suddenly invents a slang metaphor on the spot: it should go without saying' (ibid.: 126). As one critic states, 'Seizing the instant when poetry is born of prose, where prose becomes a poem, this was [Genet's] obsession' (Delvaille 1993, p. 61). Jackson both rendered the poetry of Genet's text, and delivered it in the off-the-cuff tone he suggests.

Jane Giles's study of Genet and cinema claims that in Miles's film, '[c]inematically oblique visuals capture the text's radical class hatred' (Giles 2002: 38). However, as this analysis illustrates, the film's cinematography highlights the play's poetry and philosophical questions of identity, rather than solely serving the social realist end of denouncing the class system.

Yoshi Oida (2002)

Since an Aristotelian plot does not constitute the central axis in Genet's theatre, other theatrical elements – textual, visual, acoustic – can communicate meaning, as many of the accounts here demonstrate. One critic said of García's version, 'How can we not admire the extent to which this staging beyond words serves the author's ends so wondrously' (J. Lemarchand, quoted in Chevalier 1998: 103). Genet himself writes in a footnote to *The Maids*, 'It is possible that the play appears like it has been reduced to a skeleton of a play. ... I suggest ... that prospective directors replace expressions that are too precise, those that make the situation too explicit, with others that are more ambiguous' (Genet 2002: 147). Certain productions remove the text entirely, the most radical example provided by the théâtre du Centaure's horseback version (December 1998). *Die Zofen*, created at the Theaterhaus Stuttgart and presented in the Pit Theatre at the Barbican in London (October 2002), was Japanese actor-director Yoshi Oida's dance adaptation of *The Maids*.[25]

As with several productions discussed here, Oida made associations between the imprisonment sensed by the Maids and that experienced by the cellmates in *Deathwatch*. Oida's intertextuality was direct rather than oblique, borrowing not only from *Deathwatch* but also from the 1950 short silent film *Song of Love*. In what has become an iconic scene from this, the only film Genet directed (see Chapter 1), one prisoner uses a piece of straw to blow cigarette smoke through the wall between two cells (for photographs see Giles 2002: 110). His neighbour lets the smoke emanating from the wall caress his face, catching it in his mouth in an act steaming with sexual innuendo. Separated by the wall, the prisoners nonetheless commune through a chink, becoming a latter-day gay Pyramus and Thisbe. Meanwhile, the Guard looks on through the spy hole with masturbatory pleasure.[26] Oida's transposition of *The Maids* into dance-theatre – a series of interrelated dance sequences – began with a silent re-enactment of this homoerotic scene. The plain dark grey set suggested first the prison cell, then the Maids' attic room, again drawing parallels between the three works. Each prisoner had a low flat bed, suggestive of the granite blocks Genet recommends in the final edition of *Deathwatch*, and each bed was covered in a white sheet which the prisoners wrapped around their waists, transforming them into maids' aprons. The association between the prisoners' incarceration and the Maids' lack of freedom in the service of Madame was underscored by the cell-like design, and by the fact that one dancer put a swooping red velvet cape over his grey uniform, transforming himself from the sober Guard into Madame, a demented, back-flipping harpy. Oida states in an interview that his play concerns imprisonment in the broadest sense: 'The maids are a symbol of a society in which we are all prisoners of culture, religion, political decisions, race, education' (quoted in Hutera 2003). The fact that the audience was seated on the stage added further to the sense of claustrophobic entrapment.

A red dustpan, brush and rubber gloves, and a long swathe of fabric and collection of hats were thrown into relief by the grey set. This minimalist scenography reflected Oida's classical training in Noh and Kabuki, where the almost bare stage accentuates the performers' greatly stylized gestures. Perhaps thanks to the fact that Genet's works are heavily inspired by Far-Eastern theatrical traditions, as this chapter demonstrates, his theatre plays an important

Figure 2   Ismael Ivo and Koffi Kôkô (left to right) in *Die Zofen* (*The Maids*), directed by Yoshi Oida (2002). Photograph © Dieter Blum

part in Japan, where many productions of plays have taken place. The bare set reflected not only Oida's Far-Eastern training, but also his 30-year collaboration with Peter Brook who, inspired by Elizabethan theatre, stages plays in what he calls an 'empty space': 'A naked area does not tell a story, so each spectator's imagination, attention and thought process is free and unfettered' (Brook 1993: 25). Moreover, the transformation by the Maids of the fabric and hats into Madame's ceremonial costumes echoed alchemical performance techniques frequently seen in Brook's theatre, where in *The Tempest* (1991), for example, a shaken glass of water becomes a sea storm. In *Die Zofen* the Maids were played by Ismael Ivo, a Germany-based Brazilian dancer who has worked in New York; and by Beninese Koffi Kôkô, who lives in Paris. The roles of the Guard and Madame were played by Vienna-based Turkish dancer Ziya Azazi. The percussion music was composed and played by the Brazilian João de Bruço. The performance, choreographed mainly by Ivo and Kôkô, contained influences as diverse as Brazilian samba, African animism, Japanese Kabuki, Sufi whirling, contemporary

European and North-American dance and performance, and gymnastics. The barely intelligible bursts of language intermittently emitted by the dancers in their native languages reflected the cosmopolitan influences composing the production. Genet describes his own theatre as 'clumsy' or 'awkward': 'it's a theatre that, if it wasn't new, was certainly awkward. And being awkward, perhaps it had something new about it. Because it was awkward' (Genet 1991: 303; 2004: 262). Equally, critical theorist Roland Barthes described the acting in Roger Blin's production of *The Blacks*, discussed in Chapter 5, as 'intelligent clumsiness' (Barthes 1960: 96); and Philippe Adrien refers to Genet's theatre as 'unsteady' (Adrien 2008: 151). Identity in Genet's theatre is composite and changing. Genet's performers must therefore alternate between different styles, tones and tempos to avoid portraying identity as a stable essence. This hybrid state of incompletion produces an impression of 'clumsiness' or 'awkwardness'. With its eclectic combination of performance styles, Oida's production certainly rendered this 'gauche' theatrical mode.

As with the Living Theatre's and other productions, the Maids and Madame were played by men. In addition, evocative of Serreau's production, the performers playing the Maids were of African origin. Identity on a range of levels, most notably gender and race, was exposed as performance, artifice. In a letter to Bourseiller, Genet speaks of Japanese theatre, where a burly man who drives a taxi by day might play a leading Noh lady by night (Genet 2002: 903). Masculine and feminine are revealed as arbitrary categories. In *Die Zofen*, the Maids' primping and preening, gently swaying hips and coquettish glances were performed incongruously by the dancers' rippling naked torsos, sinewy bare feet and breathtakingly vigorous moves. Girlish playfulness turned into macho wrestling, teasing into fighting. Stereotypes associated not only with gender but also with skin colour were blurred and deconstructed. The Valet in Genet's *The Blacks* says, of Blacks, 'They have a strange beauty. Their flesh is weightier' (Genet 2002: 485; 1960: 19). People of African origin are frequently stereotyped by European culture as bearing innate talents for sport, music, dance and sex. Fanon warns that Blacks are aligned with the physical, to exclude them from intellectual spheres (Fanon

1967: 117, 123). Since Oida's dancers self-consciously revealed the vigorous thrusts of their majestic bodies to be performance rather than instinct, there was less risk of them being exoticized.

It is apt to end the section on *The Maids* in performance with *Die Zofen*, since it could not be more aesthetically removed from the first ever production, by Jouvet.

Figure 3   Koffi Kôkô in *Die Zofen* (*The Maids*), directed by Yoshi Oida (2002). Photograph © Dieter Blum

Deathwatch in production

As with *The Maids*, directors of *Deathwatch* have for the main part recognized that, whilst the play's location denotes a familiar social setting – a prison – any naturalism is *faux* naturalism.[27]

Jean Marchat (1949)

Presumably disappointed by the naturalism that dominated Jouvet's production of *The Maids*, Genet himself collaborated with Jean Marchat, more known as a distinguished French actor than director, for the première of *Deathwatch* at Paris's théâtre des Mathurins (February 1949). Photographs reveal a cell with steps leading to a door made of iron bars. Rather than painting a realist image – constructing an illusion of the social reality of a prison, and concealing the artifice of that illusion – the scenography self-consciously drew attention to its own theatricality. The décor, a box set depicting dungeon-like walls made from large stones, was painted onto a backdrop with obvious, heavy-handed brushstrokes (for photographs see Boyer and Boyer 2006: 150–1). Whilst the box set, with its invisible fourth wall, is often associated with realist representation, here the bare walls of the theatre were visible around it (Spade 1949: 4, quoted in Genet 2002: 1022). To employ terminology developed by Ubersfeld, the box set was referential, since it denoted a prison cell, whilst the theatre walls were non-referential since, as with the case of Elizabethan theatre, they did not reference anything in particular but were simply the theatre walls (Ubersfeld 1982: 175). The very first production of *Deathwatch* thus shattered realist illusion with its juxtaposition of the referential and non-referential, which drew attention to the play's status as theatre rather than reality. The costumes too did more than simply denote the reality of prison life. The cellmates' striped shirts were low-cut and figure-hugging, their trousers tight and their feet bare, their uniforms thus becoming aestheticized signifiers of the homoerotic undercurrents running between the men. Rather than understanding the play as an account of French prison life, spectators were encouraged to reflect on complex themes at the heart of the human experience, such as identity and gender.

Alexandre Arcady (1970)

Two decades later *Deathwatch* was staged by French actor-director Alexandre Arcady, better known for his films than for his theatre work, at Paris's théâtre Récamier (September 1970). This production also highlighted the play's artifice (for a summary of reviews see Genet 2002: 1024–5). Rather than prison uniforms, the costumes comprised jeans and shorts, into which the actors changed on stage. This partly produced a Brechtian *Verfremdungseffekt* – a device that indicates that the representation on stage is but theatrical illusion (Brecht 1964: 219); and also emphasized the importance in

Deathwatch of dressing and undressing. Lefranc, according to Maurice, tries five or six times to put on Yeux-Verts's jacket (Genet 2002: 14; 1989: 122). Since identity for Genet is composed of layers of shifting social influences, it is often symbolized by clothing. Lefranc thinks he can acquire Yeux-Verts's anti-hero image simply by donning his jacket. The fact that identities are projected onto individuals by social influences was emphasized further when Bernard Rousselet, playing Yeux-Verts, removed all his clothes for the moment where Genet indicates, 'the actor will have to invent a kind of dance which shows Green Eyes trying to go backwards in time' (Genet 2002: 18–19; 1989: 131–2). Yeux-Verts explains the lengths to which he went to avoid being a murderer: 'I tried every form and shape so as not to be a murderer. Tried to be a dog, a cat, a horse, a tiger, a table, a stone! I even tried, me too, to be a rose!' (Genet 2002: 18; 1989: 131). The fact that Rousselet danced naked perhaps indicated that even when he removed all his clothes, Yeux-Verts could not be whom he wanted to be, but had to submit to his predestined role as assassin and convict. As scholar Timothy Mathews states in a chapter on Genet, his characters enjoy no acute insight, or detached moment of awareness (2000: 164). Self-perception in Genet's world is never free from the determination of society, establishment and duty.

The production, like Adrien's *The Maids*, was partly aestheticized and partly realist. The musical prologue incorporated sounds of slammed iron doors and clanking chains, and the set comprised scaffolding poles and planks that sketched out a prison cell, rendering the complex linear formalization that Genet describes. The inmates' only means of escape from this network of lines and traps was via fantasy, Arcady illustrating this by projecting slides and films – prefiguring his cinema career – of their daydreams. Since cinema has long been considered an incarnation of dreams, the use of multimedia was appropriate (see Metz 1977: 99–137).

Jean-Baptiste Sastre (1997)

Nearly 50 years after the première, the young French director Jean-Baptiste Sastre presented *Deathwatch* at Paris's théâtre de la Bastille (December 1997). Sastre, who also staged *The Screens* in 2004 (see

Chapter 6), has a reputation for his radically anti-naturalist stagings, whether of classics by Shakespeare or of modern works by Artaud. His production made no concessions whatsoever to naturalism, even if it did employ the earlier edition of the text. Sastre's scenography dispensed entirely with set and properties. The stage floor was removed to create a pit in which the cellmates circled like caged animals, whilst the Guard paced the perimeter. Most notably, the performance style drew attention to the actors' bodily and vocal presence, rather than simply communicating the text. The inmates, equidistant from each other and facing the audience, stood almost totally immobile. Rather than making physical contact, for example when Lefranc lunges towards Maurice (Genet 2002: 27; 1989: 151), they suggested touch by winding their bodies round each other in slow motion. To the older edition of *Deathwatch*, Sastre thus applied Genet's updated stage directions, where he describes how 'The movements of the actors should be either heavy or else extremely and incomprehensibly rapid, like flashes of lightning' (Genet 2002: 5; 1989: 103). Not only body, but also voice, was stylized. Reminiscent of the theatre of one of France's most innovative contemporary directors, Claude Régy, with whom Sastre has worked, speech was slow, intonation monotone. In *Le Langage dramatique*, theatre theoretician Pierre Larthomas explains how intonation follows a particular melodic line, depending on whether the utterance is an assertion, question, order or exclamation. The voice's pitch is also inflected, depending on whether the speaker's mood is aggressive, suspicious, cheerful (Larthomas 1972: 51). Instead of respecting these interlocutory conventions, vocal delivery was inspired by Genet's recommendations: 'If they can, the actors should deaden the timbre of their voices' (Genet 2002: 6; 1989: 104). The recited, scripted nature of the prisoners' speech, like the naked dance in Arcady's production, perhaps symbolized the ways in which their identities were inescapably predetermined.

Yoshi Oida states in interview, 'Freedom can be found in art. It gives people the chance to analyse how we are prisoners, and to discover how to go towards liberation' (quoted in Hutera 2003. In many productions described here, the creative beauty of Genet's texts, which gives rise to such a great diversity of styles and approaches that a production history of his plays constitutes a veritable history of modern theatre, counterbalances the sense of imprisonment presented in the plays.

5 Key productions and issues surrounding production
The Balcony, *The Blacks*

The last chapter concluded by arguing that the creative originality which Genet's early theatre inspires amongst theatre artists compensates for the plays' nihilistic themes of imprisonment and hopelessness. His later theatre – *The Balcony* and *The Blacks* are discussed here – analyses the same theme of identity, but escapes the confinement of prison cell or bedroom, opening onto wider vistas that accommodate social phenomena such as political and military power, religion and race. Despite the seemingly obvious politics of these later plays, however, they can only problematically be considered as *littérature engagée* – politically committed writing the duty of which is to solicit social transformation in the spectators, and in the world (see Sartre 1976: 101). Genet ends a text on the Dutch painter Rembrandt, in which he also reveals, in abstruse terms, his philosophy of identity, by undermining his own argument: 'what I have just written is false' (Genet 1968: 25; 2003: 99). This caveat applies to his theatre, where he presents political themes, simultaneously laughing at anyone who might perceive them as a political programme. This chapter discusses this 'awkward' disequilibrium, this hybrid combination of social issue and carefree celebration, in relation to Genet's designs for scenography, costumes and acting style, and analyses the extent to which directors attain Genet's unsteady balance between politics and play.

The Balcony: set, acting, costumes

As with Genet's earlier plays, *The Balcony*'s naturalist traits must be treated with circumspection.[1] The opening stage directions itemize the contents, notably a jug and yellow armchair, of a Bishop's sacristy (Genet 2002: 264; 1991a: 1). The brothel owner Madame Irma's bedroom is later described in equally naturalist terms: 'Very elegant .... Tall lace hangings suspended from the flies. Three armchairs. Large bay window, left' (Genet 2002: 285; 1991a: 22). The location where the revolutionaries meet also appears literal rather than metaphorical: 'The décor represents a square, with panels of shadow. Quite far back, one can make out the façade of the "Grand Balcon", shutters closed' (Genet 2002: 310). In *The Maids*, opening and closing windows and curtains symbolizes a freedom beyond the sisters' grasp. In *The Balcony*, scenographic details do not appear to bear significance beyond their naturalist depiction of location.

Chapter 4 describes how certain productions, notably Marchat's *Deathwatch*, employed a set-within-a-set, to shatter realist illusion by showing the audience that they were watching a play rather than a 'slice of life'. In *The Balcony* Genet recommends that free-standing screens be erected to denote the décors of Irma's various fantasy suites: red satin for the Bishop's sacristy; brown for the Judge's chamber; green for the General's battlefield. The enormous Spanish crucifix painted in the sacristy suite is '*trompe l'oeil*', and the Bishop's mitre is made of 'gingerbread', that the prostitute-playing-the-sinner nibbles (Genet 2002: 264–5; 1991a: 1). These details might appear anti-naturalist, but in fact they are coherent with the logic of the play's narrative, since they contribute towards making the brothel mock-ups of a sacristy, chamber and battlefield.

The performance style could also be construed as naturalist. In 'How to Perform *The Balcony*' – prefatory stage directions published five years after the première, in response to what Genet considered to be misunderstandings of the play – he writes that in the first four tableaux, actors must employ two opposing tones: exaggerated and natural (Genet 2002: 258). He stipulates opposing tones in order to denote when customers and prostitutes enact erotic scenarios and when they play themselves. In the following example, the

Bishop's pomp and customer's profanities alternate bathetically: 'For Christ's sake, leave me alone. Fuck off! I'm searching my soul. (*Irma shuts the door.*) The majesty, the dignity, that illumine my person ...' (Genet 2002: 269; 1991a: 6). Like the scenography, the acting style could therefore be understood as naturalist, since it corresponds realistically with the brothel customers' actions and behaviour.

Costumes too appear naturalist. In 'How to Perform *The Balcony*', Genet recommends that they be immediately recognizable by the audience:

> What was wanted in France was a judge who resembled those in our assize courts, not a bewigged judge; the General needed a star-studded kepi or one encircled by oak leaves; he should not look like some kind of lord admiral.... The photographers ... must wear the outfits and adopt the mannerisms of the trendiest young people of the time and country in which the play is being performed.
>
> (Genet 2002: 259; 1991a: xii–xiii)

Genet takes a backhand swipe here at Peter Brook's Paris première of *The Balcony* at the théâtre du Gymnase (May 1960). The Queen's ermine-trimmed robes, Judge's full bottom wig and General's bicorne hat would have been more politically meaningful in Britain, rather than in France, where they no doubt appeared exotic, almost quaint (for photographs see Boyer and Boyer 2006: 151). Genet, who formed his opinion based on newspaper articles, perceived Brook's production to be frivolous, describing it as an 'operetta' (Genet 2002: 936). Genet advises that the costumes resonate, as in *The Maids*, with contemporary society. Significantly, the most recent addition to the brothel's list of authority figures that clients can enact is the Police Chief. He represents authoritarian rule in modern nation states more immediately than the Bishop, Judge or General, as French psychoanalytic theorist Jacques Lacan indicates (Lacan 1998: 265). Genet's aim that the production bear contemporary social and political relevance via the costumes might therefore also align *The Balcony* with naturalism.

Any apparent naturalism is, however, deceptive. The first version of *The Balcony*, drafted in 1956, contains particularly poetic scenes which would render a directorial recourse to naturalism problematic. A *tableau vivant* – scene where immobile actors create a living picture – bearing three figures on the brothel staircase, glides across the stage. In another scene, as if in a dream, they float, bleeding, down from the flies (Genet 2002: 369, 391; 1991a: 49–52). On a literal level, they might be wounded revolutionaries or counter-revolutionaries. However, their names – Blood, Tears, Sperm – are allegorical rather than everyday. The 1956 version contains further poetic features. As the Queen's Envoy departs, the ruined brothel suites pass across the stage (Genet 2002: 403), perhaps blasphemously recalling medieval church processions where episodes from the Gospels were depicted in living scenes borne on floats. The earliest draft of *The Balcony* contains both these abstract visual scenes and acoustic ones. After the Police Chief visits Irma, the stage directions state:

> The stage moves from left to right, as before, but between this scene and the next there is a fairly long space of time in which the darkness is broken up by flashes, bursts of machine-gun fire, vague cries and sighs.
>
> (Genet 2002: 393; 1991a: 52)

This idea was developed in Moriaki Watanabe's production at Tokyo's Setagaya Public Theatre in June 2001 (he had previously staged *The Maids*), where the black-out between scenes was interrupted by crackling machine-gun fire and thundering explosions, interspersed with Bach's Toccata, Mahler's Symphony Number Three, Marlene Dietrich's *Lili Marlene* (see Corvin and Dichy 2002: 1158). Watanabe's acoustic effects, like Genet's original play-text, presented non-literal scenes, the metaphorical interpretation of which was left to the audience.

Genet removed some of these poetic scenes from subsequent editions of *The Balcony*, which was confusingly uncharacteristic since, as Chapter 4 recounts, Genet's revisions generally rendered his plays more, rather than less, naturalist.[2] The final version nonetheless contains features that would scupper a naturalist staging, the Police

Chief's fantasy mausoleum suite providing a striking example. Genet's directions appear meticulous:

> Something like the interior of a tower, or of a well. The wall is circular; its stones are visible. At the rear, a staircase leading downwards. In the centre of the well there seems to be another well, with the first few steps of another staircase.
>
> (Genet 2002: 341; 1991a: 88)

The more these details are analysed, the less they stand up. Does the mausoleum loom like a tower, or plummet like a well? Does this tower/well contain, or just 'seem' to contain, another tower/well? Is the second staircase inside or outside this second tower/well? Is the mausoleum contained within the brothel, or does it join the brothel to the outside world? Is it real, or is it just another of Irma's fantasy suites? Genet's stage directions, again, mock the director seeking a user's guide and, with their illogical practicalities, obstruct naturalist scenographic design. So too do other details. Notably, the opening directions state, 'On the right-hand partition, a mirror in a carved and gilded frame reflects an unmade bed which, if the room were logically arranged, would be in the auditorium, in the front row of the stalls' (Genet 2002: 264; 1991a: 1). The unmade bed is positioned amongst the spectators, thereby abolishing any naturalist imaginary fourth wall, and drawing attention to the play's artifice. Moreover, since the same bed is visible throughout the first five tableaux, which each depict a different location, a naturalist spatial logic is disrupted.

Genet's instructions for scene changes also highlight the play's artifice. He specifies in 'How to Perform *The Balcony*', 'I want the scenes to follow one another, the sets to shift from left to right' (Genet 2002: 258; 1991a: xi). This direction is not necessarily followed by directors. Brook had a revolving stage, which Genet criticized (Genet 2002: 258; 1991a: xi). Genet equally criticized Víctor García, whose production of *The Maids* had enthralled him (see Chapter 4) but whose *The Balcony*, staged in a 20-month run from 1969 at São Paolo's Ruth Escobar Theatre, did not. It took place inside a 20-metre steel and plastic vertical funnel located within the emptied theatre, and illuminated from every angle with harsh white light.[3] The actors scuttled up and down metal ladders between transparent platforms or metal cages, both of which moved up and down the funnel, or else clung to the walls; Irma, suspended from a rope, clambered up and abseiled down; a mass of virtually naked bodies collided at the bottom and writhed up a spiral ramp (White 1994: 622). The sense of entrapment conveyed by the funnel was extended to the spectators who, perched on scaffolding galleries around it and peering voyeuristically through pierced openings, had little room for manoeuvre. Genet, who went to Brazil to see the production, was not impressed: 'It was stupid. [García] had a vertical layout, whereas it is a horizontal play' (quoted in Sobczinski 1986: x). For Corvin, the recommended sliding scene changes resemble the panning shot of a camera, and testify to Genet's desire to introduce a filmic quality to theatre (Corvin and Dichy 2002: xxxiii, 1176). The playwright certainly demonstrated a keen interest in cinema (see Giles 2002: 15–24). However, Genet adds that the sets must give the impression of amassing in the wings (Genet 2002: 258). This effect exposes the artifice of the production by drawing attention to the off-stage mechanics of theatre. Watanabe highlighted this theatricality by other means, with a large trapdoor centre-stage, into which properties for one tableau disappeared and from which properties for the next appeared. Moreover, the accumulation of sets in the wings blurs the boundaries between inside and outside, play and reality, illustrating further Genet's belief in the omnipresence of appearance. In addition to exposing theatricality on and off stage, Genet's rather obscure insistence on the 'horizontality' of the play might possess other connotations. In French director Jean Boillot's production, which premièred at the Avignon Festival in June 2001, doors, armchairs, piano, mirror and balcony entered and exited on concealed rails running along two walkways either side of the semi-circular stage (for photographs see Malgorn 2002: 62, 68–9). These sliding sets recommended by Genet and staged by Boillot may symbolize the layers of social influence that construct the shifting identities populating Genet's world.

Not only the bed and scene changes, but also the mirror in Genet's scenography disrupts naturalist illusion, since it reflects the spectators, thereby highlighting their presence at the performance. Mirrors feature prolifically in Genet's literature: his dance piece *'adame Mirror* even contains the word in its title.[4] In *The Balcony*, the Bishop entreats:

> Have I made myself clear, mirror? Golden image! Ornate as a Mexican cigar box – and I want to *be* Bishop in solitude, in appearance only... And in order to destroy every vestige of function, I'm going to create a scandal.
>
> (Genet 2002: 269; 1991a: 6)

The General exclaims, 'Waterloo! General! Man of war, in full dress. Behold me in my pure appearance. With no contingent at my back. Simply myself – I appear' (Genet 2002: 282; 1991a: 19). In Tableau Four, the Customer-playing-a-Little-Old-Man offers flowers to a prostitute in front of three mirrors (Genet 2002: 284; 1991a: 21). In the 1960 version, the scene between the revolutionaries takes place in a café containing wall-to-wall mirrors at which they frequently glance (Genet 2002: 424: 1991a: 52). The General's boots, like Madame's shoes in *The Maids*, are patent. Genet changes Irma's jewellery from pearls in the 1956 version to diamonds, presumably because they are more reflective (Genet 2002: 298). In the last tableau, the back wall of the stage is a mirror (ibid.: 325). Mirror reflections symbolize the self-image that people, particularly those in power, seek to project. This image, as the Bishop and General note here, need bear no relation to the mundane realities of the individual behind it; just so long as it appears noble, triumphant, resplendent. The revolutionaries are no less immune to the image's seductive powers, as Chapter 3 explains. Chantal, one of Irma's prostitutes, defects from Le Grand Balcon to enlist with the insurgents. Her name contains the French noun *chant* meaning 'song'. She has become an anthem, a slogan. Roger, another revolutionary, confirms in the 1956 version that Chantal's image has taken precedence over her reality: 'You'll be what you've always dreamed of being: an emblem' (Genet 2002: 312; 1991a: 73). Genet illustrates visually how the image bears little relation to the reality it claims to represent, when the Little Old Man's three mirror reflections are played by three different actors. Watanabe's production emphasized this dislocation of appearance from reality, since the back of the whole stage was a huge tilting mirror which cast ever-changing images of the characters (for photographs see Genet 2002: 1378). In the January 1996 production at the théâtre de Châtillon, staged by French director Laurent Gutmann, who also staged *Splendid's* (2004), the bare arena-like stage was surrounded by exposed machinery that lowered and raised a metallic curtain in which the spectators could see themselves (Corvin and Dichy 2002: 1157). In Terry Hands's 1987 revival of his 1971 production (discussed presently) the aluminium curtain curving around the Barbican's thrust stage also reflected the audience. Genet holds up a mirror, and obliges the public to see itself for what it is: image, appearance, performance.

Genet also disrupts naturalist illusion with the play's title, *The Balcony*. Balconies are a salient motif across Genet's theatre.[5] In *The Balcony*, a balcony is the location where the newly appointed figureheads appear, where Chantal is shot, and which lends its name to both brothel and play (Genet 2002: 324; 1991a: 74). The balcony constitutes a building's façade upon which occupants face the public. 'Façade' can mean an architectural frontage, or a pretence, a public show. In the scenes preceding and ensuing the new government's appearance on the balcony, the spectators witness the devastation wrought upon the brothel by the insurgents (Genet 2002: 315, 325; 1991a, 57, 74). The balcony scene, however, presents a front of control and calm, as the Queen and her entourage appear on it in pristine condition. Pomp and ceremony conceal abuse and incompetence, balconies therefore representing the projection of public image in Genet's works.

The term 'balcony' is relevant, too, because it highlights the tendency towards performativity and role-play in the general public. Internationally acclaimed Catalan director Lluís Pasqual's April 1991 production at the Odéon-Théâtre de l'Europe sat the audience on the stage whilst the play took place in the auditorium, from which the seats had been removed.[6] Actors used the public entrances to the auditorium to enter and exit the performance area, and the chandelier that Genet describes as being present throughout the play was the Odéon's own. The space usually occupied by spectators became the site of performance, thereby insinuating that the audience was complicit in the same act of role-playing as the brothel customers. Moreover, the Grand Balcon's balcony, on which the new Queen Irma and her entourage emerged, was the auditorium circle, which had been decorated with a canopy capped with a huge crown (for photographs see Genet 2002: 1377). As Pasqual's production highlighted, 'balcon' in French denotes the raised tier of the auditorium. Genet writes, 'for the gods, the top galleries, the 'house' – dress circle, orchestra, boxes – was an initial spectacle ... which their gaze had to pass through before perceiving the spectacle on-stage' (Genet 2002: 853; 1972: 22, translation modified). The auditorium is a spectacle in itself, of who is situated spatially lower but socially higher than whom. At the end of *The Balcony* Irma warns spectators that they are no less preoccupied with image and performance than her fantasist clients, telling them to go home, where nothing will be any more real than in the theatre (Genet 2002: 350; 1991a: 96). Genet unmasks everyday life as play-acting. The difference between actor and audience is practical, not fundamental. Characters on stage are in fact more 'honest' than people in the auditorium, since they openly enact their fantasies. For this reason, Irma refers to the Grand Balcon as 'the most honest House of Illusions' (Genet 2002: 290; 1991a: 28, translation modified). Everyone, whether inside or outside Irma's fantasy factory, on stage or in the stalls, is included in Genet's universalizing ontology of charade. Pasqual writes in the programme, 'The impossibility to distinguish true from false, the ultimate "undecidability" that undermines any formal system, precipitates the minute fault line that causes upheaval in our fragile yet persistent lives' (Pasqual 1991). By exploiting the polysemy inherent in the term 'balcony', Pasqual displayed this undecidability.

References to Spain in *The Balcony* provide a means for understanding how the play may appear to be naturalist, but is in fact allegorical. Irma and Carmen are Spanish forenames, and the mausoleum is named the Valle de los Caídos (see Aslan 1973: 64). Genet explained in a press conference with *L'Express* magazine after the play's première directed by Peter Zadek (discussed presently), 'My point of departure was situated in Spain, Franco's Spain, and the revolutionary who castrates himself was all those Republicans when they had admitted their defeat.' He clarifies, however, that his play is not a historical account of Francoist Spain: 'And then my play continued to grow in its own direction and Spain in another' (quoted in White 1994: 476). For many 1950s and 1960s European audiences, for whom Franco's military dictatorship was a living reality, Genet's evocation of Spain would have suggested repressive authoritarianism. However, since his stage directions indicate that set and costumes must reflect society contemporary to the play's staging, Genet shifts the focus from history to myth and metaphor. The play exposes the dynamics and theatrics of power not only in fascist Spain, but anywhere. After all, Genet changed the play's title from *España* to *The Balcony* (Genet 2002: 1161). Joseph Strick's 1963 film adaptation (discussed presently) opens with a newsreel montage depicting civil unrest in a variety of locations from Argentina to England, consequently portraying the conflict between popular uprisings and authoritarian repression as a universal process rather than a historically specific event.

Certain directors and designers have attained this precarious balance between the socially specific and the metaphorical. Theatre theoretician and director Herbert Blau, who contributed towards introducing European avant-garde theatre to the USA, staged *The Balcony* at the San Francisco Actor's Workshop (March 1963). Blau responded to Genet's direction that the three figures of authority be heavily made up. The Bishop wore traditional robes, but his face was decorated with linear make-up evoking stained-glass windows. Watanabe's production responded to Genet's suggestion that the three figures be 'excessive, but should not be unrecognizable', and that they display 'gigantic proportions' by wearing *cothurni* and body-padding (Genet 2002: 259; 1991a: xii). They wore conventional costumes – by European standards – except for their circus stilts and Kabuki make-up of chalk-white foundation, black angular eyebrows and vermilion lipstick. Similarly, Brook's actors were mounted on high *cothurni*. Young French director Sébastien Rajon, who staged *The Balcony* at the Athénée-Théâtre in May 2005 (discussed presently), took Genet's idea of elevating the three figures to new 'heights', mounting them and the Queen on vertiginously high unicycles with stabilizers hidden underneath their skirts. Boillot's production distanced itself from simple cultural specificity not through the hyperbolic use of stilts and exaggerated make-up, but through overt stylization. Rather than being starched stiff like an Episcopal cape, the Bishop's white robes were diaphanous (for photographs see Genet 2002: 1379). Chapter 3 alludes to *The Balcony*'s quality of weightlessness. People and objects are turned to air, since they are replaced by their appearances. The lightness of the Bishop's costume in Boillot's production highlighted this ephemerality. In addition, it abounded in blasphemous and perverse connotations, since its gossamer panels spread like wings or a wedding dress train, affording the Bishop the appearance at once of an archangel and of a bride. In each of these cases familiar costumes are amplified, distorted or aestheticized, provoking a rupture with verisimilitude and with any one social context.

The following detailed accounts analyse the extent to which various productions have achieved an unstable equilibrium between social comment and abstraction.

Peter Zadek (1957)

Because certain scenes were construed as sexually provocative and disrespectful to the Church, *The Balcony* did not initially find a French producer (White 1994: 481). The première was staged by Zadek in 1957 at London's Arts Theatre Club, a private establishment excepted from the Lord Chamberlain's censorship laws, which forbade blasphemy, indecency and unfavourable representations of living persons.[7] Zadek seemed to view this exemption as a *carte blanche* to take the play's brothel setting literally. According to Genet, who attended rehearsals – which he disrupted, and from which he was banned – lace-clad prostitutes were draped across the décor (ibid.: 481–2). Numerous productions have emphasized sensuality in *The Balcony*. In Pasqual's production, agile men and semi-naked women populated the stage. The play's salacious potential was also exploited in Rajon's production with Carmen's conical brassiere, and in Hands's, where a corset exposed the breasts of the prostitute-playing-the-General's-Horse, performed incidentally by the well-known British actor Helen Mirren. It is for individual spectators to decide whether female nudity in these productions and Zadek's constituted a facile means for seducing the audience, or if it underscored, in Hands's words, 'the relationship between sex, politics, power and corruption' (Hands 2006: 207). Genet explained in *L'Express*, 'My play *The Balcony* takes place in a "house of prostitution", but the characters belong as little to the reality of a brothel as the characters in *Hamlet* belong to the world of the court.' He continued, 'The real theme of the play is illusion. Everything is false, the General, the Archbishop, the Police Chief, and everything must be treated with extreme delicacy' (quoted in White 1994: 481). Sex, like any other element in the play, becomes a means with which to expose the images and appearances at play in daily life, rather than a literal, realist end in itself, which it became in Zadek's production.

Zadek represented not only sex, but also politics, literally (Kanters 1960). During the General's role-play the stage was criss-crossed with barbed wire, allusions being made to British imperialist activities in the 1950s such as the aggressive attempt to seize the Suez Canal from Egyptian control, and the violent suppression of uprisings between Greeks and Turks in Cyprus. Reference to the British royal family was also direct, as the Queen bestowed the Order of the Garter, the highest British honour, upon one of her subjects (Aslan 1973: 68). Genet insists in 'How to Perform *The Balcony*' that 'the play should not be performed as if it were a satire on this or that. It is – and must therefore be performed as – the glorification of the Image and the Reflection' (1991a: xiii). For cultural critic Theodor Adorno, Brecht's satire of Adolf Hitler, *The Resistible Rise of Arturo Ui*, in which a Chicago gangster attempts to control a cauliflower racket by exterminating the opposition, trivializes the awful reality of such an oppressor, 'strip[ping] it of its horror and diminish[ing] its social significance' (Adorno 1980: 184). Genet would concur, since he says of Zadek's production, 'The characters have become grotesque, disgusting clowns' (quoted in White 1994: 482). For Genet, an exaggerated theatrical style must render the politics of his play oblique, rather than producing caricature or satire.

Genet admits in 'How to Perform *The Balcony*' that Zadek's production had some merit: 'the actress playing the horse lovingly drew his moustaches on [the General] with a bit of charcoal' (Genet

2002: 259; 1991a: xii). Here, a piece of charcoal transforms a brothel client into the illustrious General. When the figures of authority are photographed in Genet's play-text, a rolled-up piece of paper becomes the General's baton, and the General's monocle placed under the Bishop's tongue becomes a holy wafer (Genet 2002: 329; 1991a: 75–6). As Chapter 3 describes, Genet reveals how power masks itself behind theatricality. Power in *The Balcony* exists in a costume or in a speech, which Zadek's production went some small way towards revealing.

Joseph Strick (1963)

Shortly after the London and Paris premières of *The Balcony*, it was adapted into a film. Strick's conceit was to locate it in arguably the world's most dominant image factory: the movie industry. He states:

> the true brothel of ideas and physicality in our world is the movie studio. There you can readily find the sets, the props, the actors and even the producers, who love to act out the role of the Chief of Police.
>
> (Strick 2004a)

After the opening montage of uprisings, the film cuts to a hangar with an immense steel sliding door: a film studio. Irma's prostitutes, one dressed as Joan of Arc, another as a saucy maid, lounge like extras waiting for their scene; workmen walk past with pieces of set. When Tableau One in Genet's play-text is finally shown, the viewer can assume that Bishop and Sinner are played by customer and prostitute, played by film actors. The artifice is emphasized when, for example, the soft organ music in the sacristy ends abruptly as the prostitute simply lifts a record-player needle.

Indeed, the film's merit is its play on the confusion between 'fictional' and 'real' scenes. The viewer sees a white clapboard cottage surrounded by a picket fence, and hears birds twittering. Irma then walks past what is in fact an enlarged photograph for a film set. Similarly, when the Queen's newly appointed dignitaries process through the streets in their limousine, the crowds, flypast and military parade behind them are so obviously a grainy two-dimensional back-projection that one wonders whether the three men have actually left Irma's film studio. Owing to these dizzying cinematographic effects, when gunfire sounds it is unclear whether it is overheard from another film studio or whether a real revolution has broken out. Genet writes, 'Do the rebels exist *inside* the brothel or outside it?' (Genet 2002: 258; 1991a: xii, Genet's italics).[8] Is the revolution real? Is Irma's brothel really sacked? Are these just more appearances, charades? Fiction becomes indissociable from the reality it threatens to dominate, an ambiguity that Strick's cinematography succeed in maintaining.

Genet worked on a treatment for the film. According to Strick, however, it was too brief, so US screenwriter Ben Maddow was enlisted to write the screenplay (Strick 2004a). Maddow's dialogue unfortunately cancels out many of the subtle ambiguities created by the visual effects. The Police Chief tells Irma in the film:

> I want you to play a game, but the best game you've ever played in your life. I want you to run the government for an hour, maybe two. You'll wear a crown, you'll wave to the people. You'll play the Queen. You can do it. You can play the Queen better than the Queen herself.
>
> (Strick 2004)

In Genet's play-text, contrastingly, the Queen's Envoy invites Irma to be the Queen in terms far more recondite than those in Strick's film. He exclaims, 'Long live the Queen, Ma'am,' and then says, 'The people, in their fury and their joy, are on the brink of ecstasy: it is for us to push them over' (Genet 2002: 320; 1991a: 64). Whilst in Genet's play-text the performance of power is evoked obliquely, in the film it is brashly direct. In addition, Strick omitted the roles of Carmen, Arthur and the Envoy, whose frequently arcane comments add further ambiguity to the play-text.

For Giles, Strick's film was unsuccessful critically and commercially because it did not appeal to the prevailing taste for realism (Giles 2002: 41). Its failure might also be owing to Strick's over-simplification of Genet's complex meditations on image, reality and identity, which eliminated much of the ambiguity and equivocalness that affords the play its theatrical impact and philosophical interest.

Terry Hands (1971)

Genet considers his play to be an exposé of appearance and theatricality in all their manifestations, whether personal or political. Unsurprisingly, given the UK's disposition since the 1950s towards socially relevant theatre, English director Terry Hands's production at London's Aldwych Theatre (November 1971) foregrounded politics. Hands, with Barbara Wright, famed for translating from the French Alfred Jarry, Eugène Ionesco and others, rendered the language more concise and prosaic; re-inserted revolutionary scenes omitted by Frechtman's translation; and, in Hands's words, created a 'very clear and coherent' political message (Hands 2006: 203). Concurrently, Colin Chambers, who helped mount the 1987 Genet season at the Barbican (only *Deathwatch*, *The Maids* and *The Balcony* were staged, before it was aborted), explains that Hands, like Genet, 'deals with politics in a mythical and non-naturalistic way' (Chambers 2006: 208). Like Brook and Watanabe, Hands included stilts, over-sized costumes and exaggerated make-up, complementing politicization with aestheticization. The characters thus incarnated, in his words, vast empires of religion, militarism and the law (Hands 2010; for photographs see Finburgh *et al.* 2006: 199–200).

Chapter 3 explains how societies, for Genet, desire to be dominated. *The Balcony* also demonstrates how societies desire spectacle and show. Goldmann claims, optimistically, that it is possible to replace an image-obsessed society with 'authentic' living, though he admits that this fails in *The Balcony* (Goldmann 1966: 101). Hands argues pessimistically that the acts and words of organized revolutionary movements cannot be immune from a fixation with image and appearance. Unlike Irma's clients, the partisans in *The Balcony* supposedly do not play-act. However, any meaningful resistance is replaced with battles of rhetoric and pretence. The Police Chief mocks, 'The revolution's a game too. ... every rebel is playing a game. And he likes his game' (Genet 2002: 305; 1991a: 44). In Rajon's production Chantal was semi-naked and bore a shaved head and no make-up, in sharp contrast to the brothel customers and staff, who wore thick make-up and wigs. Moreover, the revolutionaries appeared in the auditorium – on the side of 'reality', not theatricality. Rajon's directorial decision seemed at odds with Genet's play-text, where Roger, as Chapter 3 notes, admits that the revolutionaries are fighting 'the combat of allegories' rather than a genuine battle (Genet 2002: 312; 1991a: 73). To illustrate how the militants play clichéd roles rather than executing authentic acts, Genet recommends that they wear masks portraying stereotypical militant traits (Genet 2002: 259–60; 1991a: xiii). Hands reflected this failure of extreme left-wing movements to effect authentic change. The revolutionaries charged around the stage, spitting and yelling like thugs, demonstrating the circularity existing between hard-line left-winger, and right-wingers which, for Hands, is epitomized when the leftist Roger chooses to play the fascist Police Chief. Hands states, '[Genet] shows you how the establishment works and then how the revolutionaries work. And what you see, of course, is that the revolutionaries are hell-bent on reproducing the very system they want to overthrow' (Hands 2006: 203). The swivel chairs on which the rebels were seated illustrated this circularity.

Hands explains how his production was inspired – in dramaturgical rather than visual terms – by the French Revolution which, with its principles of citizenship and inalienable rights that were imposed via a totalitarian Reign of Terror, for him represents all failed left-wing rebellions. Marc encapsulated Robespierre's ruthless efficiency, and Roger represented Danton's weakness for compromise (ibid.: 204). Genet certainly wished *The Balcony*'s political dimensions to be prominent, and therefore condemned US-based Panamanian director José Quintero's March 1960 production at New York's Circle in the Square Theatre (at the time, the longest-running Off-Broadway show), which 'quite simply cut everything to do with the revolution' (Genet 2002: 257; 1991a: xi). However, Hands's production perhaps over-emphasized political debate, whereas Genet's play pirouettes away from rationality, with its puzzling arguments that lead perplexingly to no conclusions.

Sébastien Rajon (2005)

Chapter 4 discusses the tradition of cross-casting that has grown around Genet's plays. In Watanabe's production of *The Balcony* only Carmen and Chantal were played by women; the other roles were played by *onnagata* – men who impersonate women in Kabuki theatre. In Gutmann's, the same young female actor played the parts of the prostitutes in the first three tableaux, and that of Envoy. In Rajon's, Irma was played by Michel Fau, who has worked extensively with French director Olivier Py, whose productions of the classics or of contemporary theatre often confuse gender categories. Rajon states that transvestism lies at the heart of Genet's theatre (Rajon 2008: 177). Genet himself explains the relevance of transvestism:

> [Tiresias] retained the male sex for seven years, and for seven more the other. For seven years a man's clothing, for seven a woman's. In a certain way, at certain moments – or perhaps always – his femininity followed in close pursuit of his virility, the one or the other being constantly asserted, with the result that he never had any rest, I mean any specific place where he could rest. Like him, the actors are neither this nor that.
>
> (Genet 2002: 873; 1972: 50)

For Genet, Tiresias, the prophet from Greek mythology who alternated between masculinity and femininity, should be the patron saint of actors, since he exposes the performed nature of these genders. Transvestism for Genet is also a dramatic theory that, like the 'awkward' acting style described in Chapter 4, fractures psychological cohesion, creating hybrid, composite characters. Fau's dizzyingly dextrous acting conveyed this 'awkwardness'.

In 'How to Perform *The Balcony*' Genet describes how, from the scene between Irma and Carmen onwards, the tone must become 'equivocal' (Genet 2002: 258; 1991a: xi). Chapter 3 notes how, from this point on, distinctions between play-acting and reality collapse. Speech-act theory can assist in elucidating this slippery 'equivocalness' of the characters' speech. For Dominique Maingueneau, speech has three origins: Speaker–L (the subject producing the sounds of speech);

Speaker–λ (the subject who positions her/himself at the origin of personal pronouns and possessive adjectives: 'I', 'my', etc.); and the Performative Speaker (the subject responsible for the effect that the utterance produces on the interlocutor; Maingueneau 1990). An example elucidates how Genet exploits this tripartite division, rendering his characters' speech 'equivocal'. Arthur, the brothel's nominal pimp, enters Irma's boudoir and describes the sex scenes in which he has just participated:

Figure 4   The characters of the Thief and Judge in *Le Balcon* (*The Balcony*), directed by Sébastien Rajon (2005). Photograph © Patric Burnier

The little geezer's buttoning up. He's pooped. Two sessions in half an hour. With all that shooting in the street, I wonder whether he'll get back to his hotel. (*He imitates the JUDGE in Scene Two.*) Minos judges you ... Minos weighs you ... Cerberus? Bow-wow! Bow-wow! (*He shows his fangs and laughs.*)

(Genet 2002: 298; 1958: 42)[9]

Speaker-L is Arthur, though a fourth origin to the utterance must be added, since in theatre Speaker-L is also the actor; and in Fau's case, Speaker-L was a man playing a woman. Speaker–λ further divides the utterance. Arthur begins by speaking as himself, recounting the customer's hazardous journey home. He then impersonates the customer-acting-the-Judge from Tableau Two, who himself mimics Minos, judge of the dead in Hades. Arthur then speaks as himself-acting-the-Judge's-Torturer, who impersonates a Cerberus – a multi-headed dog that prevents people from escaping from Hades. Speaker–λ is an intricate imbrication of Arthur-as-himself, customer, Judge, Minos, Torturer, Cerberus. In Rajon's production Arthur depicted the instability of his status visually when he lay on the bed in the auditorium. Arthur, who is to play a corpse in the Police Chief's mausoleum suite, is shot dead. Or is his assassination part of another role-play? Arthur, the real-false corpse, lay in the real-false space between stage and auditorium.

Arthur's utterance is stratified further by its performative effect on the interlocutor. When he impersonates the Judge, the object pronoun – 'Minos judges *you*' (our emphasis) – could denote both the Thief and his present interlocutor, Irma. Arthur repeats lines from the moment in the role-play when the Judge overwhelms the Thief, possibly to subordinate Irma, for whose affection he competes with the Police Chief. *The Balcony*'s characters are denounced by some as muddled and incoherent (Coe 1968: 256; Dumur 1986). This criticism fails to appreciate the way in which Genet demonstrates how the subject derives from multiple, contradictory sources which render psychological character analysis or performance virtually impossible.

Fau somersaulted between tones and styles, conveying the multiple, clashing sources from which Irma's, like Arthur's, dialogue derives. Fau states, 'What's beautiful about Madame Irma is that she is all

Figure 5   The characters of Carmen and Irma (left to right) in *Le Balcon* (*The Balcony*), directed by Sébastien Rajon (2005). Photograph © Patric Burnier

roles, combined in one – all women, all female roles, even all of humanity, in all its hues and shades' (Genet 2008: 192). Irma, as Chapter 3 notes, is an exceptional figure in Genet's theatre. She plays, often simultaneously, brothel madam; brothel-madam-playing-

Queen; Police Chief's heartless whore; Police Chief's pining lover; theatre usher showing the audience the exit. According to Genet's directions, in Tableau Five alone she is to be 'conciliatory', 'wise', 'disconcerted', 'shocked', 'severe', irritated'... the list goes on.[10] Considering these descriptions as indications of psychological mood is problematic, since they are profuse and often contradictory. To portray Irma's identity as complex and shifting, Fau adopted an 'awkward' acting style. Rajon, who describes Irma as 'a hybrid being', explains how Fau '[allied] ferocity with delicacy, the sublime with the grotesque' (Rajon 2008: 179). For Lavaudant, Genet's language leaps 'From Racine to Claudel, from Rabelais to Jarry, from soap opera to airport novel' (Lavaudant 1985: 5).[11] Fau's performance drew from the ceremony of Kabuki; the austerity of classical tragedy; the lyricism of Paul Claudel (France's most poetic twentieth-century playwright); the clowning of the burlesque; the frivolity of vaudeville comedy.[12] For Philippe Adrien, whose production of *The Maids* is discussed in Chapter 4, the gravity of Genet's philosophical and political themes, and the solemnity of his lyricism, must be offset by humour and levity.[13] Fau's performance, which was matched by that of few other members of the cast, achieved this 'awkward' combination.

Conclusion

Genet claimed that *The Balcony* 'served as a step in achieving more beautiful plays' (Genet 2002: 912). This is perhaps borne out by the fact that stagings are often uneven, as these accounts illustrate. A production of *The Balcony* must be of contemporary political relevance, and a timeless allegory on the power of the image; it must be philosophical and fantastical; serious and puerile; sensuous and sterile; grandiloquent and flippant; ceremonious and derisory. Genet himself summarizes these 'awkward' contradictions in a letter to Frechtman: '[*The Balcony*] should be a satire but also a joyous festival, a true carnival that the public would revel in', and it 'should be staged with seriousness and a smile' (ibid.: 936). To directors, actors and designers, Genet throws down the gauntlet!

The Blacks

Introduction

Of all Genet's plays, *The Blacks* treats social and political issues – racism and colonialism – most frontally. Yet this and *The Screens* are his most poetic works. The tension between political content and its disavowal is reflected in the title, *Les Nègres, Une clownerie*. The literal translation of *Les Nègres* is 'The Negroes' or 'Niggers', terms that immediately connote racial discrimination, as Chapter 3 states.[14] The subtitle, *clownerie*, means 'fooling around' or 'practical joke' as well as 'clown show'. In *The Balcony* it is never clear whether the revolution is 'real' or another fantasy role-play. Likewise, here, it is never clear whether the off-stage trial and execution of a black man who has betrayed his black comrades are 'real' or scripted into the 'clown show'. Moroccan author Tahah Ben Jelloun writes about Genet's theatre, 'I was fascinated and exasperated by the power of appearance, woven with invisible threads, that governed this world' (Ben Jelloun 1993: 29). Genet's 'clown show' is, however, more than just a whirligig of derision. Since its tone is mocking, it avoids vindicating a black culture, politics or position. This is in itself political, since Genet rejects any fixed ideologies. *The Blacks*'s draft title was *Foot-ball*. A football is made from black and white patches stitched side-by-side. When kicked, black and white blur. Like any other aspect of identity in Genet's ontology, 'blackness' and 'whiteness' are social constructs, and the boundaries between these supposed opposites are porous. Genet recommends that the theatre curtain for the production be made of black, not red, velvet (Genet 2002: 478; 1960: 7). Black identity, like a curtain, can be drawn back to reveal its theatrical, performative nature. Directors of *The Blacks* are thus confronted with the play's immediately recognizable political content, and with the fact that, as with all his plays, Genet destabilizes any clear message, leaving the tasks of clarifying and concluding to the reader/spectator.

Set and acting

Staging *The Blacks* might first involve understanding where it is located. Genet proposes in 'How to Perform *The Blacks*', published in 1960, that the play might take place 'in the open air ... The Court is seated on an added horizontal branch in a broad-leafed tree' (2002: 473–4). One reason for the outdoor setting might be to exaggerate the racist association between Blacks and the virgin forest which, as Chapter 3 highlights, conjures phantoms of fear in the memory of white colonials. The famed German director Peter Stein seized upon this imagery in his production at West Berlin's Schaubühne (June 1983), where the fictional jungle dweller Tarzan swung across the stage. However, it is never clear whether *The Blacks* is actually set in a jungle or not. Village claims that he entered his victim Marie's shop to escape the intense heat, suggesting that the play-within-a-play that the Negroes enact for the White Court indeed takes place in Africa. Yet Village's victim Marie is knitting a balaclava, hardly suitable in hot climes (Genet 2002: 507; 1960: 59). Moreover, the path Village takes to her house is lined with hazelnut trees and brambles – European rather than African flora (Genet 2002: 518; 1960: 83). The colonials might have attempted to re-create a European landscape of lawns and orchards, but they surely would have planted roses or geraniums, not brambles. This European vegetation then gives way to the dust and cactuses through which the Court travels to avenge the victim's murder, which in turn cedes to a tropical forest, evoked by the sounds of frogs, owls and lions. The Queen compounds the confusion by asking, 'But we're in France, aren't we?' (Genet 2002: 525; 1960: 96, translation modified). By avoiding the specificity of one geographical location or historical period, the play's themes of anti-colonialism and racism adopt global and timeless significance, referring as readily to the 1950s decolonization of Africa as to today's problems with cultural tolerance, which the 2007 London production (discussed presently), illustrates.

By avoiding a naturalistically grounded location, Genet also reveals how space in the play is theatrically constructed. In his letter to Pauvert, he elucidates his concept of theatricality:

> On a stage almost the same as our own, on a dais, imagine recreating the end of a meal. Starting from this single elusive fact, the greatest modern drama has been expressed for two thousand years, every day, in the sacrifice of the Mass.... Under the most familiar appearance – a crust of bread – we devour a god.
>
> (Genet 2002: 817; 2003: 38)

As Chapter 2 explains, the Host is both a wafer and Christ's body. Genet aspires throughout his theatre to the simultaneity of the Catholic Mass which, for him, is of the highest theatricality. In *The Blacks* he deploys a green screen behind which Village's murder of the white woman takes place (Genet 2002: 478; 1960: 7). The Queen's Governor watches with binoculars, even though this murder is just a few metres away (Genet 2002: 516; 1960: 80). Virtue, too, plays on the simultaneity of the screen's actual proximity and the distance it symbolizes. When Bobo explains that Village is taking such a long time to return from the murder because Marie's house is far away, Virtue retorts, 'What do you mean far away? It's behind the screen' (Genet 2002: 518; 1960: 83). In the 1955 manuscript Bobo conflates the real screen and imaginary forest: 'I shall try to retrace his steps, from the screen into the heart of the forest' (Genet 2002: 553). Genet's screen, like the Host, is highly theatrical: it is simultaneously a flat piece of canvas and an endlessly mutable landscape. Genet highlights the transformatory potential both of décor and of actor. The Governor trumpets like a bugle, Negroes imitate the sounds of the forest, the Missionary lows like a cow (Genet 2002: 498, 523, 539; 1960: 44, 92, 121). This theatrical transformation of people and things is significant for several reasons. First, as this chapter has stated, it exposes the mechanisms of artifice with which theatre is constructed. Second, Genet liberates his theatre from naturalism's need to evoke places and objects literally, rendering staging efficient and economical. Third, this accentuation of theatricality bears political significance, by highlighting that all discourses in our socialized world are produced by humans, not least racial discourses. By transforming black actor into white authority figure, black actor into Negro, Negro into forest or horse, Genet demonstrates that identity is not an essence; it is a constantly shifting process. There is therefore nothing stopping Blacks one day from becoming dominant, and the Court members from becoming dominated. The fact that the Valet metamorphoses into a cow that is sent to the abattoir indicates this possibility.[15]

Genet emphasizes anti-naturalist, theatricalized acting in the play in other ways. Chapter 3 notes the 'heightened precision' that characterizes Genet's theatre. In *The Blacks* Genet recommends that actors orchestrate their movements and voices. When the white woman's murder is recounted, the Court members wipe away a tear and sob in unison, to which the Negroes respond with perfectly orchestrated laughter, repeated on numerous occasions (Genet 2002: 482; 1960: 14). When Village enacts the murder, the Negroes clap their hands, stamp their feet and recite their lines in time (Genet 2002: 514; 1960: 74). Movement is synchronized, singing orchestrated, laughter coordinated. To emphasize this formalization, Archibald 'should gesticulate like an orchestra conductor, sometimes handing over to one person, sometimes to another' (Genet 2002: 473). This orchestration highlights a heightened precision in performance, a self-conscious stylization of movement and voice. Moreover, it becomes a kind of Brechtian *gestus* – a physical expression of the political relationships between people (Brecht 1964: 139). In her famous essay 'Can the Subaltern Speak?', Indian Marxist literary theorist Gayatri Spivak questions the representation in western discourses of the third-world subject. Many political theorists, according to her, speak of *the* third world, as if it were a monolithic block where all individuals share uniform consciousness. She argues that individuals are 'irretrievably heterogeneous', and discourses must reflect this (Spivak 1988: 272, 284). Rather than attempting to represent the inevitable heterogeneity of people of African origin, Genet takes the opposite tack, stereotyping his characters to the extreme. He obliges them to perform identical movements and utter identical sounds, thus parodying or critiquing stereotypes that reduce the difference of individuals to sameness. Genet critics Boisseron and Ekotto borrow from French philosopher Henri Bergson's theory that when people repeat actions or words nonsensically, the organic flexibility that characterizes humanity becomes rigid and mechanical, and they become automatons

(Boisseron and Ekotto 2004: 100). By instructing his characters to repeat the same movements and words, Genet highlights the dehumanizing properties of the stereotypes that Spivak reproves.

So, in *The Blacks* as in *The Balcony*, dramatic elements such as scenography and performance style bear multiple metaphorical connotations that can potentially enrich readings and stagings of the play.

Roger Blin (1959)

The Blacks was premièred in October 1959 at Paris's théâtre de Lutèce. Blin's production, with an Anglophone cast, then transferred in 1961 to London's Royal Court, where Genet saw it. His admiration for Blin's directing and for scenographer André Acquart's set and costumes is clear from his comment, mentioned in Chapter 3, that photographs of this production must always be published with his play (Genet 2002: 474). Moreover, the numerous stage directions that Genet added to the final edition of *The Blacks* actually describe Blin's production.

Genet explains in his preface to *The Blacks* that he had been asked to write the play for black actors (Genet 2002: 836; 2010: 228). Blin's cast was indeed black. Some actors had previously worked with the Griots, a France-based black company who promoted black literature; one, Bachir Touré, was relatively famous; others were amateur; all were from various African and Caribbean Francophone countries. Blin explains how he struggled to render the various accents intelligible, but that he did not attempt to standardize them (Blin 1986: 132). Since the dialogue was difficult for the audience to understand, actors communicated more through broad gesture, dance-like movement, colourful *commedia dell'arte*-style half-masks worn by the Court members, and expressive voice. Blin describes the deep, resonant timbres of some actors, the ethereal voices of others (ibid.: 138). He did not, however, trivialize the play's hard-hitting racial politics with his carnival of festive folklore. As with García's *Las criadas*, discussed in Chapter 4, the play's politics were rendered blatantly evident by the climate of decolonization and immigration in which it was staged.[16] Moreover, the diversity of accents in itself bore a political dimension. In his preface Genet condemns shows by black performers that provide inoffensive amusement to gratify bourgeois audiences (Genet 2002: 836; 2010: 228). By speaking each with their own accent, the actors were not compliant with the norms of bourgeois French pronunciation.

The variety of accents, and also the clashing modes of delivery that Blin cultivated, emphasized the 'gauche' performance style that Genet integrates into his play. Blin explains:

> [Genet's] writing is completely poetic, but cannot be played in a poetic style. Genet's texts are completely devoid of sentimentality, but are extremely moving. I think the emotion comes through when his texts are played with great aggression and harshness.
>
> (Blin 1986: 193)

No tidy paradigm unites the clashing styles in Genet's plays. On the one hand, actors are to produce clownesque laughter; on the other they must 'imitate tragedians, especially French tragediennes' (Genet 2002: 474). On the one hand, the white Queen and black matriarch Felicity joust for supremacy; on the other they 'talk to each other like two women exchanging recipes' (Genet 2002: 531; 1960: 107). Blin conveyed this collision of styles not least when the Negroes first entered the stage to a Mozart minuet, to which they danced a ballet with comical hops and skips (Blin 1986: 134). This 'awkward' clashing, which destabilizes the fixity of character, identity and race, exposing them as fluid and mobile, was a founding principle in Blin's production.

The fact that the text was not entirely comprehensible enabled spectators to hear the rhythmic musicality of Genet's writing. Genet expert Mairéad Hanrahan writes, 'On every level, it is the excess of language – where it becomes music, or exceeds good sense – that this writing celebrates' (Hanrahan 1997: 115). One example from scores, provided by Archibald's incendiary speech to the Negroes, illustrates the melodiousness of Genet's theatrical prose:

> ARCHIBALD: I order you to be black to your very veins. Pump black blood through them. *Let* Africa circulate in them. *Let*

Negroes negrify themselves. *Let* them persist to the point of madness *in* what they're condemned to be, *in their* ebony, *in their* odor, *in their* yellow eyes, *in their* cannibal tastes. *Let* them not be content with eating Whites, but *let* them cook each other as well. *Let* them invent recipes for *shin-bones, knee-caps, calves, thick lips, everything. Let* them invent unknown sauces. *Let* them invent *hiccoughs, belches* and *farts* that'll give out a deleterious jazz. *Let* them invent a criminal painting and dancing.
(Genet 2002: 502–3; 1960: 60–1, our italics)

Frechtman's translation adheres closely to the structure of Genet's dialogue. The repetition of similarly structured sentences in Archibald's speech – 'Let' + noun + verb – creates rhythm. Musicality is enhanced further by the repetition of 'in' + 'their' + noun/relative clause ('in their ebony'; 'in what they're condemned to be'); and by the repetitions of body parts ('shin-bones', 'knee-caps'); and bodily functions ('hiccoughs', 'belches'). Since the actors' diction was not immediately clear in Blin's production, words and syllables were freed from their strictly semantic function, their acoustic sonority becoming palpable.

Rather than relying essentially on dialogue, Blin's production communicated both through the incantatory rhythms of Genet's text, and via the visual. The Court members had, according to Genet's descriptions, which reproduce Blin's and Acquart's designs, 'superb gown[s]'; 'sublime uniform[s]' (Genet 2002: 479: 1960: 8). The Queen, for example, wore a shimmering white robe and gold tiara, and was attended to by a Valet in blue silk britches, stockings and lace ruffed shirt (for photographs see Boyer and Boyer 2006: 167–77). The Negroes, conversely, displayed 'the very height of bad taste', the men sporting black tuxedos with brightly coloured shoes, the women wearing 'heavily spangled evening gowns suggest[ing] fake elegance' (Genet 2002: 478; 1960: 8). Indeed, their dresses resembled those of saloon girls from a Western that had been decked in aprons, braid and bunting. Redonnet suggests that their mismatching costumes afford the play a carnivalesque air, both because they convey a sense of ebullient abandon and because they are subversive (Redonnet 2000: 200–9). Russian literary critic Mikhail Bakhtin explains how carnival marks a time when habitual rules and regulations are undermined. Literatures are carnivalesque when they overturn conventional hierarchies, fools becoming wise, kings becoming beggars. For Redonnet, Genet's costumes, inspired by Acquart's designs, are carnivalesque, since the Negroes deform European fashions in an act of subversion. Acquart's costumes could be described not only as carnivalesque, but also as 'awkward'. Fanon explains, 'not only must the black man be black; he must be black in relation to the white man' (Fanon 1967: 110). The Negroes' self-image is constructed from the clichés projected onto them by the Whites, just like the costumes that had been thrown together for the show.[17] The motley mismatchings of black tie and multicoloured shoes, ball gown and bare feet, symbolized the composite, refracted nature of the Negroes' identities.

Both Acquart's costumes and his scenography were semiotically charged. The white flooring and scaffolding of poles and platforms, bearing a few chairs, were thrown into relief by the black background and harsh lighting. As with the set of black activist and director Robert Hooks's production at the John F. Kennedy Center in Washington D.C. (June 1973), which comprised black and white platforms, the colour scheme reflected the play's central theme of race (Tribby 1973: 513).[18] In Blin's production, white ropes hung against the black backdrop, evoking a ship's rigging, thus alluding to the transatlantic slave trade, a facet of the play also underscored in Alain Ollivier's January 2001 production at the Studio-Théâtre de Vitry, where the stage was divided into two-storey wooden stalls evoking either a slave galley, stables – which recalled the treatment of slaves as cattle – or prison cells (see Chapter 4 for the motif of prisons in Genet's works). In Blin's production the scaffolding was wrapped in white rags, which in part conjured the barnacled piles of a pier, perhaps the one under which the Negroes find the tramp whose body they use in their ceremony; and evoked the 'vines or bending branches' with which the Court descends from the balcony to cross the jungle (Genet 2002: 474). The division of space was also significant. The scenography comprised several levels, the Court located on a raised platform left of centre-stage which they accessed via a raised walkway traversing the auditorium; the Negroes on ground level; Marie's grocer's, represented by a curtain and shop entry bell, in between (Blin 1986: 134, 139). The balcony – the seat of power – epitomized genteel civilization and security whilst, as the Queen's Governor describes, the lower level, where the murder was enacted, represented savagery, danger and madness (Genet 2002: 523; 1960: 91). For Savona, the Court's descent to stage level marks the decline of white imperial power, and Felicity's ascent to her throne on an adjacent platform announces the resurgence in African pride (Savona 1983: 121). This view, whilst valid, upholds the binary oppositions of white and black, civilized and savage. In Blin's production, when Virtue recited a tirade on behalf the snoozing Queen, she sat directly below her, so the monarch's body appeared on the top level whilst her voice was heard from the bottom level; when Marie-played-by-Diouf was murdered, she was taken to the upper level, presumably to heaven, suggesting that the Court represented death rather than power and vitality (Genet 2002: 498, 520; 1960: 44, 88). Dichotomies of powerful and powerless thus became increasingly confused. Blin also divided the stage horizontally, into the space in front of the screen where live action occurred; behind the screen where narrated action happened; and in the wings where a real trial supposedly took place. However, this spatial separation also collapsed, since the boundary between the fiction behind the screen and the 'fact' on stage, between the 'real' off-stage trial and the Negroes' enactment of the murder, became increasingly porous, as this chapter has illustrated. Blin's production, which inspired theatrical spatialization in Genet's text, thus compartmentalized space, only to reveal that, like the distinctions between black and white, these categorizations were arbitrary. The multiplication of perspectives rendered by the diversity of vertical and horizontal planes thus incarnated the complexity of viewpoints that Genet's play-text perpetuates.

Blin succeeded in striking the balance recommended by Genet between being evasive and precise (in Dichy and Peskine 1986: 12), and the production, while no doubt contentious for 1950s European audiences, played to packed houses, received dithyrambic reviews, and won the Grand Prix de la Critique for best new play (see White 1994: 499).

Ultz and Excalibah, and Cristèle Alves Meira (2007)

Blin's production foregrounded Genet's playful exposure of the artifice of theatre without underestimating the play's politics. Genet insists in his directions that at least one white spectator be present (Genet 2002: 475; 1960: 4). Chapter 3 argues that the spotlight illumination of this spectator emphasizes the artifice of the whole play, and of the images the Negroes portray of themselves. Conversely, this white person could indicate that the opposition between Black and White is a live confrontation, a point that Chapter 3 also makes, in relation to the Genetian concept of the 'wound'. Genet explained to Jerzy Lisowski, Polish translator of *The Blacks*, why he refused to authorize an all-white production:[19]

> if, a couple of days before their execution, prisoners on death row – real ones – could play, in the prison yard, in the presence of their judges and their executioners, a play about the treachery of their relationships with each other and with their judges and executioners, the dramatic emotion to which such a performance would give rise would be nothing like what usually happens in theatre.
>
> (quoted in Federman 1970: 702)

As we have stated, the political relevance of Blin's production would have been patently obvious to 1950s audiences. Blin states in the 1980s, however, 'I do not know if the show would have the same impact today' (Blin 1986: 147). *The Blacks Remixed* at the Theatre Royal Stratford East, London in October 2007, co-directed by the versatile and prolific British theatre designer Ultz and UK hip-hop DJ Excalibah, demonstrated that Genet's play can still have relevance today.

The production appeared initially to have little contemporary bearing. A police sergeant or magistrate might have better conveyed the oppression of Blacks in the UK today than the Judge, Missionary and Governor in their Victorian colonial uniforms. The Queen – a lookalike of Elizabeth II – was contemporary, but since today's monarch is more a figurehead than a politically powerful leader,

Figure 6   The characters of (left to right) Diouf, Villagem Felicity, Ville de Saint Nazaire, Snow, Bobo and Virtue in *The Blacks Remixed*, directed by Ultz and Excalibah (2007). Photo © Jake Green

references to racism in contemporary Britain were not immediately obvious. The political relevance of the production became apparent when one noted that it took place in October, namely during the annual British Black History Month which remembers events and people from Africa and its Diaspora that have been omitted from official discourses; and in 2007, the 200th anniversary of the abolition of the slave trade. The pertinence of the colonial costumes became obvious when, as the Court took their place on their balcony, a portrait of Queen Victoria and then the word 'APOLOGIZE' flashed on a screen.

These, and the belt buckle reading 'slave' worn by Village, brought into sharp focus the theme of slavery discussed in Genet's play and, significantly, Britain's involvement in the slave trade. Moreover, rather than appearing in a middle-class theatre like the Almeida in Islington or the Royal Court in Sloane Square, the play was staged in Stratford, where the effects of colonialism and slavery are evident today in the demographic, which originates predominantly from

Britain's ex-colonies in the West Indies, Asia and Africa. Kerry Michael, the theatre's artistic director, writes, 'theatre in our country is still controlled by a white elite … At best they are finding it hard to give up real power, at worst they have no intention of doing so' (Michael 2007).[20] The audience at *The Blacks Remixed* was predominantly 'black', as word spread amongst the local community – historically excluded from 'highbrow' theatre – that the play concerned their history and identity, and was not just a remote piece of art about colonialism by a canonical playwright – something of which Blin's Royal Court production, with its predominantly white audience, could have been accused.

Genet's play-text recommends that the Court's costumes be elegant and the Negroes' vulgar, something that the Stratford production reversed: the Court members, not the Negroes, looked affected and ungainly, since the black actors wore thick white greasepaint, affording their faces the lifelessness of corpses, which indeed they become when the Negroes in Genet's play-text kill them (Genet 2002: 539; 1960: 122). The Stratford production adapted Genet's stage

Figure 7　The characters of (left to right) the Missionary, Valet, Queen and Governor in *The Blacks Remixed*, directed by Ultz and Excalibah (2007). Photo © Jake Green

direction that instructs the Negro Bobo to paint Village's face black before he enacts the murder scene: '[Bobo] applies the colours in the same way that a painter applies paint to canvas, stepping back to appreciate her work. The other Negroes, like visitors in a museum, also appreciate it, their heads cocked to one side' (Genet 2002: 473). Race is socially constructed with words and images, as a painting is constructed with brushes and oils: both are artifice. Genet highlights this further: '[Bobo] can use black, yellow, red and white polish'. This make-up could reinforce racial stereotypes by conjuring tribal face paints, as could the shoeshine box where Bobo stores her paints, which might draw associations between Blacks and manual labour. But as fast as Genet reinforces stereotypes, he undermines them. Far from being an essential feature, colour is an arbitrary category that bears multifarious meanings depending on cultures and societies, as Felicity's words illustrate: 'Walk gently on your white feet. White? No, black. Black or white? Or blue? Red, green, blue, white, red, green, yellow, who knows? (Genet 2002: 515; 1960: 77).[21] The black actors in the Stratford production reversed Genet's stage direction, here demonstrating through the use of face paint the relativism not of 'blackness' but of 'whiteness', as the Court, played by black actors, painted their faces white.[22] Towards the end of the play, instead of removing white masks as Genet recommends, the Court smeared their make-up, partially revealing their black skin, and highlighting the shifting and layered nature of racial identity.

Grace in the Stratford production was the preserve not of the Court, but of the Negroes – played by some of the UK's leading rappers, singers and performance poets – who were full-blooded, athletic and attractive. The literary agency of Rosica Colin, who originally worked with Frechtman and then in the 1960s took control of the English translation and production rights of Genet's works, allowed *The Blacks* to be adapted, or 'remixed'. Robert David Macdonald's unpublished translation, used in the Stratford production, provided prosaic, literal dialogue, which was then complemented by singing, raps and poetry which, the slam poet Kat François explains, were improvised each night (François 2007). Numerous critics perceive *The Blacks* as a celebration of the vitality of black culture. For Tom Driver, Genet no longer conjures

Figure 8   Village in front of the catafalque in *The Blacks Remixed*,
directed by Ultz and Excalibah (2007). Photo © Jake Green

the frivolous chimeras of his previous plays: 'Narcissism, impulsive
attraction to form, and ontological nihilism give way to a kind of
ontological affirmation. Outside the self's hall of mirrors there is
"something". We may call it energy. However wild and terrifying, it
is "there"' (Driver 1966: 40–1). Lewis Cetta interprets the Negroes'
exit from the stage to Mozart's *Don Juan* as an expression of their
unrepressed libertine pleasure (Cetta 1970: 511–25). However,
Fanon warns against the essentialist associations drawn, notably by
the 1930s *négritude* movement founded by Martinican Aimé Césaire
and Senegalese Léopold Senghor, both politically committed poets,
between Blacks and musicality, sensuality and nature: 'one had to
distrust rhythm, earth-mother love, this mystic, carnal marriage of
the group and the cosmos' (Fanon 1967: 123–5). As Fanon states,
these generalizations, whilst they appear positive, can reinforce racist
clichés about the black impulse towards sex and violence: 'Negroes
are savages, brutes, illiterates. But in my own case I knew that these
statements were false' (ibid.: 117). The actors playing the 'Negroes'
in the Stratford production appeared to present a confident black
culture, with their rhythmical, lithe, vigorous moves. But as fast as
they constructed black identities on stage, they countered readings

like those of Driver and Cetta by highlighting that they were simply acting out stereotypes.

Blatant stereotyping was evident in the costumes. Virtue resembled a girl gangster, in her tight black jeans and top, 'bling' gold jewellery and belt; Felicity was the African 'earth mother', in her batik dress and headscarf; Diouf was the evangelical preacher, in his sharp dark suit; Village, in his low-rise jeans, gyrated his hips provocatively and removed his top to reveal his toned torso; Ville de Saint Nazaire wore a hoodie – an immediate reference to urban audiences of teenage delinquency. They thereby emphasized the racist associations made between Blacks, crime and sex, which Genet's play-text notes when the Governor says, 'You can say what you like about them, but [the Negroes] are terrific fuckers' (Genet 2002: 516; 1960: 80). The audience both revelled in the prodigious song and dance, and was reminded that gangster rapper, R&B vocalist or gospel singer are racial typecasts. Snow showed up the audience's complicity in stereotyping when she snarled, 'You think we're savages? We'll give you savage.' Archibald says in Genet's text, 'Since they merge us with an image and drown us in it, let the image set their teeth on edge!' (Genet 2002: 495; 1960: 39). It became apparent that the rappers and hip-hop dancers were performing the roles expected of them rather than celebrating what one might simplistically term 'black' culture. The production, like Genet's plays themselves, set the audience up to believe something which was then torn down. Moreover, the references to racial stereotyping and prejudice exposed not merely discrimination in general, but discrimination in 21st-century Britain. The pall that lay over the murdered girl's coffin, and which Diouf wrapped around himself when playing her, highlighted the allusions to racial prejudice that the production made: it was the St George's Cross, an emblem widely associated with British nationalism.

The improvised MCing, rapping and slamming sat somewhat uncomfortably in a formal theatrical venue. Maddy Costa of *The Guardian* wrote, 'There are several awkward scenes during which all momentum is lost' (Costa 2007). *The Blacks* was staged at the same time at Paris's Athénée-Théâtre by newcomer Cristèle Alves Meira. Aesthetically, the Paris production was far more slick. Costumes were kitsch, camp and stylish: the Queen, with towering blond *ancien régime* wig, décolleté lamé bodice, cream skirts that only just concealed her buttocks and white platform shoes, was a disco-diva Marie-Antoinette. Costumes complemented each other chromatically, so that the Queen's ensemble was offset by Archibald's cream jacket, white trilby, black trousers and glittery shoes. Certain references to black cultures were made, for instance by the inclusion of *krumping*, the energetic US street dance, but these were essentially decorative. Alves Meira states that her main interest in the play was its use of ceremony rather than politics (Alves Meira 2008: 163). The production's utilization of masks and its precise analysis of the different sources of the characters' utterances, discussed in this chapter with reference to *The Balcony*, enabled the audience to distinguish clearly between instances when Blacks played 'Negroes', white power figures, or themselves. This emphasis on role-play was highlighted self-consciously from the start, when the partially raised safety curtain revealed the cast putting on their costumes. But whilst the Paris production was accomplished in aesthetic terms, it lacked the political punch of the Stratford production. There was a near-total absence of any reference to contemporary society, even though Paris's black population rivals that of London's relatively in size, and problems with racism are no less pressing. The only exception was the blinding beam of a searchlight and deafening sound of helicopters, which evoked gangland under police surveillance. But for the Athénée's essentially white audience, seated in a safe Parisian district, the resonances of this dramatic effect would have been very different from the impact on audiences at, for example, the théâtre Gérard Philippe, located in Paris's predominantly black and Arab *banlieus*, which are often in a near state of war with the police. The Paris production, with its farcing and abstract time and space, emphasized the *clownerie* dimension to Genet's play, thereby emasculating its political force, which the Stratford production, whilst not as polished, successfully seized. Kerry Michael describes the artists in the Stratford production as 'self-defining; they use words, music, rhythm and structure on their own terms without apology'. In his preface to the letters of George Jackson, a self-educated black author on death row, Genet warns, 'the black man ... writes a masterpiece, it is his enemy's

Figure 9   The characters of (left to right) the Judge, Queen, Missionary, Governor and Valet in *Les Nègres* (*The Blacks*), directed by Cristèle Alves Meira (2007). Photo © Yann Dejardin

language and treasure which is enriched by this additional jewel he has so hatefully and lovingly carved' (Genet 1991: 68; 2004: 53). The elegant Paris production risked becoming a 'jewel' in the crown of bourgeois culture, whilst the Stratford production exhibited an unapologetic refusal to conform to what the mainstream considers to be accomplished or presentable.

The concept of betrayal is central to Genet's philosophy of being. He writes, 'Real fidelity is often to do the opposite of those to whom one vows fidelity' (Genet 1991: 196; 2004: 169). Unlike Alves Meira's production, Ultz's and Excalibah's was not a word-for-word rendition of the play. Chapter 4 described two productions of *The Maids* – García's and Oida's – that drastically modified Genet's stage directions or text, or abandoned them altogether. The creative team of Ultz and Excalibah succeeded with bravura in appropriating and radically updating Genet's text, rendering it acutely relevant to the communities for whom they staged it. Perhaps some of the most powerful productions of Genet's plays are able to understand and convey the depth of his philosophical, political and aesthetic ideas, without necessarily reproducing his every word 'faithfully'. After all, Genet himself declares in *Prisoner of Love*, 'Anyone who hasn't experienced the ecstasy of betrayal knows nothing about ecstasy at all' (Genet 1992: 59).

6 Key productions and issues surrounding production

The Screens

Introduction

Owing to its contentious subject matter, *The Screens*, like *The Balcony* (see Chapter Five) was not premièred in France. The theme of an Arab country battling for independence from colonial rule was far too incendiary for most French theatres to accept since, when Genet first completed *The Screens* in 1961, France was still fighting against pro-independence forces in its colony Algeria, during a bitter war which lasted until 1962. The play premièred in May 1961 at the Schlossparktheater in Berlin, in a production by German director Hans Lietzau, who had staged *The Balcony* in 1959. It was subsequently staged in Vienna, Stockholm and London, where Brook, who had previously directed *The Balcony*, staged the first twelve tableaux at the Donmar Rehearsal Rooms.[1] *The Screens* was finally presented to French audiences in April 1966 at Paris's Odéon-Théâtre de l'Europe in a production by Roger Blin, who had already staged *The Blacks* (see Chapter 5).

Even in 1966, four years after the end of the Algerian War, certain scenes provoked outrage amongst critics, furious that public money had been spent on denouncing the State. Indeed, in October 1966 André Malraux, the then Culture Minister, had to defend the production in a parliamentary debate (Genet 2002: 971–80). Most infamous is the scene where French soldiers pass wind over their shot Lieutenant's body, in order that his last breath be 'a little French air' in the words of Roger, one of the soldiers (Genet 2002: 700; 1962: 153, translation modified).[2] Coordinated by Jean-Marie Le Pen, until recently leader of France's far-right Front National party, commandos and paratroopers who had served in the Algerian War and former members of the Organisation armée secrète (an underground far-right body that used assassinations and bombings in an attempt to stop Algeria gaining independence) rioted outside the theatre and sabotaged performances, jumping from the balconies and attacking the actors, until the iron curtain was lowered and the artistic director, Jean-Louis Barrault, restored calm and called for the performance to resume.[3]

There is perhaps another reason why, even though *The Screens* is arguably Genet's masterpiece, it is one of his least-staged plays. Blin and numerous other contemporaries of Genet remark that the playwright disliked the theatre, and rarely frequented it (Blin 1986: 183). Chambers states, '[Genet's] writing is enormously imaginative and experimental, but virtually impossible to stage. Genet is a visionary – he's not interested in the grubby side of theatre, like actually putting on the show' (Chambers 2006: 210). Whether or not Genet had an aversion to theatre cannot be verified. It is, however, clear that his imagination, notably in *The Screens*, is not constrained by the mundane practicalities of staging. Taking over five hours to perform, *The Screens* contains nearly 100 characters, and requires highly sophisticated stage machinery to mobilize the multiple acting levels that Genet proposes. In Frédéric Fisbach's 2002 production, lest anyone thought that the lengthy first half was the whole play, two stagehands walked on at the beginning of the interval with a sign warning, 'It's not finished'! *The Screens* is both long and dense. Genet cites amongst his influences Charles Baudelaire, Stéphane Mallarmé and Arthur Rimbaud, all three of whom revolutionized French poetry in the nineteenth century with their radically iconoclastic attitude towards versification and their vivid, often hermetic imagery (Genet 1991: 332; 2004: 150). Genet's dialogue in his theatre is as tightly wrought over several thousand lines as it would be in a sonnet. Blin notes that *The Screens* 'never gives any respite. Unlike what usually happens in theatre, it doesn't allow the spectator to listen to beautiful sentences that are a little empty' (Blin 1986: 193). Language in *The Screens* is not only intense but also often opaque. Eminent French director Patrice Chéreau, who staged the play at the théâtre des

Amandiers just outside Paris (September 1983), admits, 'for the first time in my life, I've staged a play in which there are pieces I'm not sure I understand' (quoted in Malgorn 1988: 89).[4] Not only the language but every aspect of the play is dense. Theatre theoretician Michael Issacharoff describes how theatre, which comprises simultaneously functioning signs – dialogue, gesture, scenography – avoids becoming a 'semiotic Babel' by carefully calibrating the different systems in order to orientate the spectator's perception (Issacharoff 1985: 147). Not this play. *The Screens* is sprawling and unruly, yet ecstatically flamboyant. Barrault, one of France's great twentieth-century directors and actors, agreed to produce it in his theatre, and Blin's production remains one of the monuments of twentieth-century French theatre, for reasons that this chapter attempts to elucidate.[5] In addition, this chapter makes reference to several other key productions, notably Fisbach's.

Roger Blin (1966)

Live performance – the most ephemeral of all the arts, which leaves few tangible remains save a few costumes, photographs and testimonies – is notoriously difficult to record. Blin's *The Screens* is the best-documented production of a Genet play.[6] The reader can consult Genet's 'Letters to Roger Blin', written whilst he attended rehearsals (Genet 2002: 845–77; 1972: 7–60). Moreover, as with *The Blacks*, Genet incorporated into his revised play-text many references to Blin's production and to Acquart's visual designs, and modified dialogue according to changes that Blin and his actors made during rehearsals (Blin 1963: 115). So much so, that Blin's production now constitutes Genet's final edition of the play, and it is impossible to separate the two.

On Brook's production of *The Screens* in May 1964, US director and critic Charles Marowitz, who worked closely with Brook before the latter moved from the UK to France in the early 1970s, states, 'The costumes and set conveyed two thirds of the play's truth' (Marowitz 1972: 57). Genet had originally entitled his play *The Mothers*, but renamed it *The Screens* (*Les Paravents*), testifying to the centrality in the play of scenography, principally the screens. One critic present at Blin's production complained that the screens were an encumbrance that overburdened the action (Cohn 1966: 286); another writes, '[*The Screens*] becomes at too many points an accumulation of *things*, of props, so that the actors and the characters they portray tend to disappear into the tiers, drawings, screens, offstage sounds, floating objects and the like' (Jacobson and Mueller 1968: 209). Perhaps for this reason, some more contemporary productions, notably French director Marcel Maréchal's at Marseille's théâtre de la Criée in November 1991, have dispensed altogether with the screens (see Maréchal 1996).[7] They are nonetheless worthy of discussion, not least in an account of Blin's production.

Chapter 5 notes that Genet's use of the actors' voices in *The Blacks* is an economical and efficient means of evoking the forest. Genet's screens constitute an efficacious way of depicting the play's panorama of scenic locations: desert road, town ramparts, village square, courtroom, brothel interior, palm or orange grove; alpine scene.... In this respect the screens resemble *periaktoi* – rotating triangular prisms used in Ancient Greek theatre, each side of which symbolically depicted a place with a simple outline, for example a column, tree, wave etc. – or else the equally minimalist and symbolic scenography in Chinese theatre, the influence of which Genet cites frequently (see Chapter 4).[8] Both traditions dispense with the accessories of everyday life favoured by naturalist theatre. Many critics understand the screens in these practical terms. For Aslan, who provides the most comprehensive illustrated account of Blin's and other early productions of *The Screens*, they delimit time and space (Aslan 1972: 60); for Marchand, they provide a scenic backdrop, and demarcate one tableau from the next (Marchand 1997: 193).[9] Blin explains how in his production, one of the Arab workers conveyed a sunset by removing a paper sun stuck to a screen, screwing it up into a ball, and throwing it to the side (Blin 1986: 200). And in Genet's text, 'with a charcoal pencil that she has taken from her pocket', Leïla draws the clock that she has stolen above a real table positioned in front of a screen representing her house (Genet 2002: 623; 1962: 62). Genet's screens thus serve the functional purpose of setting the scene.

Screens played a central role in Blin's production (for photographs see Boyer and Boyer 2006: 181–205). The stage filled gradually with

27 screens, designed by Acquart's son Claude, until they constructed what Blin describes as a 'town' (Blin 1986: 196). However, the screens both in Genet's play-text and in Blin's production serve not merely as a backdrop; they are a crucial participant in the play's action. In the play-text, the Arab rebels set the colonial Sir Harold's plantation ablaze by engulfing painted trees in painted flames (Genet 2002: 632; 1962: 72). Blin explains how the Arabs crept on stage, hiding behind their backs little candles with which they gave the impression that they were setting the trees alight. Fabric flames, manipulated by threads, then danced up and down the screens (Blin 1986: 215). In Genet's play-text the rebels celebrate the atrocities they commit against the colonials by bespattering a white screen with graffiti. One, who rapes a colonial virgin, daubs the screen in red paint. Another, who hacks off a westerner's feet, draws the stumps. 'Let's see the smell ...', cries the rebel leader Kadidja. He 'draws above them a few spirals of smoke' (Genet 2002: 658; 1962: 97). The stage is transformed into a fresco of atrocities evocative of Pablo Picasso's *Guernica*.[10] Even Maréchal, who dispensed with screens, still staged this scene, unravelling huge rolls of paper onto which rebels sprayed images with aerosols. Maréchal no doubt borrowed the idea from Blin, who states that spray cans were better suited than paint to creating this 'formidable uproar', where actors climbed onto each other's shoulders and splattered every last corner of the variously sized screens, located on three levels, in red and black scribbles of the revolt: a gun, a blood-streaked dagger, a trampled heart, a burning car ... (Blin 1986: 219).[11] The screens thus not only set the scene, but also narrate the action.

In his instructions to Blin, Genet insists that depictions of time, space and action via the screens must not be mimetic – the Ancient Greek term for imitation or mimicry. Genet writes, 'I believe that a sex maniac, who had never seen an orange tree in his life, nor even an orange, could invent a truer orange tree than anyone else (Genet 2002: 847; 1972: 13).[12] Later, he clarifies:

> All I'm doing is trying to encourage you in your detachment from a theatre which, when it turns its back on middle-class conventions, goes in search of its models: gestures, tone, in the

visible life and not in the poetic life, that is, the one we sometimes find near the confines of death.

(Genet 2002: 848; 1972: 15)

Genet entreated Blin and his designers to avoid what he terms 'worldly beauty' or 'prettiness'. In other words, they had to resist flattering the audience's lethargy with recognizable forms copied from daily life (Genet 2002: 846; 1972: 12–13). Instead, they must be inspired by 'death'. He explains earlier in his letters, 'If we maintain that life and the stage are opposites, it is because we strongly suspect that the stage is a site closely akin to death, a place where all liberties are possible' (Genet 2002: 845; 1972: 11–12). Genet wishes theatre to resemble death because, since the realm of death is unknown to the living, it constitutes a blank space across which the imagination can range freely. On Claude Acquart's screens, daylight was represented by sunflower yellow across which white diamond shapes radiated; a town was depicted with a naïve sketch of brown ramparts flanked by an emerald, indigo and gold palace. Other screens – uniform panels of fuchsia pink, midnight blue or earthy brown whose vibrancy was accentuated by the black backdrop – avoided mimetic representation altogether, becoming abstract panels of tone and texture.

Like the actors' voices that create the forest in *The Blacks* (see Chapter 5), the screens both evoke a scene and reveal the artifice of that theatrical evocation. According to Genet's stage directions, as *The Screens* begins, the stage is flooded with a harsh blue light. However, the first words of the play, exclaimed by Saïd, are, 'Rose. (*A pause.*) I said rose! The sky's already pink as a rose' (Genet 2002: 578; 1962: 11). From the start, the spectator must suspend disbelief and accept artifice: the sky is pink because Saïd says it is pink, even if it looks blue. Equally, spectators believe the screens to be a town wall or colonial plantation, knowing that they are only wooden frames covered with paper. Genet heightens this dual effect by stipulating that real objects be placed next to the screens: 'wheelbarrows, cheese grater, bicycle, gloves, etc.' (Genet 2002: 856; 1972: 25). The pictures are nothing more than paint, and yet they possess the same representational capabilities as the real objects beside them.[13] The characters' actions underscore further this theatrical duality. For example, an Arab worker at Sir Harold's plantation 'comes crawling in. He blows on the fire drawn at the foot of the trees'; another 'stirs it with his hand'. And the unwitting Sir Harold swears he can smell marmalade (Genet 2002: 635; 1962: 75). The characters' words and actions lead the spectator to believe that the plantation is ablaze, even if the fire is just a paper sketch. Blin's production played on this simultaneity of belief and disbelief both with the plantation scene and in other ways. For example, as Leïla traced the outline of her clock on a semi-transparent screen, a stagehand behind the screen followed her finger and drew the clock with a spray can on the other side of the screen. Sometimes the finger took the lead, sometimes the spray can (Blin 1986: 214). The spectator thus oscillated between being absorbed by the illusion and being reminded that it was but theatrical illusion. Blin thus created the effect of the Eucharist that for Genet lies at the heart of theatricality (see Chapter 5).

Blin demystified theatrical production not only with his use of screens but also with his scene changes. Genet recommended darkness between tableaux (Blin 1986: 38). He explains that the contents of each tableau should be minimal, but sufficiently strong so that during the darkness, spectators can use their imagination and sensibility to see with clarity what has been omitted (Genet 1986a: 20). Blin, an experienced director, explains that blackouts tend to interrupt a performance's rhythm. He therefore opted for scene changes reminiscent of those that Genet recommends in *The Balcony* (see Chapter 5). As a screen entered from one side of the stage, another exited from the other. Moreover, the actors pertaining to each scene entered and exited by walking behind the screens, thus emerging and disappearing as if by magic (Blin 1986: 205–6). Scenes were assembled and dismantled before the audience's eyes, exposing the artifice inherent in the process of producing meaning in theatre.

As Chapter 5 explains with reference to *The Blacks*, this use of theatricality highlights the artifice of meaning not only in theatre but also in life. The term scenography derives etymologically from the Greek *skene*, 'scene' and *graphein*, 'to draw', 'write' or 'create'. Genet's screens illustrate how meaning is not innate or permanent; it is written or produced. Signification is anchored in nothing more concrete than the artifice of words and symbols, as Genet demonstrates in this play: platforms and planks are erected and become a village fort; a crude sketch is drawn and becomes a clock; Saïd and his mother make the sound of an approaching storm and it begins to rain. Derrida states in *Writing and Difference*, 'Being is a Grammar; and ... the world is in all its parts a cryptogram to be constituted or reconstituted through poetic inscription or deciphering' (Derrida 1978: 76). In the absence of absolutes, meaning can be created and renewed, in a constant, playful cycle. This impermanence applies to realities both within the theatre and beyond. In the 1961 version of *The Screens*, while pinning multicoloured medals onto a huge mannequin, the colonial wife Madame Bonneuil says, 'in the past, so I've been told, the national holiday only had three colors, but now it has an incalculable number' (Genet 1961: 127; 1962: 103). Colonial authority, symbolized here by the *bleu-blanc-rouge* of the tricolore, has been replaced by an inclusive rainbow of colours, which potentially welcomes a postcolonial plurality of peoples, cultures and classes. Genet celebrates the possibility for constant renewal both of theatrical meaning and of meaning, truth and reality in general. As with *The Blacks*, he enables the possibility for a renewal of power too (see Chapter 5).

Screens were central to Blin's production, as were the multiple stage levels. When Genet's play-text begins, the stage comprises one unified acting space. A platform is erected in Tableau Five upon which first the prison, then the court are situated. A third level appears in Tableau Eleven, and by the end of the play the scenic space is split into four levels, the upper three of which are divided into three sections, affording a vast, versatile acting space. Craig, cited in Chapter 4 as the founder of modern stage design, writes, 'I suppose it offends no one to admit that unless unity reigns "chaos is come again"' (Craig 1962: 97). Genet and Blin ignored the prevalent preference for minimalist simplicity, favouring a baroque profusion of scenic elements. In Acquart's design, horizontal flights of steps linked the stage to the platforms, and platforms to each other. Whereas the steps joined acting areas, lighting effects separated them, since Blin alternately illuminated one area whilst the others remained in darkness. For Aslan the play therefore appeared like flashes in a dream (Aslan 1972: 19). Chapter 4 observes the relationship drawn by theorists between dream and film, and Aslan describes Blin's lighting effects as cinematic, since he cut abruptly from scene to scene. In addition, Blin's centrifugal dispersal of space prevented the play's narrative from congealing into a whole. As Chapter 3 explains, *The Screens* is splintered into isolated dramatic moments. Genet notes:

> Each scene, and each section within a scene, must be perfected and played as rigorously and with as much discipline as if it were a short play, complete in itself. Without any smudges. And without there being the slightest suggestion that another scene, or section within a scene, is to follow those that have gone before.
>
> (Genet 2002: 856; 1972: 25)

When *The Screens* begins, each tableau is a singular event. As it progresses, each tableau is fragmented into a delirious kaleidoscope of images, colours, sounds. The continuity of plot and character cede to a contiguity between dissolute poetic fragments. In Blin's production no unifying paradigm focused the spectator's view, since the narrative was displaced from level to level and section to section, thanks to the lighting effects. Moreover, as Chapter 5 remarks with reference to Blin's *The Blacks*, Genet stratifies space, only to reveal the random nature of this segmentation. When they die, colonial soldiers, Arab rebels, Arab traitors, Arab prostitutes, betrayed wives … all tear through the same paper screens and emerge on the same platform. Genet thus exposes discourses of identity – national, cultural, political, ethical – to be as fragile and porous as his tattered screens. 'The object, and the style of this work, is the *fragment*', writes Derrida in his study of Genet (Derrida 1974: 135). Both Genet's play-text and Blin's production thus divide space in order to present *The Screens*'s fractured narrative. Concurrently, they demolish the boundaries they erect, highlighting the arbitrariness of all categorization.

Genet also explodes unity with his prismatic approach to colour, which was mainly inspired by Blin's costumes, designed by Acquart and made by Acquart's wife, Barbara. Whilst, as Chapter 4 observes,

Genet's first play *Deathwatch* limits colour to black and white, *The Screens* becomes a celebration of 'violent', bright colours (Genet 2002: 578; 1962: 11, 62). The Arab customers at the brothel, those working for Sir Harold, the agitators and their wives, wear, according to Genet's play-text, shirts that are 'red, green, yellow, blue' or 'of bright and clashing colors' (Genet 2002: 584, 596, 650, 708; 1962: 17, 29, 90, 163). Saïd wears 'green trousers, red jacket, tan shoes, white shirt, mauve tie, pink cap'. His mother wears a 'violet satin dress, patched all over in different shades of violet. Big yellow veil', which goes down to her toes, each of which is painted 'a different – and violent – color; (Genet 2002: 578; 1962: 11). Colonials too take part in this pageant of colour. Monsieur Blankensee has a red moustache and whiskers, black-and-yellow striped trousers and a purple dress-coat (Genet 2002: 629; 1962: 30). In Blin's production the soldiers were not exempted from this iridian celebration, and sported apple green instead of khaki uniforms. Indeed, numerous productions, from the very first through to today, have been marked by their multicoloured visual aesthetic. Aslan notes how multicolour characterized Swedish director Per Verner-Carlsson's Stockholm production at the Stadsteater (April 1964); and in Jean-Baptiste Sastre's production at Paris's théâtre national de Chaillot (January 2004), reams of fabric in boldly patterned primary colours hung from the flies as if in an Arab *souq*, demonstrating how certain details – here multicolour – are inherited from one production to the next (see Sastre, in Finburgh *et al.* 2006: 193–8).

Colour in Genet's play-text and in Blin's production most notably characterizes the make-up. The Mother's toes are to be multicoloured. Genet describes the rest of her body:

> Her hair of tow. A white face, made up with ceruse, and very elaborate wrinkles – blue, mauve, purple ...; finally, the tendons of the neck made very prominent. Her hands as white as her head, and the wrinkles, or rather the veins, extremely visible. The same for her legs, up to her knees.
>
> (Genet 2002: 856; 1972: 27)

Genet also provides a sketch of Kadidja's make-up, where tiger stripes radiate from her nose, reflecting her ferociousness as a rebel leader.[14] In Blin's production the prostitutes were also painted emerald green; the Arabs, all of whom save Saïd were played by European actors, wore a thick band of black make-up above their eyes and a couple of crosses on each cheek, in a crude depiction of facial hair; Ommou's face resembled the cratered surface of the moon, perhaps symbolizing her matriarchal status, since in many cultures the moon is female (*la lune*), something that Genet highlights in another play, *The Penal Colony* (Genet 2002: 801–3); Madame Blankensee's cheeks were decorated with little squares resembling the national flags that her fellow colonials defend. Finally, when a character died, her/his face was painted white, and across it was drawn a large black Omega (Ω) – the last letter of the Greek alphabet, which is often used to denote finality or death (Blin 1986: 185–9). In his letters Genet entreats Blin and the artists who collaborated with him not to design costumes and make-up that simply prettify the actors: 'No face should retain the conventional beauty of feature which is played up all too often on both stage and screen' (Genet 2002: 576; 1962: 10). And he advises that Maria Casarès, arguably the greatest tragedian in France during the second half of the twentieth century, who agreed to play the Mother, should 'look at herself in a mirror, to make faces in it without indulgence, and to discover, in this new uglified face, a beauty' (Genet 2002: 877; 1972: 57). Like the screens, costumes and make-up must be inspired by the imagination rather than merely emulating everyday life. For this reason, no doubt, they are often highly stylized both in the play-text and productions.

The Arabs' crudely painted facial hair might have given the impression that Blin resorted to clichéd representations of North Africans. However, references to the Arab world were, as in Genet's text, subtle, carefully avoiding orientalism – the European imperialist tradition of stereotyping the 'East' as either 'a place of romance, exotic beings, haunting memories and landscapes', or else as dark and perilous, or as both (Said 1995: 1). Genet's play-text does make several references to North African geography and costume: palm groves, cacti lining desert roads, turbans. Blin's production also alluded to the Maghreb. The Acquart family's rich colours, notably ochres, oranges and purples, suggested North African textiles; Madani carried a little moth-eaten carpet, evoking a Muslim prayer rug; Leïla's costume – a shapeless mass with a jagged hoop skirt that deformed her silhouette, and a black hood containing only openings for her eyes and mouth – could have referenced the *burqa*, the Muslim garment that conceals women's faces and bodies; Saïd's three 'Mothers' wore great swirling gowns patched from remnants that one might find in a *souq*.[15] Acquart's and his wife's costumes thus referenced North Africa but, along with their son's screens and his make-up design, resisted an orientalizing aesthetic. First, set, costumes and make-up were obliquely inspired by North Africa, but did not provide a naturalistic copy. Genet writes, 'A few details here and there should remind one of Algeria, but the general style will be of great nobility' (Genet 2002: 846; 1972: 12).[16] Secondly, they avoided 'prettifying' the 'East'. In *Prisoner of Love* Genet describes how the colours and motifs of the Palestinian refugee camps where he resided weave visually into an oriental rug of patterns and tones (Genet 1986: 24–5). Critic Donna Wilkerson-Barker notes Genet's condemnation of glossy magazine photojournalism that exploits this photogenic richness in order to depict these places of shambolic misery as joyous and carefree (Wilkerson-Barker 2003: 68–70). Blin's and the Acquarts' designs certainly were exultant in their flamboyance and creativity, but they avoided cultivating the cliché of 'conventional beauty' against which Genet warns. Genet describes, in his letters to Blin, that the costumes for *The Screens* should be 'full, with trains and drapes, even if all this has dust and straw clinging to it' (Genet 2002: 846; 1972: 12). Blin describes how André Acquart 'succeeded in rendering the poverty of a people with luxuriant costumes that could have been made by a great designer' (Blin 1986: 199).[17] Blin's jubilatory depiction of the anti-colonial struggle afforded the Arabs grace and nobility whilst accentuating their abjection and misery, thereby refusing to reassure audiences with harmless, decorative depictions of an exoticized East.

Blin's description of Acquart's costumes as an eclectic mix of grime and haute couture illustrates the hybrid, 'awkward' aesthetic to which this book makes frequent reference. Nathalie Prats, Maréchal's costume designer, describes how, taking her lead from Genet's text, she derived inspiration from a hybrid variety of sources:

> My starting point was to follow to the letter Genet's stage directions, which always direct the artist's freedom in the direction of outrageous oppositions. East-west, tradition-modernity, poverty-wealth, costume-mask. A kind of counterpoint that leaves a great place for the imagination.
>
> (in Maréchal 1991)

According to Genet's directions, the Arab rebels are 'dressed either in a European, or in an Oriental, multicoloured fashion'. The Court Usher wears a combination of North African and European items: a turban, European jacket, and *djellaba* – Maghrebi robe (Genet 2002: 610; 1962: 46). The Acquarts' costumes included a range of cultural influences. Warda wore a stiff silver and gold robe resembling a kimono, which journalist Gilles Sandier describes as a 'glorious carapace' or a 'multicoloured and golden catafalque' (Sandier 1966: 70). Her face, neck and hands were scored with crabby wrinkles and veins, and her purple hair was combed into a metre-high beehive penetrated in every direction with hatpins. Her ceremonial robe and pierced hair, that resembled a black magic doll, elevated her from prostitute to high priestess, emphasizing Genet's desire to transform sawdust into gold dust, explained in Chapter 4. The soldiers wore cowboy hats and unbuttoned jackets revealing their casual white shirts, the former projecting their machismo, the latter feminizing them. This, too, illustrated the porous boundaries in Genet's world between supposedly opposing categories – here, masculine and feminine. Chapter 5 notes how in *The Blacks*, the hotchpotch of garments worn by the Negroes symbolizes the composite nature of their identities. Genet asks 'What exactly is a black? First of all, what's his color [*sic*]?' (Genet 2002: 475; 1960: 3). Equally, he asks, 'what is Arabness?' (Genet 1991: 179; 2004: 153). The assortment of influences from which Acquart's costumes derived ensured that neither Arab identity, nor for that matter any identity, was represented as stable, certain, knowable.

The 'awkward' combination of costumes was complemented by the actors' performances. Genet suggests frequent alternations in the tempo or pace of movement and voice. Tableau One is 'allegro' (Genet 2002: 582). In Tableau Two, the prostitutes' voices are first 'drawling', then the pace picks up until speech is delivered so fast that it is barely comprehensible (Genet 2002: 584–8; 1962: 18). And in Tableau Nine, Genet advises 'a slight calm, and a silence, then, without any warning, the mad explosion of the Gendarme' (Genet 2002: 864; 1972: 38). Finally, the graffiti scene and the final tableau are to be played extremely fast. Statuesque poise alternates with frenzied alacrity, generating an awkward hybridity of vocal delivery and corporeal expression. Moreover, Genet recommends a further dislocation, this time between voice and body. He writes to Blin:

> It is preferable, when the voice has found its true inflections, to discover the gestures which will then reinforce it, gestures which will no longer be familiarly granted the voice but will, perhaps, be in opposition to it – for example, to an inflection of deep regret a very light-hearted gesture of the hand and foot – in such a way that the whole forms a long succession of unstipulated agreements – broken but always harmonious, freeing the actor from the temptation of the commonplace.
>
> (Genet 2002: 877; 1972: 56–7)

The actor's performance should be syncopated or, in Blin's words, 'in counterpoint' (Blin, 1963: 115). As chapters 2 to 5 illustrate, Genet's characters possess no identifiable or established personality. With the actors' jarring, jagged performance styles Blin presented identity as multiple and precarious. Delgado remarks that Casarès's rendition of the Mother drew from both classical tragedy and avant-garde performance, describing it as 'both pragmatic and superstitious, wily and stubborn' (Delgado 2003: 107–10). Delgado quotes journalist Guy Dumur, who recalls how Casarès 'squat[ted] like an Arab woman, contort[ed] like a gypsy woman, bark[ed] like a dog' (Delgado 2006: 143). Blin also presented identity as unfixed by casting actors in multiple parts. Whilst, as Chapter 5 describes, Genet insisted that *The Blacks* be performed by black actors, he requested that the Arabs in *The Screens* be played by actors of European origin (Blin 1986: 191). This was no doubt because *The Screens*, more than any of Genet's plays, dismantles all identities, even identity itself (Said 1995: 235). Blin cast each actor in several roles partly because Genet's list of characters is unaffordably long, and also to emphasize Genet's anti-identitarian logic. Since the same actors played Arab rebels and European soldiers, the difference, as in *The Balcony*, between revolutionary and imperial power was not inherent or essential, but became academic.

The 'gauche' performance style cultivated by both Genet and Blin prevented actors from having recourse to a naturalist aesthetic. Genet is adamant that actors do not 'let themselves slip back into the movements and gestures that are theirs off-stage' (Genet 2002: 851; 1972: 19). Casarès recounts:

> [Genet] wanted us all to recreate each and every word of the text.... each word, each gesture had to be reinvented so that, by progressing from invention to invention, we would approach the secret world that he invites us to discover, by living it.
>
> (Casarès 1986: 50)

Many moments in Genet's play-text cannot be represented naturalistically. For example, when the Gendarme who comes to raid Saïd's shack enters stage-left, Leïla faces stage-right (Genet 2002: 624; 1962: 63). Later, 'The dead will look down, although the scene they are watching is played above' (Genet 2002: 697; 1962: 149).[18] Instead of complacently using everyday gestures and intonations, actors must constantly invent new modes of moving and speaking. Genet insists that the acting must 'be extremely precise. Very taut. No useless gestures' (Genet 2002: 576; 1962: 10). Even the most farcical or frenetic scenes must be acted with ceremony. He advises, 'The scenes where the characters arse about or fart on stage, must be played by very great actors – kinds of clowns – with great boldness and lightness. Chinese actors would know how to do it' (Genet 2002: 941). Blin's production was marked by the actors' precise stylization of every gesture and word. Saïd, Leïla and the Mother worked with him for four months before the two-month rehearsal period began, and the entire cast contemplated and calculated their every move. Casarès even recounts how Genet wanted to ban the sound of footsteps:

> One evening, some actors were rehearsing a passage from the play where they had to walk on stage backwards, one behind the other ... and their shoes made a terrible din on the hollow wooden platform.... Suddenly, we heard a sort of bark from the back of the auditorium: 'Without noise!' It was the voice of Jean Genet, who was attending the rehearsal. 'Don't worry,' cried Madeleine Renaud [Barrault's wife, who played Warda], 'we'll put felt on their soles.' And Genet exclaimed, 'No! We'll put nails on their soles, and they'll come on without making a sound.' ... And when they started over, their approach, their attitude, their breathing, their performance, the very movement of the scene was different, transposed, transfigured and ... silent. Theatrical magic had galvanized everything, and even the nasty old wood on which they walked began to live.
>
> (Casarès 1986: 51).

As with *The Maids* and *Deathwatch*, Genet wishes that the act of walking be renewed on stage (see Chapter 4). The stylization of every step and sound enabled the actors to transform simple walking, and even the flooring underneath their feet, into poetry. In Fisbach's production (discussed presently) Saïd, played by a dancer, sometimes fell forwards, did a few press-ups, and flipped onto his back; or else he walked as if on a tightrope.[19] Leïla pirouetted, her skirts spinning outwards; the Mother charged like a bull or strutted like a cockerel. Each had a non-naturalistic way of moving across the stage. Both in Blin's and in Fisbach's productions, this highly precise ritualistic performance drew attention to the actors' bodies and voices, which were not mere vehicles employed to communicate the play's plot or characters; they became a tangible material presence of mass, movement, colour, texture, sound. Finally, by highlighting the physical presence of lyrical gestures and musical words, attention was drawn away from narrative and character, fragmenting the play further into an array of isolated poetic moments.

Poetry, hybridity and physicality also characterized the use of voice in Blin's production. Playwright Valère Novarina, France's foremost proponent today of the actor's voice and its rhythms, writes, 'the language coming out of me alive from my mouth in an invisible ribbon is the very matter of which I am' (Novarina 2003: 42). Both Genet and Blin foreground this materiality. Chapter 5 analyses a speech from *The Blacks* to illustrate the musicality of Genet's prose. Through the repetition of syntactical structures, or of individual words and sounds, Genet incorporates rhymes and cadences into his prose.[20] He also adds directions on how to articulate this rhythmical text, recommending, as he does with movement, that the voice discover or invent new modulations that do not have recourse to the everyday: 'The director, taking into account the various tonal qualities of the different actors' voices, will have to invent a manner of speaking which ranges from murmurs to shouts' (Genet 2002: 855: 1972: 24). Actors must find a vocal tone that 'comes from somewhere else, not the larynx: this is a difficult music to find' (Genet 2002: 846: 1972: 12, translation modified). In his play-text Genet gives examples. Sir Harold's labourers 'speak in a very fragile voice that at times falters, and at times is falsetto'. Sir Harold and Monsieur Blankensee speak 'in a very high-pitched voice: they almost scream, enraged, like General Franco on Spanish radio' (Genet 2002: 600, 636). Genet introduces more vocal modes by suggesting that Saïd sing his lines when taunting Leïla about her ugliness; that the wives of the Arabs who visit Warda's brothel sing their embittered grievances; that the dead French soldier Pierre sing about the beloved Boulogne that he will never see again (Genet 2002: 594, 708, 715; 1962: 28, 164, 175). The alternations between falsetto shrieks, gentle whispers and melodious tunes contribute towards the 'gauche' aesthetic discussed in this book. Blin's actors certainly emphasized the materiality of the actors' voices. Casarès describes how she approached the Mother's dialogue as if it were a jazz tune (quoted in Aslan 1972: 128). Blin describes her range of voice: 'It was unbelievable. She could laugh for a very long time and using every different tone. Her laugh was always beautiful and expressive' (Blin 1986: 183). He also describes how Germaine Kerjean, who played Kadidja, had 'an extraordinary voice and laugh', and how Paule Annan, with her 'voice which was faltering, broken, blank, quite singular and quite moving', succeeded in bringing to life Leïla, a faceless heap, through subtle modulations of the voice (ibid.: 188–90).

The hieratic tone and meticulous precision of Blin's production did not prevent humour. Blin remarks that Genet's play is packed with gags. Notably, the scene where the Mother tangles the soldier Pierre in his tunic straps whilst helping him into it, was performed like a wrestling match, and roused peals of laughter from the audience (ibid.: 200–2). Genet himself indicates that light-heartedness must pervade any production of the play. For example, when the Arab women chase the Mother from Si Slimane's funeral, 'the audience should know that it's a game', and 'each actor must say her lines as if, inside, a huge laugh was about to burst out' (Genet 2002: 609). And Leïla's and the Mother's evocation of a farmyard through their 'cock-a-doodle-doos' and 'oinks' is 'underscored by laughter that is as prominent as the noises themselves' (ibid.: 595). Genet instructs Blin, '[i]n short, treat everything as a joke' (Genet 2002: 856: 1972: 25). With *The Blacks*, as Chapter 5 explains, Genet exposes his own theatre as a *clownerie* – a farce that laughs at itself rather than laying claim to any truths. With *The Screens* Genet exposes life itself as a *clownerie*. In Genet's world, truths are questionable, realities are movable, identities are unstable. So nothing can be taken entirely seriously. The Mother, between guffaws, goes some way towards elucidating this:

> Those are the truths that are false!... ha! ha! ha! ho! ho! ...
> Those are the truths you can't carry to their extremes... ho! ho!
> ho! ... without seeing them die and without seeing yourself die of
> laughter, that you've got to exalt.
>
> (Genet 2002: 700; 1962: 155)

Certain critics, notably Sartre (in Genet 1989: 31) and Genet critic Hédi Khélil, interpret the absence of certainty in Genet's world in pessimistic terms. 'Too bad,' writes Khélil, 'if certain critics persist in seeking in Genet's text a glimpse of hope whilst despair is total' (Khélil 2001: 147). But from this potential despair at the fact that no unequivocal truths exist, Genet derives hope, even jubilation. Maréchal affirms this promise of optimism offered by *The Screens*:

'Despite its seriousness, *The Screens* is never heavy. It possesses the playfulness of a child. It is traversed by a sacred jubilatory joy that makes it fundamentally and essentially a monstrously optimistic poem' (Maréchal 1991). Uncertainty enables endless creative potential, since truths, realities and identities can be perpetually reconfigured. For this reason, Genet's stage directions recommend that actors exercise a constant *va-et-vient* between 'an enormous outburst of laughter interrupted by a sob that returns to the original laughter' (Genet 2002: 610).

Blin's production has entered French theatrical folklore, mainly owing to the civil unrest with which it is associated. But for critics and spectators alike, it was most of all a colossal monument to theatrical creativity, originality and poetry, as this critic testifies:

> an exceptional mastery of scenic space: the diversification of acting areas; the scrupulously organized movement of around one hundred actors; the screens that moved silently and with ceremony, cutting the dramatic action like golden razorblades; the sheer scale; the stupefying beauty of the whole thing.
>
> (Paget 1966: 8)

Fisbach (2002)

Fifty years after it was written, does *The Screens* still provoke outrage? Does it still bear political relevance? Or is it but a pageantry of poetic forms? Frédérich Fisbach's production at the théâtre du Quartz in Brest (April 2002), which transferred to Paris's théâtre National de la Colline before going on an extensive tour and was then restaged at the Avignon Festival (June 2007), demonstrated how politics today might reside precisely in the form rather than in the content of *The Screens*.[21]

Every aspect of *The Screens*, from its absence of narrative linearity and convincing characters to its abstract scenography, obstructs a naturalist representation. Fisbach, renowned for staging both the classics and contemporary plays in highly innovative and often iconoclastic ways, explored a vast and varied array of representational means in his production of *The Screens*, most notably puppetry.[22]

Every role except for Saïd, Leïla and the Mother, who were performed by actors, were played by Japanese *ningyo joruri*, otherwise known as *bunraku* puppets (for photographs see Finburgh 2007: 2–28).[23] The audience followed the 30 or so puppets with binoculars. Using puppets had the advantage of reducing costs, since only six puppeteers were needed to operate the large number of characters. The benefits of using puppets were not simply financial. Genet states in his letter to Pauvert that puppets might be better suited to his theatre than actors (Genet 2002: 817; 2003: 38). Not being human, they are not tempted to resort to everyday gestures and tones. For Erwin Piscator, the theatre director who, along with Brecht, attempted to transform 1920s and 1930s German theatre into a revolutionary Marxist tool through aesthetic innovation, puppets represent the mutation of humans into unthinking automatons (Piscator 1980: 264). In interview, Fisbach suggested that the puppets embodied quite the opposite: a riotous celebration of human creative potential (Fisbach 2007). In his production, when Si Slimane flew into a rage at having

Figure 10   Three Japanese puppeteers with the puppets of Warda, Ommou and the Sergeant (left to right) two French *Gidayus*, and the character of the Mother (far right) in *Les Paravents* (*The Screens*), directed by Frédéric Fisbach (2002). Photograph © Pascal Victor

been woken from the dead by the Mother, the puppet literally flew over her as she lay on his grave; and whereas Blin's characters symbolized their deaths by drawing Omega signs on their faces, Fisbach's simply rose and floated ten centimetres above the stage. The constraints implicit in the human body, which, even if it avoids naturalism, is not free to perform without limits whatever it desires, were thus overcome by Fisbach. Moreover, the puppets produced the theatrical thrill of the Eucharist (described in Chapter 5) that Genet advocates. Just as the Host is both a wafer and the body of Christ, the puppets were both a collection of strings, pieces of wood and fabric, and an Arab rebel, prostitute, colonial sergeant or plantation owner. In Fisbach's production the actor playing the Mother pulled off Pierre's head when strangling him in his tunic straps, crying, 'little soldier from France ... what does one do with these things?' as she tangled up his strings (Genet 2002: 679; 1962: 124). These words, from Genet's play-text, highlighted the theatrical dualiy of the

Figure 11   The character of Saïd, the puppet of Sir Harold, and a puppeteer in *Les Paravents* (*The Screens*), directed by Frédéric Fisbach (2002). Photograph © Pascal Victor

puppets: Pierre was both a military character in the play and a 'little' puppet made of 'things': strings and bits of wood.

Traditionally, *ningyo joruri* puppets are ventriloquized by a *gidayu*, who chants the voices of all the characters. In Fisbach's production, two French actors, Valérie Blanchon and Christophe Brault, played the voices of around 90 characters. They sat like musicians behind lecterns that bore their scripts, or followed characters around the stage. With the range of a philharmonic orchestra, they voiced everything from the flies at Si Slimane's funeral, to the pompous English plantation owner Sir Harold, to his horse Bijou, to the half-witted Gendarme, to the haughty Warda, to the camped-up Sergeant. Their agile somersaulting between voices emphasized the jubilatory playfulness which, states Genet, subtends the play. Moreover, it contributed towards the 'awkward' representation of characters. The puppets were operated by puppeteers – sometimes more than one per puppet. Whilst their black clothing and head veils would have camouflaged them had the background been black, here they were far from inconspicuous, since Fisbach set them against light backdrops. Moreover, they sometimes wore *geta* – Japanese wooden elevated sandals – that clicked as they hopped and skipped when working the puppets, drawing further attention to themselves. Thus, the characters were composed of the puppets, their clearly visible puppeteers, and the *gidayus*, who provided their voices. Genet warns that those who are inspired by the 'Orient' run the risk of 'do[ing] it like ordinary women practicing yoga', but this was not the case here (Genet 2002: 817; 2003: 38). Fisbach's use of Japanese puppets possessed value far in excess of mere entertainment or decoration. The hybrid, 'gauche' representation of characters served to highlight the multiple sources, discussed in Chapter 5, from which the Genetian subject derives. Moreover, Fisbach explains that he held separate rehearsals for the puppets and for the three main characters, and that the two groups only came together for the final month of rehearsals (Fisbach 2010: 325). This process heightened the impression of heterogeneity, since two distinct performance registers confronted each other on stage

This dislocation or 'awkwardness' was amplified by the acoustics, costumes and scenography. Characters' voices already derived from a separate source from their bodies, namely the *gidayus*. In addition, the *gidayus*' voices were sometimes fed live through a sort of oscilloscope, which translated the volume of their voices, notably that of the dead villager Si Slimane, into a fluctuating horizontal line on a screen. In addition, when the Mother and Leïla hummed 'a kind of chant' whilst waiting for Saïd outside the prison, their melody was recorded live, and played back in a continuous loop over the top of their live voices (Genet 2002: 603; 1962: 37). Sound technologies therefore refracted the characters' utterances into a polyphonic chorus, which again illustrated the multiple sources from which the speaking subject derives.

Costume and make-up drew from an eclectic range of origins. The puppets' faces were painted in the *bunraku* style, similar to the *kabuki* make-up described in Chapter 5, whilst their costumes made an assortment of cultural references. Warda wore a kimono; Kadidja's dress was more North-African; the Mother's patched tent-like robes referenced both cultures; the soldiers wore French legionnaires' uniforms, incongruous with their Japanese features. As for Saïd, he wore a T-shirt which, since it was figure-hugging and flesh-coloured, gave the impression that the red flowers and breaking blue waves, which resembled a traditional Japanese woodblock print, were a tattoo. Numerous characters across Genet's works, from Yeux-Verts in *Deathwatch* to Pierrot in *Miracle of the Rose*, are tattooed. Tattoos, like lace, which also features heavily across Genet's *oeuvre*, simultaneously conceal the skin and expose it; they are both costume and body. Like the Catholic Host, they provoke the thrill of duality that, for Genet, should lie at the heart of theatre. Moreover, tattoos reveal how the body itself is a costume, emphasizing further the point that Genet makes across his theatre, that identity is a performance, a costume; it is worn, discarded, swapped, like an item of clothing. Finally, Leïla's dress, which resembled an *ancien régime* bodice and underskirts, had one padded hip and a padded hood, the uneven lumpiness of which made a visual echo with her eyes, which Saïd describes: 'Your lazy eyes, your hazy eyes, one looking off to Rio de Janeiro and the other staring into the bottom of a cup' (Genet 2002: 642; 1962: 83). A grotesque cross between Velasquez's *Infanta Margarita* and Picasso's *Dora Maar*, her cockeyed grace illustrated

Genet's 'awkward' aesthetic, which exposes identity as an assemblage of parts.

Finally, the play's quite minimalist scenography was as heterogeneous as its performers and costumes. It was arranged over two levels backed by a single screen, onto which were projected nonspecific landscapes, words from the play-text, and short films of certain scenes – for example Said's trial for theft – and behind which sometimes actors appeared in silhouette. The multifarious media – actors, puppets, puppeteers, *gidayus*, sound technologies, projected images, film – simultaneously constructed character and location in a celebration of theatrical possibility, and deconstructed them by self-consciously exposing the modes and means with which they were constructed.

Unlike Blin's, Fisbach's production caused no riots and no parliamentary debates. So is *The Screens* still politically potent? The Gendarme's naming of the Mother and Leïla as *racaille*, meaning 'riffraff', certainly had resonances when Fisbach's production was re-staged in 2007. This derogatory term had been used in 2005 by the current French President Nicolas Sarkozy to refer to disaffected youths, mainly of African origin. His remark sparked riots in

Figure 12   The *Gidayus* (far left and right), the Mother's shadow, and a projected photograph of the puppet of Si Slimane in *Les Paravents* (*The Screens*), directed by Frédéric Fisbach (2002). Photograph © Pascal Victor

deprived areas across France. It was clear that the discriminatory treatment of North Africans by certain elements of French society exposed in *The Screens* had simply shifted from the pro-independence context of Algeria in the 1960s to the immigrant context in France today. As Fisbach states in interview, '*The Screens*, like all great poems, is reactivated when it comes into contact with the present' (Fisbach 2007).

However, perhaps the politics of Fisbach's production lay more in its aesthetic form than in its political content. Fisbach's polychromatic plethora of dissipated, stratified visual and acoustic signs was more than an avant-garde exercise in style. He explains, 'Today, mass media employ a means of telling and representing the world that follows a strict regime of communication and consumption' (ibid.). Since the *raison d'être* of mass culture, notably of television, whose main representational format is naturalism, is its rapid production and consumption, the concept of challenging the consumer's creativity or imagination is not a priority. Fisbach's directorial practice creates a rupture with the bland words and images with which humans and their societies are represented in everyday dominant media. Fisbach thus locates himself within a lineage of French theatre-makers dating back to the beginning of the twentieth century, when playwright Alfred Jarry, father of French anti-naturalist avant-garde theatre, condemned commercial theatre where, for him, people '[suffer] from a dearth of sensations, for their senses have remained so rudimentary that they can perceive nothing but immediate impressions' (Jarry 1997: xxxiii). Closer to today, for contemporary playwright Roland Fichet, a political theatre 'does not represent a restored world of delivered humans in a renewed society, but enables spectators to see, hear, understand and speak differently' (in Milin 2002: 17). Fisbach's production, like Genet's playwriting, was thus of political consequence because it searched for new representational modes which would provoke in the spectator a renewed way of apprehending and comprehending the world (see Fisbach 2010: 325).

Genet's last play is a laboratory for research into formal possibility, and directors of *The Screens* often rise to the challenge of diversifying their representational means. People, events, time and space are represented by Genet with every possible theatrical element: screens, platforms, levels, costumes, make-up, hairstyles, manners of walking, tempos, sounds, vocal pitches and rhythms. Genet describes *The Screens* as 'a new joy, a new festivity, and God knows what besides' (Genet 2002: 877; 1972: 57). Still today, Genet's plays are 'new' and radical, and in turn, frequently inspire 'new' and uncompromising innovation and expansive imagination in the artists who stage them.

Notes

1 Life and politics

1 For information on Genet's literary interests see Corvin 2006: 27–31.
2 The pseudonym was Nano Florane. As Moraly explains, Nano is a diminutive of Jean and Florane a reference to the flower of the broom plant (broom in French is *genêt*).
3 White's footnote mistakenly assigns this to 'The Criminal Child'; in fact, the statement appears at the end of the interview Genet gave to Antoine Bourseiller in 1981, reprinted in *L'Ennemi déclaré* (1991: 217–26; 2004: 186–93).
4 Michel Corvin, a leading authority on Genet's theatre, has also written highly original, perceptive and accessible introductions to the French Gallimard Folio edition of each of Genet's plays (see Bibliography).
5 'Le Funambule' was performed by Pierre Constant at Paris's Maison de la Poésie in January 2008; 'Quatre heures à Chatila', directed by Alain Milianti, was staged at the Volcan in Le Havre in March 1991; *Flowers*, an adaptation of *Our Lady of the Flowers* by Lindsay Kemp, was premièred between 1968 and 1974 (see Hargreaves 2006).
6 *Splendid's*, *Elle* and *The Penal Colony* are not discussed in production. For information on productions of *Splendid's*, see Nordey 1995, Bradby 1997, Corvin 2010; on *Elle*, see Corvin 2010.

2 Key early plays: *The Maids, Deathwatch, Splendid's*

1 The first French publication of *The Maids* in book form contained two very different texts: one, previously published in the literary review *L'Arbalète* in May 1947, a long version, and the second published for the first time in 1954, which was the shorter version

that had been produced by Jouvet in April 1947. Since the English
translation is of the 1947 version, we provide references here to that
original French version.

2   We reference Genet's 1988 edition of *Deathwatch*, published in his
Théâtre complet, and the English translation, which is of an earlier
version.

3   Key late plays: *The Balcony, The Blacks, The Screens*

1   References are made to Genet's final French version of *Le Balcon*,
published in the Pléiade *Théâtre complet* (Genet 2002), and to
Hands's and Wright's English translation (Genet 1991a) of an earlier
version. Genet's final version is not translated into English.

2   For an account of this immense project, see Moraly 1996.

3   Symbols of emptiness permeate the play, from the Mother's empty
suitcase in Tableau One to Saïd's empty trousers with which Leïla
dances, and Sir Harold's empty glove. In the final moments of the
play the Arab soldiers retreat into the wings; the remaining living
characters 'remove the screens and objects which they brought in at
the beginning of the scene'. Next, the dead leave the stage, taking
their paper screens. Then 'The Mother leaves last, with her armchair.
The stage is empty. It's all over' (Genet 2002: 737; 1962: 201).
Everything, including Genet's own play, is revealed as a chimera
concealing a void.

4   The Mother is more preoccupied with her image than her son and
sister-in-law. She insists on carrying Saïd's presents to his wedding so
that her son can arrive fresh at the function. She also abstains from
eating the roast chicken she is carrying even though she is hungry, lest
the wedding guests think she rears one-legged chickens (Genet 2002:
579–80; 1962: 14). When she dies she is canonized, since she is
enthroned on a gilt and velvet chair (Genet 2002: 713; 1962: 173).
However, unlike the other characters, whose images continue to
inspire the living, the Mother's is forgotten. Warda tells her that she
has been completely forgotten by the living (Genet 2002: 714; 1962:
174). The Mother thus occupies an intermediary space between the
characters who are obsessed with appearance, and Saïd and Leïla
who reject it altogether.

5   Leïla is perhaps the play's real hero, since she escapes appearances
altogether. In the 1958 draft of the play a villager says of her, 'she is
nothing' (Genet 2002: 740). Whilst Saïd's end is tangible in that he is
shot, Genet describes Leïla as simply dissolving into her dress, a
detail he borrowed from Blin's staging of the play described in

Chapter 6 (Genet 2002: 702, 706). Indeed, rebellious roles are frequently given to women in Genet's theatre: Claire and Solange in *The Maids*; Snow, Bobo and Felicity in *The Blacks*; Leïla, the Mother, Kadidja and Ommou in *The Screens*.

4   Key productions and issues surrounding production: *The Maids, Deathwatch*

1   Richard Webb (1982) provides a comprehensive account of Genet's plays in production from 1943 to 1980.
2   Corvin identifies in *The Maids* the exposition (introduction of the plot and characters), peripetaeia (unexpected event), and *dénouement* (resolution of the plot). He concludes that Genet systematically contravenes each of these French classical conventions (in Genet 2002: 1062–3). For detailed definitions of the components of French classical theatre, see Scherer 1950.
3   Unlike Norway or Germany, France never had a tradition of naturalist theatre. However, André Antoine's théâtre-Libre, opened in Paris in 1887, sought to put Zola's theories on naturalism into practice (see Sarrazac and Marcerou 1999).
4   See Appia 1960; Craig 1962.
5   For information on the evolution of *mise en scène* in France see Whitton 1987: 49–123; Pavis 2007: 13–28.
6   In Chapter 2 we reference Genet's 1947 version of *The Maids*, since it is translated into English. Here, we reference the 1968 edition, since it is most frequently staged.
7   In Marcel Delval's production mentioned presently, Madame's curtains, and that separating stage from auditorium, were identical, highlighting further the theatricality of her behaviour. For an explanation of 'theatricality' in Genet's theatre see Bradby 2006: 34–6.
8   For a detailed account of the semiotic value of a range of objects in *The Maids*, see Khélil 2004: 48–50; Chevalier 1998: 43–8.
9   For a summary of numerous productions of *The Maids*, see Chevalier 1998: 111–12.
10 For information on Jouvet see Bradby 1991: 3–7.
11 For information on Serreau see Bradby 1991: 144–5.
12 Genet also states in 'How to Perform *The Balcony*' that, should a female actor refuse to utter the obscenities in his play-text, her part must be given to a man (Genet 2002: 258). This comment, which might be seen to typecast women as prudish and men as brash,

alludes to Marie Bell who, when playing Irma in Brook's 1960 production, omitted all profanities from her dialogue.

13 For information see de Cecatty 2007.

14 One of Genet's first plays in draft form, *Hélioglobale*, is named after a Roman emperor whose absence from the public eye was interrupted only by rare appearances in women's clothing. For information on gender in Genet's works see Bersani 1994 and 1995: 157–60; Hanrahan 1997; Éribon 2001; Stephens 2009; Vannouvong 2010.

15 It is relevant that one of the stage properties was a screen, possibly denoting the impact that *The Screens*, Genet's most non-naturalist play, retrospectively had on productions of his other plays.

16 For information on García see Whitton 1987: 163–79.

17 For detailed accounts of this production, see Delgado 2006: 143–57; Whitton 1987: 175–8; Magedera 1998: 20–6; Compte 1975.

18 Studies of mirrors in Genet's works include Coe 1968: 3–30; Went-Daoust 1979: 23-42.

19 For information on the multiple voices into which Genet's characters are split see Finburgh 2004.

20 *Las criadas* was not censored, because the officials left Madrid's Teatro Reina Victoria, where it was created, before it began. Fearing potential controversy, the theatre's director cancelled the run anyway. The play was therefore clearly perceived as political.

21 Other minimalist productions include Tania Balachova's (1954); Alfredo Arias's (2001).

22 Extracts from Adrien's and other contemporary productions of Genet's plays can be viewed on the Institut national de l'audiovisuel website: www.ina.fr

23 See Carlson 2009: 26–45.

24 See Giles 2002: 36–40 for information on other film versions of *The Maids*.

25 For information on Oida see Oida 1992; 1997; 2002: 65–70.

26 An intertextual reference to *Un chant d'amour* is also made at the beginning of Miles's film, where the Detective's eye is seen through a spyhole in Madame's door.

27 Naturalist productions have nonetheless been staged, for example by Claude Mathieu (1978) in Paris's Coupe-Chou Théâtre, which is located in a cellar the walls of which constituted the décor.

5 Key productions and issues surrounding production: *The Balcony*, *The Blacks*

1 See Chapter 4 for a definition of naturalism.

2   Genet's letters to Frechtman reveal how he was never happy with *The Balcony*, which he revised constantly, sometimes rendering it more narrative, sometimes less (Genet 2002: 939).
3   For information see Whitton 1987: 168–70, 176.
4   For information on this ballet in production see Webb 1982: 445.
5   In *The Maids* Claire secretly parades on the balcony dressed as Madame, and in the final scene Solange proclaims her defiant speech from the balcony. In *The Blacks*, the White Court sits in a gallery or balcony, and in *The Screens* the Blankensees adorn a mannequin in colonial medals on their balcony.
6   For further information on Pasqual and on this production see Delgado 2003: 182–224. Italian director Giorgio Strehler's production at Milan's Piccolo Teatro in May 1976 also located the audience on the stage.
7   In a letter to Frechtman, Genet lists the cuts demanded by the Lord Chamberlain (Genet 2002: 906).
8   In his November 1969 staging at the théâtre du Gymnase in Marseille, Bourseiller followed this instruction. The problem, according to critics, was that the production's oniric quality foreclosed on eventual social critique (in Genet 2002: 1152).
9   Since this passage is omitted from Hands's and Wright's translation, Frechtman's is used here.
10 Marchand provides an inventory of Genet's recommendations for tone in Tableau Five (Marchand 1997: 58).
11 For information on Lavaudant see Bradby and Sparks 1997: 52–4.
12 This hybridity was complemented by the actors' make-up: Kabuki face paint, eighteenth-century beauty spots, and prosthetic foreheads referencing celebrity plastic surgery.
13 See Corvin 2006 for a discussion of humour in Genet's theatre.
14 We employ 'Negro' here to denote the black actors who play out racial stereotypes before the White Court.
15 In Blin's production (discussed presently) the Queen lifted her skirts to reveal dolls representing the Court members, which were then hung up. The literal shrinking of white power was obvious (Blin 1986: 139).
16 Most reviews of the play in the 1950s and 1960s in France and in the UK referenced its contemporary political context (see Webb 1992: 52–63). See Chapter 3 for historical details.
17 Blin explains that this exposure of the play's 'construction' was intentional, and that he had also wanted the actors to construct the set during the play, but that this was not practical (Blin 1986: 135).

18 For information on the use of black and white in the play see Savona 1983: 121.

19 Despite this, numerous productions have taken place with white actors, notably Stein's, which contained only one black actor, who played Felicity. Before the show, the audience followed the actors into the wings to see them put on black make-up, thus showing the constructed nature of race (Godard 1984). Alves Meira's production (discussed presently) had a mixed cast. Five decades after Genet wrote *The Blacks* it is still rare in France, Germany or the UK to see any production containing over a dozen black actors, except for dance, which simply proves the point made by the Stratford production (discussed presently) that black culture is seen more as entertainment than as serious art. Black directors are even rarer, and the production of *The Blacks* at St Mark's Playhouse in May 1961 attracted criticism because its director, Gene Frankel, was white. See White 1994: 504–8 and Warrick 2006: 131–42.

20 Michael notes, 'London is over 30% non-white. But how many theatres do you walk into that have that kind of demographic in their audience?' (quoted in Logan 2007).

21 In Jean-Louis Thamin's production at Bordeaux's théâtre du Port de la Lune (February 1988), the (white) actors were painted green (see Genet 1988b: 241–52).

22 By 'whiting up' they also parodied the 1960s British made-for-television series *The Black and White Minstrel Show*, where white singers and dancers in blackface performed clichéd black musical numbers.

6 Key productions and issues surrounding production: *The Screens*

1 There has been no major UK production of *The Screens*. There have been two important productions in the USA: Peter Sellars's site-specific community-based 1998 *The Screens/Los Biombos* (see Rauch and Jeffries 2006); and JoAnne Akalaitis's October 1989 production at the Tyrone Guthrie Theatre, Minneapolis (see Akalaitis 2010).

2 References are made to Genet's final French version, published in the Pléiade *Théâtre complet*, and to Frechtman's English translation (Genet 1962) of an earlier version of the play.

3 For a comprehensive account of the protests, including testimonies from directors, actors and designers, see Dichy and Peskine 1986. For further details see Blin 1986: 174–83; Lavery 2010: 168–94.

4 For information on the production see Bradby 2006: 40–2. It is no surprise that Chéreau staged *The Screens*, since his productions habitually draw arresting visual images and political force from texts, whether classic or contemporary. For information on Chéreau see Fancy 2010.

5 For information on Barrault see Bradby 1991: 23–30.

6 For a detailed account see Blin 1986: 174–230.

7 Maréchal has always been particularly drawn towards poetic playwrights, from the early twentieth-century Paul Claudel, to Genet, to the contemporary Valère Novarina. For further information on Maréchal see Knapp 1995: 26–9.

8 For information on scenography in Ancient Greek and in Chinese theatres see Ley 2006: 23–4 and Riley 1997: 12–15, respectively.

9 Other readings are more analytical. For example, for critic McMahon the screens mask the truth, so that Sir Harold, for instance, cannot accept that both his plantation and his power are under threat (McMahon 1963: 263). Savona provides a useful inventory of the screens' different functions (Savona 1983: 141–2).

10 Picasso painted this mural in response to the 1937 bombing, ordered by General Franco, of civilians in the Basque town of Guernica in Spain.

11 In Fisbach's production, stagehands evoked the arson attack on Sir Harold's plantation by sticking pieces of red paper onto drawings of trees on screens. To depict the insurrection, members of the cast daubed sketches of the atrocities onto Perspex screens. Standing behind the screens, the actors could soon no longer be seen through the dripping red paint.

12 Acquart indeed tried this, and the asylum inmates' orange trees were 'the dull academic drawings of good students' (White 1994: 562)!

13 Since everything on Genet's stage must be aestheticized, he describes how these objects 'will also be interpreted larger than life, made of stronger material (the cheese grater out of cast iron), heavier' (Genet 2002: 856; 1972: 25). Or else, an actor could draw a black line around them on the ground, highlighting their status as theatrical properties rather than everyday objects.

14 This design was realized in Verner-Carlsson's Stockholm production (for photographs see Aslan 1972: 36).

15 The Mother's was in regal purples which portended her enthronement amongst the dead; Kadidja's was in flaming oranges which reflected her revolutionary ardour and referenced the arson attack; Ommou's was in tertiary earth colours, resonating with her commitment to baseness and abjection.

16 Whilst Genet and Blin were insistent that the play did not become a historical documentary of a specific period, Genet recommends that some of the colonials' costumes reference the 1840s (Genet 2002: 652: 1962: 91). This is significant, since the French conquest of Algeria took place between 1830 and 1847. Therefore, *The Screens* combines abstract poetry with direct politics in a similar way to *The Balcony*, explained in Chapter 5.

17 In Lietzau's production, designed by Jürgen Rose, the set, composed of stacked crates, was ramshackle and wan (for photographs see Aslan 1972: 51). The set in Sastre's production became increasingly littered with reams of torn material. The backdrop in Chéreau's production was a tattered cinema screen (for photographs see Boyer and Boyer 2006: 209). Rather than emphasizing the play's colourful exuberance, these productions focused on the counter-motif of decrepitude and decomposition that Genet underscores in his letters to Blin: 'And the ruin! I almost forgot the ruin! The ruin of the teeth cultivated with Warda's needle, and the total shambles of the play itself' (Genet 2002: 848; 1972: 15).

18 UK director Walter Donohue, who staged *The Screens* in a translation by Howard Brenton at the Bristol Old Vic (March 1973) states that the play was a huge challenge for British performers, owing to the latters' essentially naturalist training (Donohue 1974: 75). Fisbach, whose production is discussed presently, states that he chose puppets rather than humans for most of the roles, since puppets can take on a vast range of non-naturalist acting styles without losing credibility with the audience, a risk that actors might run (Fisbach 2010: 326).

19 Blin's Saïd, played by the actor Amidou, also emulated a tightrope walker (Thévenin 1986: 5). This is perhaps no coincidence, given that for Genet, the metaphor of the ideal artist is the tightrope walker, who is prepared to leap into the unknown (Genet 2003: 69–83).

20 For a detailed study of textual rhythm in *The Screens* see Finburgh 2002a.

21 For detailed information on the production see Fisbach 2010: 323–32; Finburgh 2007: 24–7.

22 For information on Fisbach see the special issue of *Alternatives théâtrales* dedicated to the Avignon Festival that he co-curated: 93 (summer 2007).

23 The puppets were from Tokyo's 375-year-old Marionette Theatre Youkiza, whose repertoire includes both contemporary European and traditional Japanese plays. The 70-centimetre-high individually crafted puppets have carved wooden heads, arms and legs, bamboo trunks, and between 30 and 40 strings. This was not the first time

that Genet's theatre was performed by puppets. Phillip Zarrilli's May 1980 production of *The Maids* at the University of Wisconsin, Madison was played simultaneously by three casts: one male, one female, one *bunraku*-like puppets. Since there was little fundamental difference between the enactment of identity by humans or by puppets, all behaviour was exposed as theatricality and performance (Weinberg 1981: 253).

Bibliography

[In cases where two dates of publication are given for one reference, the second date, in square brackets, refers to the original date of publication.]

Adorno, T. (1980 [1961]) 'Reconciliation under duress', trans. Rodney Livingstone, in *Aesthetics and Politics: Debates between Ernst Bloch, Georg Lukács, Bertolt Brecht, Walter Benjamin and Theodor Adorno*, London, New York: Verso: 155–76.

Adrien, P. (2008) 'Entretien', in F. Ekotto, A. Renaud and A. Vannouvong (eds) *Toutes les images du langage*, Fasano: Schena Editore: 151–61.

Alternatives théâtrales (2007) dossier on Frédéric Fisbach at the Avignon Festival: 93.

Alves Meira, C. (2008), in F. Ekotto, A. Renaud and A. Vannouvong (eds) *Toutes les images du langage*, Fasano: Schena Editore, 2008.

Appia, A. (1960 [1921]) *The Work of Living Art: A Theory of the Theatre*, trans. H. D. Albright. Coral Gables, FL: University of Miami Press, 1960.

Akalaitis, J. (2010) 'Interview with JoAnne Akalaitis' in C. Lavery (2010) *The Politics of Jean Genet's Late Theatre: Spaces of Revolution*, Manchester: Manchester University Press.

Aristotle (1996 [c. 335 BCE]) *Poetics*, trans. M. Heath, London: Penguin.

Artaud, A. (1964) 'Le Théâtre d'après-guerre à Paris' in *Œuvres complètes d'Antonin Artaud* vol. IV, Paris: Gallimard.

Aslan, O. (1972) '*Les Paravents* de Jean Genet', *Les Voies de la création théâtrale*, 3: 13–107.

——(1973) *Jean Genet*, Paris: Seghers.

Barthes, R. (1960) '*Le Balcon* de Genet: mise en scène de Peter Brook au théâtre du Gymnase', *Théâtre populaire* 38: 96–8.

Ben Jelloun, T. (1993) 'Une crépusculaire odeur l'isole', *Magazine littéraire* 313, September: 29–30.

Bersani, L. (1994) 'The gay outlaw', *Diacritics* 24.2–3: 5–18.

——(1995) *Homos*, Cambridge, Mass.: Harvard University Press, 1995.

Biner, P. (1968) *Le Living Theatre*, Lausanne: La Cité-L'Âge d'homme.

Blin, R. (1963) 'Interview by Bettina Knapp', *Tulane Drama Review* 7.3: 111–25.

——(1986) *Souvenirs et propos*, Paris: Gallimard.

Boisseron, B. and Ekotto, F. (2004) 'Genet's *The Blacks*: "And Why Does One Laugh at a Negro?", in M. Hanrahan (ed.) *Genet* special issue of *Paragraph* 27.2: 98–112.

Boyer, É. and Boyer, J.-P. (eds) (2006) *Genet*, Tours: Farrago.

Bradby, D. (1991) *Modern French Drama*, Cambridge: Cambridge University Press.

——(1997) 'Genet's *Splendid's*', in B. Read (ed.) *Flowers and Revolution: A Collection of Writings on Jean Genet*, London: Middlesex University Press: 145–55.

——(2006) 'From theatricality to performance theory: *The Screens*' in C. Finburgh, C. Lavery and M. Shevtsova (eds) *Jean Genet: Performance and Politics*, Basingstoke: Palgrave Macmillan: 34–43.

Bradby, D. and Sparks, A. (1997) *Mise en scène: French Theatre Now*, London: Methuen.

Brecht, B. (1964) *Brecht on Theatre: The Development of an Aesthetic*, ed. and trans. John Willett, London: Methuen.

Brook, P. (1993) *There are No Secrets*, London: Methuen.

Carlson, M. (2009) *Theatre is More Beautiful than War: German Stage Directing in the Late Twentieth Century*, Iowa City: University of Iowa Press.

Casarès, M. (1986) 'Extrait d'un article paru dans *Masques*', in A. Dichy and L. B. Peskine, (eds) *La Bataille des Paravents*, Paris: Le théâtre de l'Odéon: 49–52.

de Cecatty, René (2007) 'La Zone invisible d'Alfredo Arias', *Alternatives Théâtrales* 92 (spring 2007): 19–20.

Cetta, L. (1970) 'Myth, magic and play in Genet's *Les Nègres*', *Comparative Literature* 11: 511–25.

Chambers, C. (2006) 'Interview with Carl Lavery', in C. Finburgh, C. Lavery and M. Shevtsova (eds) *Jean Genet: Performance and Politics*, Basingstoke: Palgrave Macmillan: 208–12.

Chevalier, Y. (1998) *En voila du propre! Jean Genet et* Les Bonnes, Paris: L'Harmattan.

Coe, R. (1968) *The Vision of Jean Genet*, New York: Grove Press.

Cohn, R. (1966) 'European theatre, Spring 1966: a sampling', *Drama Survey* 5.3: 286–92.

Compte, C. (1975) '*Les Bonnes* de Jean Genet dans la mise en scène de Víctor García', *Les Voies de la création théâtrale*, 4: 257–78.

Corvin, M. (2000) 'Préface', in J. Genet, *Les Paravents*, Paris: Gallimard: i–xxxvi.

——(2001) 'Préface', in J. Genet, *Les Bonnes*, Paris: Gallimard: i–xxxv.

——(2002) 'Préface', in J. Genet, *Le Balcon*, Paris: Gallimard: i–xxvi.

——(2005) 'Préface', in J. Genet, *Les Nègres*, Paris: Gallimard: i–xxxiv.

——(2006) 'Préface', in J. Genet, *Haute surveillance*, Paris: Gallimard: 7–34.

——(2006a) 'Genet lecteur', in E. Boyer and J.-P. Boyer (eds) *Genet*, Tours: Farrago: 27–31.

——(2006b) 'Jean Genet "In his Humour"', in C. Finburgh, C. Lavery and M. Shevtsova (eds) *Jean Genet: Performance and Politics*, Basingstoke: Palgrave Macmillan: 23–33.

——(2009) 'Préface', in J. Genet, *Le Bagne*, Paris: Gallimard: 7–25.

——(2010) 'Préface' and 'Mise en scène', in J. Genet, *Splendid's et Elle*, Paris: Gallimard: 7–36; 188–98.

Corvin, M. and Dichy A. (2002) 'Introduction', and 'Notices et Notes', in J. Genet, *Théâtre complet*, Paris: Gallimard: xi–lxxviii; 993–1362.

Costa, M. (2007) '*The Blacks*', *The Guardian*, 20 October. Online. Available at: www.guardian.co.uk/stage/2007/oct/20/theatre3.

Cournot, M. (1991) 'En voilà du propre', *Le Monde*, 27 September.

Craig, E. G. (1962 [1911]) *The Art of the Theatre*, London: Mercury.

Delgado, M. (2003) *'Other' Spanish Theatres: Erasure and Inscription on the Twentieth-Century Spanish Stage*, Manchester: Manchester University Press.

——(2006) '*Las criadas*, Jean Genet and Spain', in C. Finburgh, C. Lavery and M. Shevtsova (eds) *Jean Genet: Performance and Politics*, Basingstoke: Palgrave Macmillan: 143–57.

Delvaille, B. (1993) 'La poésie comme salut', *Magazine littéraire* 313, September: 61–2.

Derrida, J. (1972) *La Dissémination*, Paris: Seuil.

——(1974) *Glas*, Paris: Galilée.

——(1978) *Writing and Difference*, trans. A. Bass, London: Routledge & Kegan Paul.

Dichy, A. (1997) 'Jean Genet: Portrait of the Artist as Warrior' in B. Read (ed.) *Flowers and Revolution: A Collection of Writings on Jean Genet*, London: Middlesex University Press: 21–4.

——(2002) 'Chronologie', in J. Genet, *Théâtre complet*, Paris: Gallimard: lxxxix–xciv.

Dichy, A. and Peskine L. B. (eds) (1986) *La Bataille des Paravents*, Paris: Le théâtre de l'Odéon.

Donohue, W. (1974) 'Genet's *The Screens* at Bristol', *Theatre Quarterly* 4:13: 75–90.

Driver, T. F. (1966) *Jean Genet*, Columbia: Columbia University Press.

Dumur, G. (1986) 'Genet le voleur de mots', *Le Nouvel Observateur*, 2 January.

Edwards, R. and Reader, K. (2001) *The Papin Sisters*, Oxford: Oxford University Press.

Éribon, D. (2001) *Une morale du minoritaire: Variations sur un thème de Jean Genet*, Paris: Fayard.

Fancy, D. (2010) 'Patrice Chéreau: staging the European crisis', in M. Delgado and D. Rebellato (eds) *Contemporary European Theatre Directors*, London: Routledge.

Fanon, F. (1967 [1952]) *Black Skin White Masks*, trans. C. L. Markmann, New York: Grove Press.

Fau, M. (2008) 'Entretien', in F. Ekotto, A. Renaud and A. Vannouvong (eds) *Toutes les images du langage*, Fasano: Schena Editore: 191–200.

Federman, R. (1970) 'Jean Genet ou le théâtre de la haine', *Esprit* 4, April: 697–713.

Finburgh, C. (2002) 'Jean Genet and the poetics of palestinian politics: statecraft as stagecraft in "Quatre heures à Chatila"', *French Studies* 56.4: 495–509.

——(2002a) 'Facets of artifice: rhythms in the theater of Jean Genet, and the painting, drawing and sculpture of Alberto Giacometti', *French Forum* 27.3: 73–98.

——(2004) 'Speech without acts: politics and speech-act theory in Genet's *The Balcony*', *Paragraph, the Journal of Modern Critical Theory* 27.2: 113–29.

——(2007) 'Un monstre bariolé: *Les Paravents* de Fréderic Fisbach', *Alternatives théâtrales* 93: 24–7.

Finburgh, C., Lavery, C. and Shevtsova, M. (eds) (2006) *Jean Genet: Performance and Politics*, Basingstoke: Palgrave Macmillan.

Fisbach, F. (2007) Unpublished interview with C. Finburgh, May.

——(2010) '*Les Paravents* joués par trois acteurs et des marionnettes', Interview with O. Aslan, *Revue d'histoire du théâtre* 247: 323–32.

Foucault, M. (1979 [1975]) *Discipline and Punish: The Birth of the Prison*, trans. A. Sheridan, New York: Vintage.

François, K. (2007) 'Interview with Harriet Gilbert', *The Word*, BBC World Service, 25 November.

Galey, M. (1970) '*Les Bonnes* de Genet', *Les Nouvelles littéraires*, 16 April: 13.

García, V. (1968) 'Déshumaniser', in *Théâtre 1968-1*, Paris: Bourgois: 71–9.

——(1970) '*Les Bonnes*', *Les Nouvelles littéraires*, 2 April 1970: 8.

Genet, J. (1950) *Un Chant d'amour*, DVD.

——(1951) *Œuvres complètes*, vol. 2, Paris: Gallimard.

——(1953) *Œuvres complètes*, vol. 3, Paris: Gallimard.

——(1958) *The Balcony*, trans. B. Frechtman, New York: Grove Press.

——(1960) *The Blacks*, trans. B. Frechtman, New York: Grove Press.

——(1961) *Les Paravents*, Décines: Barbezat.

——(1962) *The Screens*, trans. B. Frechtman, New York: Grove Press.

——(1963) *Les Nègres*, with photographs by E. Scheidegger, Décines: L'Arbalète.

——(1966) *Œuvres complètes*, vol. 3, Paris: Gallimard.

——(1968) *Œuvres complètes*, vol. 4, Paris: Gallimard.

——(1972) *Reflections on the Theatre and Other Writings*, trans. R. Seaver, London: Faber.

——(1979) *Œuvres complètes*, vol. 5, Paris: Gallimard.

——(1982) *The Thief's Journal*, trans. B. Frechtman, New York: Grove Press.

——(1986) *Un captif amoureux*, Paris: Gallimard.

——(1986a) 'Lettre de Jean Genet à Jean-Louis Barrault', in A. Dichy and L. B. Peskine (eds) *La Bataille des Paravents*, Paris: Le théâtre de l'Odéon: 56.

——(1988) *Lettres à Olga et Marc Barbezat*, Décines: L'Arbalète.

——(1988a) 'Rembrandt's Secret', trans. R. Hough, in *Rembrandt*, Madras, New York: Hanuman Books.

——(1988b) *Les Nègres au Port de la lune* (writings by Genet and a collection of critics), Bordeaux: Éditions de la différence.

——(1989) *The Maids and Deathwatch*, trans. B. Frechtman, London: Faber.

——(1990) *Fragments ... et autres textes*, Paris: Gallimard.

——(1991) *L'Ennemi Déclaré*, ed. A. Dichy, Paris: Gallimard.

——(1991a) *The Balcony*, trans. T. Hands and B. Wright, London: Methuen.

——(1992) *Prisoner of Love*, trans. B. Bray, Hanover, New Hampshire: Wesleyan University Press.

——(1995) *Splendid's*, trans. N. Bartlett, London: Faber.

——(2002) *Théâtre complet*, ed. M. Corvin and A. Dichy, Paris: Gallimard.

——(2003) *Fragments of the Artwork*, trans. C. Mandell, Stanford, Ca.: Stanford University Press.

——(2004) *The Declared Enemy: Texts and Interviews*, trans. J. Fort, Stanford, Ca.: Stanford University Press.

——(2010) 'Preface to *The Blacks*', trans. C. Finburgh, in C. Lavery, *The Politics of Jean Genet's Late Theatre: Spaces of Revolution*, Manchester: Manchester University Press: 227–34.

Giles, J. (2002) *Criminal Desires: Jean Genet and Cinema*, London: Creation Books.

Godard, C. (1984) 'Les Nègres', *Acteurs* 21, October–November: 25.

Goldmann, L. (1966) 'Le théâtre de Jean Genet et ses études sociologiques', *Cahiers Renault-Barrault* 57: 90–125.

Gontard, D. (1987) *Nô Kyôgen*, Paris: Hitzeroth.

Hands, T. (2006) 'Interview with Terry Hands', in C. Finburgh, C. Lavery and M. Shevtsova (eds) *Jean Genet: Performance and Politics*, Basingstoke: Palgrave Macmillan: 201–7.

——(2010) Unpublished interview with C. Finburgh (October).

Hanrahan, M. (1997) *Lire Genet: Une Poétique de la différence*, Montreal: Presses Universitaires du Montréal.

Hargreaves, M. (2006) 'Dancing the impossible: Kazuo Ohno, Lindsay Kemp and *Our Lady of the Flowers*, in C. Finburgh, C. Lavery and M. Shevtsova (eds) *Jean Genet: Performance and Politics*, Basingstoke: Palgrave Macmillan: 106–16.

Hutera, D. (2003) 'Preview of a mesmerisingly erotic version of Jean Genet's *The Maids*', *The Times Online*, 17 November. Online. Available at: http://entertainment.timesonline.co.uk/tol/arts_and_entertainment/article1018485.ece

Issacharoff, M. (1985) *Le Spectacle du discours*, Paris: Corti, 1985.

Jackson, G. (2003) 'Interview with Glenda Jackson', on *The Maids*, DVD bonus.

Jacobson, J. and Mueller, W. R. (1968) *Ionesco and Genet: Playwrights of Silence*, New York: Hill & Wang.

Jakobson, R. and Halle M. (1956), *Fundamentals of Language*, The Hague: Mouton.

Jarry, A. (1997 [1896]) *Jarry: The Ubu Plays*, trans. C. Connolly and S. T. Watson, London: Methuen.

Kanters, R. (1960) 'Le Chef-d'oeuvre scandaleux: *Le Balcon* de Jean Genet et Peter Brook', *L'Express*, 26 May.

Khélil, H. (2004) *Figures de l'altérité dans le théâtre de Jean Genet: Lecture des* Nègres *et des* Paravents, Paris: L'Harmattan.

Knapp, B. (1995) *French Theatre since 1968*, New York: Twayne.

Lacan, J. (1998 [1958]) 'Sur *Le Balcon* de Genet', in *Le Séminaire*, vol. 5, *Les Formations de l'inconscient*, ed. J.-A. Miller, Paris: Seuil: 264–69.

Larthomas, P. (1972) *Le Langage dramatique*, Paris: Armand Colin.

Lavaudant, G. (1985) *Le Balcon* programme note, *Comédie-Française* 143–4.

Lavery, C. (2003) 'Ethics of the wound: a new interpretation of Jean Genet's politics', *Journal of European Studies* 33.2: 161–76.

——(2006) 'Reading *The Blacks* through the 1956 preface: politics and betrayal', in C. Finburgh, C. Lavery and M. Shevtsova (eds) *Jean Genet: Performance and Politics*, Basingstoke: Palgrave Macmillan: 68–78.

——(2010) *The Politics of Jean Genet's Late Theatre: Spaces of Revolution*, Manchester: Manchester University Press.

Lehmann, H.-T. (2006 [1999]) *Postdramatic Theatre*, trans. K. Jürs-Munby, London: Routledge.

Ley, G. (2006) *A Short Introduction to the Ancient Greek Theater*, Chicago: University of Chicago Press.

Logan, B. (2007) 'Do the White Thing', *The Guardian*, 17 October. Online. Available at: www.guardian.co.uk/world/2007/oct/17/race.uk

McMahon, J. (1963) *The Imagination of Jean Genet*, New Haven: Yale University Press.

Magedera, I. (1998) *Jean Genet: Les Bonnes*, Glasgow: Glasgow French and German Publications.

Maingueneau, D. (1990) *Pragmatique pour le discours littéraire*, Paris: Bordas.

Malgorn, A. (1988) *Jean Genet, Qui êtes-vous?* Lyon: La Manufacture.

——(2002) *Jean Genet: Portrait d'un marginal exemplaire*, Paris: Gallimard.

Marchand, A. B. (1997) *Genet: Le Joueur impénitent*, Montreal: Les Herbes Rouges.

Maréchal, M. (1991) *Les Paravents* at the théâtre de la Criée programme note.

——(1996) 'Autour des *Paravents*: Entretien avec Marcel Maréchal', in M.-C. Hubert, *L'Esthétique de Jean Genet*, Paris: Sedes: 181–91.

Marowitz, C. (1972) 'Notes sur le Théâtre de la Cruauté, Les Paravents', *Obliques*, 2: 56–9.

Mathews, T. (2000) *Literature, Art and the Pursuit of Decay*, Cambridge: Cambridge University Press: 153–91.

Metz, C. (1977) *The Imaginary Signifier: Psychoanalysis and the Cinema*, trans. C. Britton *et al.*, Bloomington, Indiana: Indiana University Press.

Michael, K. (2007) *The Blacks Remixed* at the Theatre Royal Stratford East, programme note.

Miles, C. (1975) *The Maids*, DVD.

Milin, G. (ed.) (2002) *L'Assemblée théâtrale*, Paris: Éditions de l'Amandier.

Moraly, J.-B. (1988) *Jean Genet, la vie écrite*, Paris: Éditions de la Différence.

——(1996) 'Le Livre impossible', *Jean Genet* special issue of *Europe*, 808.9: 134–43.

Nordey, S. (1995) 'Stanislas Nordey, metteur en scène de *Splendid's*', *Théâtre/Public* 123: 5.

Novarina, V. (2003) *La Scène*, Paris: P.O.L.

Oida, Y. (1992) *An Actor Adrift*, London: Methuen.

——(1997) *The Invisible Actor*, London: Methuen.

——(2002) 'An Interview with Yoshi Oida by David Bradby and David Williams', in D. Bradby and M. Delgado (eds) *The Paris Jigsaw: Internationalism and the City's Stages*, Manchester: Manchester University Press: 65–70.

Olivier, J.-J. (1971) '*Les Bonnes*', *Combat*, 3 March.

Paget, J. (1966) '*Les Paravents* de Jean Genet – sublime!', *Combat*, 23, 24 April: 8.

Pasqual, L. (1991) *Le Balcon* at the Odéon-Théâtre de l'Europe, programme note.

Pavis, P. (2007) *La Mise en scène contemporaine: origines, tendances, perspectives*, Paris: Armand Colin.

Piscator, E. (1980 [1929]) *The Political Theatre*, trans. H. Rorrison, London: Methuen.

Pucciani, O. (1972) 'La Tragédie, Genet et *Les Bonnes*', *Obliques* 2: 11–22.

Puzin, C. (1998) Les Bonnes, Le Balcon, *Jean Genet*, Paris: Nathan.

Quirot, O. (1989) 'Mortel simulacre', *Le Monde*, 28 December.

Rajon, S. (2008) 'Entretien', in F. Ekotto, A. Renaud and A. Vannouvong (eds) *Toutes les images du langage*, Fasano: Schena Editore: 177–89.

Rauch, B. and Jeffries, L. (2006) 'An Interview', in C. Finburgh, C. Lavery and M. Shevtsova (eds) *Jean Genet: Performance and Politics*, Basingstoke: Palgrave Macmillan: 187–91.

Redonnet, M. (2000) *Jean Genet, le poète travesti: Portrait d'une œuvre*, Paris: Grasset.

Regnault, F. (1983) *Les Paravents* at the théâtre des Amandiers, programme note.

Riley, J. (1997) *Chinese Theatre and the Actor in Performance*, Cambridge: Cambridge University Press.

Said, E. (1995 [1978]) *Orientalism*, London: Penguin.

——(1995) 'On Genet's late work', in J. E. Gainor (ed.) *Imperialism and Theatre*, London: Routledge: 230–42.

Sandier, G. (1963) '*Les Bonnes* de Jean-Marie Serreau', *Arts*, 24 Sept.

——(1966) 'Genet un exorciste de génie', *Arts*, 27 April: 69–70.

Sarrazac, J.-P. and Marcerou, P. (1999) *Antoine, l'invention de la mise en scène: Anthologie des textes d'André Antoine*, Arles: Actes Sud-Papier.

Sartre, J.-P. (1952) *Saint Genet, comédien et martyr*, in J. Genet, *Œuvres complètes*, vol. 1, Paris: Gallimard.

——(1976 [1973]) *Sartre on Theatre*, trans. F. Jellinek, London: Quartet.

Sastre, J.-B. 'An Interview', in C. Finburgh, C. Lavery and M. Shevtsova (eds) (2006) *Jean Genet: Performance and Politics*, Basingstoke: Palgrave Macmillan: 193–8.

Savona, J. (1983) *Genet*, London: Macmillan.

Scherer, J. and Scherer, C. (1993) *Le Théâtre classique*, Paris: Presses Universitaires de France.

Serreau, J.-M. (1973) *Les Bonnes* at the théâtre des Amandiers, programme note.

Sheringham, M. (1993) *French Autobiography: Devices and Desires. Rousseau to Pérec*, Oxford: Clarendon, 1993.

Sobczinski, J. (1986) 'Rencontre au pays d'Azzedine', *Le Monde*, 20 April 1986: x.

Spivak, G. C. (1988) 'Can the subaltern speak?', in C. Nelson and L. Grossberg (eds) *Marxism and the Interpretation of Culture*, Urbana, Chicago: University of Illinois Press.

Stanislavski, C. (1980 [1924]) *My Life in Art*, trans. J. J. Robbins, London: Eyre Methuen.

Stephens, E. (2004) 'Disseminating phallic masculinity: seminal fluidity in Genet's fiction', in M. Hanrahan (ed.) *Genet* special issue of *Paragraph*, 27.2: 85–97.

——(2009) *Queer Writing: Homoeroticism in Jean Genet's Fiction*, Basingstoke: Palgrave Macmillan.

Strick, J. (2004) *The Balcony*, DVD.

——(2004a) 'Memoir by Joseph Strick', on *The Balcony*, DVD bonus.

Thévenin, P. (1986) 'L'Aventure des *Paravents*', in A. Dichy and L. B. Peskine (eds) *La Bataille des Paravents*, Paris: Le théâtre de l'Odéon: 5–11.

Tribby, W. (1973) '*The Blacks* by Jean Genet', *Educational Theatre Journal* 25.3: 513–4.

Ubersfeld, A. (1982 [1977]) *Lire le théâtre*, Paris: Sociales.

Vaïs, M. (1978) *L'Écrivain scénique*, Montreal : Presses de l'Université de Québec.

Vannouvong, A. (2010) *Jean Genet: les Revers du genre*, Dijon: les presses du réel.

Warrick, J. (2006) '*The Blacks* and its impact on African American theatre in the United States', in C. Finburgh, C. Lavery and M. Shevtsova (eds) *Jean Genet: Performance and Politics*, Basingstoke: Palgrave Macmillan: 131–42.

Webb, R. C. (1982) *Jean Genet and his Critics: an Annotated Bibliography, 1943–1980*, Metuchen, NJ: The Scarecrow Press.

——(1992) *File on Genet*, London: Methuen.

Weinberg, M. (1981) '*The Maids* by Jean Genet. University of Madison, 2 May 1980', *Theatre Journal* 33:2, 253–4.

Went-Daoust, Y. (1979) 'Objets et lieux dans *Le Balcon* de Jean Genet', *Neophilologus* 63:1, 23-42.

——(1980) *Le Symbolisme des objets et l'espace mythique dans le théâtre de Jean Genet*, Oegstgeest: Drukkerij de Kemenaer.

White, E. (1994 [1993]) *Genet*, London: Picador.

——(1995) 'Introduction', in *Splendid's*, trans. N. Bartlett, London: Faber.

Whitton, D. (1987) *Stage Directors in Modern France*, Manchester: Manchester University Press.

Wilkerson-Barker, D. (2003) *The Space of the Screen in Contemporary French and Francophone Fiction*, New York: Peter Lang.

York, S. (2003) 'Interview with Susannah York', on *The Maids*, DVD bonus.

Zola, É. (1968 [1881]) *Le Naturalisme au théâtre*, Paris: Cercle du Livre précieux.

Index